IMMACOLATA CALABRESE & SILVANA RAMPONE

Cross-Curricular Resources
for Young Learners

OXFORD
UNIVERSITY PRESS

OXFORD
UNIVERSITY PRESS

Great Clarendon Street, Oxford OX2 6DP

Oxford University Press is a department of the University of Oxford.
It furthers the University's objective of excellence in research, scholarship,
and education by publishing worldwide in

Oxford New York

Auckland Cape Town Dar es Salaam Hong Kong Karachi
Kuala Lumpur Madrid Melbourne Mexico City Nairobi
New Delhi Shanghai Taipei Toronto

With offices in

Argentina Austria Brazil Chile Czech Republic France Greece
Guatemala Hungary Italy Japan Poland Portugal Singapore
South Korea Switzerland Thailand Turkey Ukraine Vietnam

OXFORD and OXFORD ENGLISH are registered trade marks of
Oxford University Press in the UK and in certain other countries

© Original work by Immacolata Calabrese, Silvana Rampone:
Cross-curricular Projects Published by Loescher Editore, Torino, 2005

© English edition by Oxford University Press 2007

The moral rights of the authors have been asserted

Database right Oxford University Press (maker)

First published 2007

2011 2010 2009
10 9 8 7 6 5 4 3 2

All rights reserved. No part of this publication may be reproduced,
stored in a retrieval system, or transmitted, in any form or by any means,
without the prior permission in writing of Oxford University Press (with
the sole exception of photocopying carried out under the conditions stated
in the paragraph headed 'Photocopying'), or as expressly permitted by law, or
under terms agreed with the appropriate reprographics rights organization.
Enquiries concerning reproduction outside the scope of the above should
be sent to the ELT Rights Department, Oxford University Press, at the
address above

You must not circulate this book in any other binding or cover
and you must impose this same condition on any acquirer

Photocopying

The Publisher grants permission for the photocopying of those pages marked
'photocopiable' according to the following conditions. Individual purchasers
may make copies for their own use or for use by classes that they teach.
School purchasers may make copies for use by staff and students, but this
permission does not extend to additional schools or branches

Under no circumstances may any part of this book be photocopied for resale

Any websites referred to in this publication are in the public domain and
their addresses are provided by Oxford University Press for information only.
Oxford University Press disclaims any responsibility for the content

ISBN: 978 0 19 442588 9

Printed in China

ACKNOWLEDGEMENTS

We are grateful to the following for permission to reproduce photographs: ©ADAGP,
Paris and DACS, London 2007, p 134 (man), Alberto Giacometti, *Walking Man*,
1960; Alamy Images, pp 30, 102, 112 (lemon, desk, cake, honey, yoghurt),
185 (Sphinx, Abu Simbel); The Art Archive/Skoklosters Stot Balsta, p 91,
Giuseppe Arcimboldo, *Emperor Rudolf II, 1552-1612, as Vertumnus*, c 1591;
The Barnes Foundation, Merion PA, p 67 (sitting child); Bayerische
Staatsgemäldesammlungen, Alte Pinakothek, Munich, p 67 (baby),
Michael Pacher, *Kirkenväteraltar* (detail); Bridgeman Art Library/©Pompeii,
Italy/Alinari, p 195, *Cave Canem, from the House of the Tragic Poet*, 1st century AD;
Berte Morisot, 1872, *Blanche Pontillon as a Baby*; The Frick Collection, New York,
p67 (woman), Jean August Dominique Ingres, *Comtesse d'Haussonville*, 1845
(detail); Galleria d'Arte Moderna, Palermo/©DACS 2007, p 13, Felice Casorati,
Gli Scolari, 1927; Solomon R Guggenheim Museum, New York, p 134 (woman),
Amadeo Modigliani, *Jeanne Hébuterne with Yellow Sweater (Le Sweater Jaune)*
1918-19; Heritage Images pp 185 (Karnak, Valley of Kings), 189 ©British
Museum, *Fowling in the Marshes*; Musée d'Orsay, Paris, pp 67 (girl) Edgar Degas,
La Famille Bellelli (detail), 134 (girl), Edgar Degas, *Grande Danseuse Habillée*,
1880; Musée du Louvre, Paris, p 67 (man in hat), Raffaello Sanzio, *Portrait
of Baldassarre Castiglione*, 1514; Museo de Antioquia, Medellin, p 134 (family),
Frederico Botero, *La Famiglia Colombiana*; Museo Nacional del Prado, p 67 (man
without hat), Jacopo Tintoretto, *Portrait of a Venetian Senator*, 1580 (detail);
Oxford University Press/Photodisc, p 112 (coffee, chips).

Illustrations by: Kathy Baxendale pp 130, 158, 167, 168, 169, 187, 190
Judy Brown p 153

THE PURPOSE OF THIS BOOK

This book is intended as a resource book for teachers of English in primary schools. It contains a range of activities which will help you to vary or expand the materials provided by course books.

It is generally recognized that linguistic diversity is as vital a component of a civilization as economic activities and religious and civil customs. It is believed that the learning of language and content in conjunction provides many opportunities for learning language indirectly; it enables children to learn more quickly and to reach a higher level of knowledge than a traditional approach does. In recent years the recognition of the potential of Content and Language Integrated Learning (CLIL), whereby the children study a subject in a foreign language, has persuaded many researchers to carry out experimental projects whose aims may be summarized as follows:

- To learn not just to use a foreign language but to use a foreign language as a tool for learning.
- To increase motivation for learning a foreign language or for learning other subjects through that language.
- To improve the effectiveness of foreign language learning and to acquire a better knowledge of other subjects.
- To provide opportunities for using the foreign language in practical and motivating contexts, while stimulating comprehension, production, and interaction in a natural way.
- To economize on time by contextualizing learning and combining strands of different subjects in the same curricula.
- To use abilities, knowledge, and skills from other disciplines (not just the linguistic ones).
- To exploit the children's mixed abilities and learning styles.
- To develop the social skills of co-operation and taking turns.

Content and language integrated experiences in primary schools do not necessarily mean teaching a whole subject in a foreign language but selecting, within that subject, some significant areas to be exploited and developed in a foreign language. One can either develop language by choosing a topic the children are studying in their own language and then integrating it with activities in the foreign language, or use foreign language knowledge which they have already acquired to teach them new content of a subject in the foreign language. A subject can be initially introduced in mother tongue and later expanded on in the foreign language, or vice versa. What is important is that there should not be a simple transposition of activities from one language to another, but that the activities in the two languages complement one another. For some examples of CLIL projects around the world, taught through English, see http://www.factworld-info/

HOW TO USE THIS BOOK

The book contains teaching plans which can be used in different contexts with children of various age groups. It is up to you to select activities and materials and to fit them into your own course syllabus, adapting them to your children's needs, and cognitive and linguistic competences.

Each teaching plan is structured according to a cross-curricular approach which makes it possible either to use all the activities or to select just some of them, in accordance with the needs of the class. An effective approach to CLIL at primary level can be summarized as follows:

a) Exploit the children's previous linguistic and subject knowledge.
b) Place the initial emphasis on listening and comprehension.
c) Facilitate foreign language comprehension by:
- creating a reassuring environment in which the children can express themselves without anxiety
- pre-teaching vocabulary
- using age-appropriate vocabulary
- reinforcing linguistic structures that have already been learnt
- using visual supports (pictures, flashcards, PowerPoint presentations, etc.), miming, and gestures
- code-switching (shifting from one language to another as a natural communicative strategy) to explain a concept, overcome a breakdown in communication, or introduce a complex topic
- constantly checking progress and providing feedback
- paraphrasing, reformulating, simplifying, and giving examples

d) Facilitate foreign language production by:
- allowing children to answer in different ways (from non-verbal answers in the early stages to verbal answers, in both mother tongue and in the foreign language, before gradually progressing to the point where children only answer in the foreign language)
- using role-play; group work; songs and games
- making posters, booklets, tables and graphs

e) Use additional activities common to both the new subject and foreign language learning (investigations, making predictions, experiments, data collection, gap filling, matching games, listening, etc.).

ASSESSMENT, SELF-ASSESSMENT, AND PORTFOLIO

The content of this book is intended to promote a kind of learning which is an active and creative building up of the child's skills through practical experience, observation, conceptualization, and experimentation. In this context, assessment should be seen as careful observation with the aim of collecting significant data in order to assess the quality of the learning process. It is important to use different assessment tools in accordance with the progress of children's learning and the context in which the children are working. These are some suggestions:

1) Make teacher's notes based on observation of children's strategies and abilities. A model table with some indicators already filled in can be found in Appendix 1. You can also download a copy from the website: www.oup.com/elt/teacher/clilyl, which you can adapt for your classes.
2) Record the skills achieved by the children at the end of a topic or a significant activity. Suggestions are given in the section entitled **Assessment** at the end of each topic as to which skills may be tested. A sample form is shown in Appendix 2. You can also download and modify a copy from the website: www.oup.com/elt/teacher/clilyl

3) Children's own reflections and self-assessment. Appendix 3 provides a table which can be given to the children at the end of a topic or significant activity (some translated versions of the form can be found on the website: www.oup.com/elt/teacher/clilyl). Explain to the children that they have to reflect upon their learning processes and the skills they have learnt and fill in the tables in their mother tongue. You will find 'I can' statements for the 'What I can do' part of the sheet in the Assessment section at the end of each topic. These should be filled in on the form before you copy it and give it to the children. Children should then decide whether they can now do each skill described and tick the smiley face (fully achieved), straight face (achieved but not 100 per cent sure of it), or sad face (not yet fully achieved) accordingly.
4) Portfolio. This should be a collection of materials selected by the child to reflect his/her individual learning process. Children should fill in a description form to accompany any piece of work they include in their portfolio. An example of this form can be found in Appendix 4 and/or you can download a model from the website: www.oup.com/elt/teacher/clilyl.
5) For additional assessment task ideas, see *Assessing Young Learners*, Oxford Resource Books for Teachers series.

In the assessment of CLIL activities it is essential to work out assessment tasks that highlight the progress that has been made both at the linguistic and content level. It is therefore necessary to use different tools, some in the foreign language and some in mother tongue, taking care to make the content comprehensible at a linguistic level in order to avoid the possibility that a lack of linguistic comprehension may compromise the assessment of the content.

No less important is the assessment of the effect of the activities on cross-curricular learning. This can be achieved by the teacher reflecting on:

a) To what extent did each CLIL activity help to introduce, reinforce, and develop curricular learning?

	Activity	Activity	Activity	Activity
Aim				
Introducing				
Reinforcing				
Developing				

b) What would I change if I did this again?
c) Which activities did not work as well as I expected?
d) Which activities worked better than I expected?
e) Which linguistic skills were/were not effectively acquired or reinforced through the subject content?
f) Which subject content was/was not effectively acquired or developed through the vehicular use of the foreign language?
g) Which learning styles did I enable or disregard?
h) Which materials did/did not work or were lacking?
i) Did I use 'open' activities? (Activities which required children to make active choices rather than selecting between given options and/or activities which required them to work co-operatively with their classmates to find the answer.)
j) Did I have any help or feedback from colleagues who teach other subjects?

HOW THE TEXT IS ORGANIZED

The material is divided into content areas, which are organized in topics.

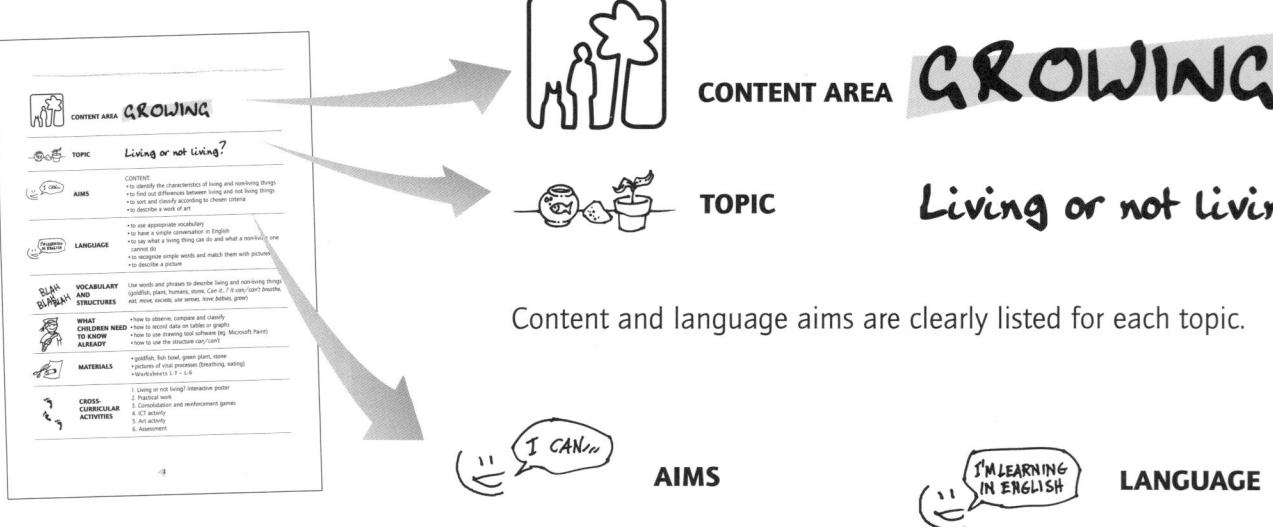

Content and language aims are clearly listed for each topic.

AIMS

LANGUAGE

Each topic provides a detailed teaching plan as well as photocopiable worksheets.

• The teaching plan

In addition to describing the suggested activities, the plan provides the language to be used in class during the activities and details of how to use the photocopiable worksheets. Often there are additional suggestions which do not require any additional photocopiable material.

2.2 EXPERIMENT

Organise the class into five groups; give a pot and some sunflower seeds to each group; four groups should fill their pot with soil and one group with sand. Tell the children to follow your instructions for preparing the pots:

 Fill a pot with soil (sand).

 Make two small holes in the soil.

 Put a seed in each hole.

 Cover the seeds with some soil (sand).

Each topic ends with extension ideas for further work on the subjects covered. These often involve other subjects such as art and information technology.

5. EXTENSION ACTIVITY: ICT

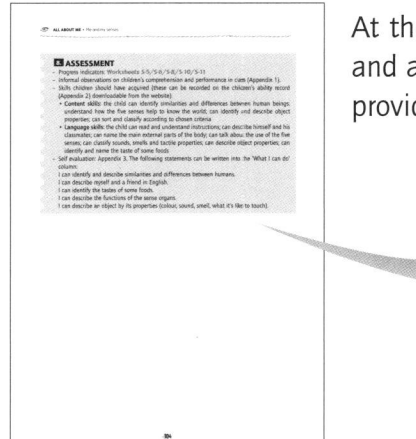

At the end of each topic relevant Worksheets are suggested for assessment and a list of the content and language skills children should have acquired is provided.

8. ASSESSMENT
- Progress indicators: **Worksheets S-5/S-6/S-8/S-10/S-11**
- Informal observations on children's comprehension and performance in class (Appendix 1).
- Skills children should have acquired (these can be recorded on the children's ability record (Appendix 2) downloadable from the website):
  • **Content skills:** the child can identify similarities and differences between human beings; understand how the five senses help to know the world; can identify and describe object properties; can sort and classify according to chosen criteria
  • **Language skills:** the child can read and understand instructions; can describe himself and his classmates; can name the main external parts of the body; can talk about the use of the five senses; can classify sounds, smells and tactile properties; can describe object properties; can identify and name the taste of some foods
- Self evaluation: Appendix 3. The following statements can be written into the 'What I can do' column:
  I can identify and describe similarities and differences between humans.
  I can describe myself and a friend in English.
  I can identify the tastes of some foods.
  I can describe the functions of the sense organs.
  I can describe an object by its properties (colour, sound, smell, what it's like to touch).

• The worksheets

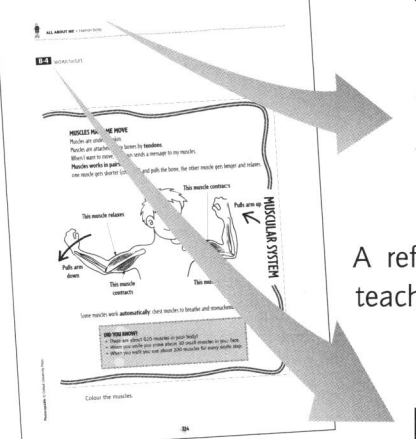

The topic to which the Worksheets refer is always clearly indicated.

ALL ABOUT ME • Human body

A reference letter and number make it easier to find the point in the teaching plan where the activity is explained.

B-4

• The symbols

`GAME` Indicates an activity based on a game, often involving movement or a craft activity.

  Indicates Information Technology.

T-3 Indicates the number of the Worksheet required. The letter refers to the content area (in this case, *Time travelling*).

APPENDIX 1

RECORD OF CHILDREN'S STRATEGIES AND ATTITUDES

Date: .... Group/class: .... Topic: ....

Description of activity: ....

Students	INTERACTION			COMPREHENSION				PRODUCTION			
	S/he is interested in the activities carried out	S/he works with the other students in carrying out the activity	S/he can work autonomously to complete activities	S/he can understand the general meaning of the subject	S/he can understand simple questions about the subject	If s/he does not understand, s/he asks for explanations in L1 or L2		S/he can answer simple questions on the subject	S/he participates and asks questions only in L1	S/he participates and asks questions in L2 as well as L1	
1.											
2.											
3.											
4.											
5.											
6.											
7.											
8.											
9.											
10.											
11.											
12.											
13.											
14.											
15.											
16.											
17.											

Key: ☺ always   ☺ sometimes   ☹ never

Comments: ....

Photocopiable © Oxford University Press

APPENDIX 2

RECORD OF CHILDREN'S ABILITIES

School .... Group/Class/Age .... Teacher .... Topic ....

Name .... Name ....
Date .... Date ....

Is capable of ... (list skills)	Achieved	Progressing	Not yet achieved	Achieved	Progressing	Not yet achieved
Forms of assessment used						

APPENDIX 3

STUDENT'S SELF-ASSESSMENT FORM

Class: _____ Name: _____

Date: _____ Activity: _____

☐ What I liked doing most: ....
....

☐ What I didn't like or found difficult: ....
....

How I worked:

☐ on my own   ☐ with the help of the teacher   ☐ with the help of the other students

☐ with commitment   ☐ without much commitment   ☐ with difficulty   ☐ without difficulty

In the group

☐ I participated actively in the work of the group

☐ I let the other students take the initiative and decide

☐ I accepted all the suggestions of the other students without discussion

☐ I tried to contribute my own ideas and suggestions to the work

☐ ....

WHAT I CAN DO	☺	😐	☹

Photocopiable © Oxford University Press

APPENDIX 4

PORTFOLIO MATERIALS: DESCRIPTION FORM

School: _____   Name: _____

Class: _____   Date: _____

Fill in this form and attach it to each assignment you put in your Portfolio

Activity type	Activity format
☐ individual	☐ worksheet
☐ in groups	☐ drawing / artwork
☐ class activity	☐ listening activity
☐ home activity	☐ video
☐ with the help of an adult	☐ practical activity
☐ without the help of an adult	☐ performance (script, photo, ...)
☐ listening	☐ research
☐ oral	other: _____
☐ reading	
☐ written or spelling	
☐ other	

What I have learnt from this assignment: _____
_____

Why I liked it: _____
_____

What I could have done better: _____
_____

Ask your teacher to add a comment:
_____
_____

Photocopiable © Oxford University Press

FURTHER READING

- AA. VV, *The Romans (Footsteps)*, London, Franklin Watts, 2001.
- S. Canizares, D. Moreton, *Frogs,* Leamington, Scholastic Publications Ltd, 2001.
- Centro Diffusione Lingue Comunitarie, *L'uso veicolare della lingua straniera in apprendimenti non linguistici*, in «Quaderni USR Piemonte» 6 (2003), Torino, MIUR – Direzione Generale USR Piemonte.
- J. Challoner, *Light and Dark,* London, Belitha Press, 1995.
- J. Challoner, *Wet and Dry*, London, Belitha Press, 1995.
- P. R. Cox, *Who Were the Romans?*, London, Usborne Publishing Ltd, 2002.
- C. Creary; G. Wilson, *100 Science Homework for Year 2*, Leamington, Scholastic Publications Ltd, 2002.
- European Cooperation Project Lingua A, *TIE-CLIL. Professional development corse*, Milano, MIUR – Direzione Regionale Lombardia, 2002.
- Geography Success, *Starter book*, Oxford, Oxford University Press, 2001.
- *Infant Projects – Child Education magazines*, Leamington, Scholastic Publications Ltd.
- S. Ioannou-Georgiou and P. Pavlou, *Assessing Young Learners*, Oxford, Oxford University Press, 2003.
- T. Jennings, *Geography Success starter. 1,* Oxford, Oxford University Press, 2000.
- T. Jennings, *Science Success starter. 1,2,3,4*, Oxford, Oxford University Press, 2000.
- A. Langley, 'My body', *Oxford First Encyclopedia*, Oxford, Oxford University Press, 1999.
- J. Lindsay, *Mummy Activity Book,* London, The British Museum, 2003.
- L. Magloff, *Watch Me Grow. Frog,* London, DK, 2003.
- S. Meredith, K. Needham, M. Unwin, *You and Your Body*, London, Usborne Publishing Ltd, 1993.
- N. Morris, *Your Incredible Body*, Great Bardfield, Miles Kelly, 2001.
- Oxford First Encyclopedia, *Animals and Plants*, Oxford, Oxford University Press, 2002.
- S. Phillips, *Young Learners*, Oxford, Oxford University Press, 1993.
- Scotland P1-P3, *Science: key stage 1*, Cheltenham, Stanley Thornes, 2002.
- A. Smith, J. Tatchell, *Flip Flap Body Book*, London, Usborne Publishing Ltd, 1998.
- G. Wilson, C. Creary, *100 Science Lessons for Year 2,* Leamington, Scholastic Publications Ltd, 2001.
- Teacher resource Key stage 1, *Science Activities 1*, Richmond, Brighter Vision, 1996.
- The Oxford Junior Atlas, *Activity book,* Oxford, Oxford University Press, 1996.
- The Science Coordination Group, *Key Stage Two: Science*, CGP, Newcastle upon Tyne, 2003.
- S. Thomas, *Skills*, Oxford, Oxford University Press, 1992.

http://www.abcteach.com
http://www.ancientegypt.co.uk
http://clilcompendium.com
http://www.cilt.org.uk/index.htm
http://www.dinosauria.com
http://www.dinosaurvalley.com
http://www.educate.org.uk
http://www.enchantedlearning.com
http://www.euroclic.net
http://factworld.info/

http://www.geography.org.uk
http://www.historyforkids.org
http://kiddyhouse.com
http://lessonplanz.com
http://www.preschoolrainbow.com
http://www.primaryresources.co.uk
http://schooldiscovery.com
http://www.teachercreated.com
http://www.tieclil.org/
http://www.ub.es/filoan/CLIL.html

CONTENT MAP

GROWING

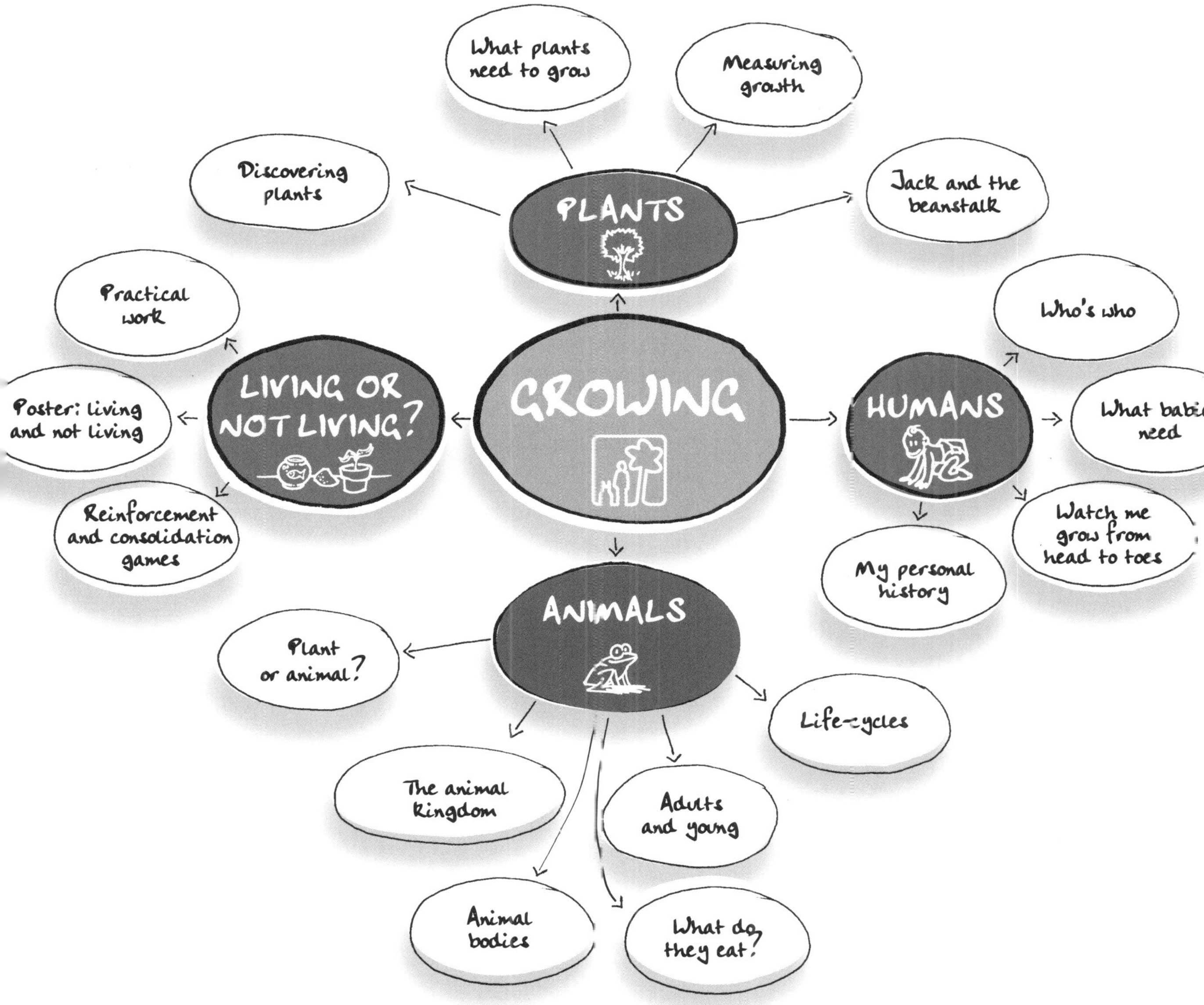

GROWING

- **PLANTS**
  - What plants need to grow
  - Measuring growth
  - Discovering plants
  - Jack and the beanstalk

- **LIVING OR NOT LIVING?**
  - Practical work
  - Poster: living and not living
  - Reinforcement and consolidation games

- **HUMANS**
  - Who's who
  - What babies need
  - Watch me grow from head to toes
  - My personal history

- **ANIMALS**
  - Plant or animal?
  - The animal kingdom
  - Animal bodies
  - What do they eat?
  - Adults and young
  - Life-cycles

 CONTENT AREA **GROWING**

	**TOPIC**	*Living or not living?*
	**AIMS**	• to identify the characteristics of living and non-living things • to find out differences between living and non-living things • to sort and classify according to chosen criteria • to describe a work of art
	**LANGUAGE**	• to use appropriate vocabulary • to have a simple conversation in English • to say what a living thing can do and what a non-living one cannot do • to recognize simple words and match them with pictures • to describe a picture
	**VOCABULARY AND STRUCTURES**	Use words and phrases to describe living and non-living things (*goldfish, plant, humans, stone; Can it …? It can/can't breathe, eat, move, excrete, use senses, have babies, grow*)
	**WHAT CHILDREN NEED TO KNOW ALREADY**	• how to observe, compare, and classify • how to record data on tables or graphs • how to use drawing tool software (e.g. Microsoft Paint) • how to use the structure *can/can't*
	**MATERIALS**	• goldfish in a fish bowl, green plant, stone • pictures of vital processes (breathing, eating) • **Worksheets L-1–L-6**
	**CROSS-CURRICULAR ACTIVITIES**	1. *Practical work* 2. Poster: *Living and not living* 3. Reinforcement and consolidation games 4. ICT (Information Technology) 5. Art 6. Assessment

GROWING • Living or not living?

1. PRACTICAL WORK

Time: 20 minutes
Materials: a goldfish in a bowl, a green plant, a stone, **Worksheet L-1**

1.1 PREPARATION

Place some objects (for example, a goldfish in a bowl, a green plant, and a stone) in different parts of the classroom (on a window-sill, on a desk, on a bookcase) before the start of the lesson.

1.2 INVESTIGATION

Invite the children to look around the classroom and name the new objects they see. Put the goldfish, the green plant, and the stone on a table and say: **Look at the fish!** Then ask the children questions, using gestures and pictures [**Worksheet L-1**] to help them understand: **Can the goldfish move? Can the goldfish breathe? Can the goldfish eat? Can the goldfish drink? Can the goldfish grow? Can the goldfish have babies?** The children may answer the questions in mother tongue; in that case translate them into English: **Yes, it moves! ... Yes, it can move!**

1.3 Ask the children: **Can you move? Can you breathe? Can you eat? Can you drink? Can you grow?** Point to a boy, then to a girl, and finally at yourself saying: **You are a boy! You are a girl! I am a woman/a man! We can move, breathe, eat, drink, grow. We are humans!**

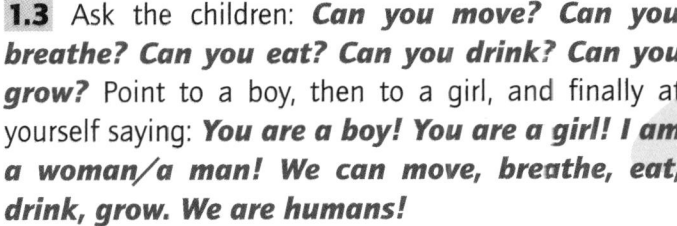

1.4 Say: **Now look at the plant! Can the plant move? Can it breathe? Can it eat? Can it drink? Can it grow? Can it have babies?** Brainstorm, in English or in mother tongue, what the children know about movement (turning towards the light), reproduction (from seed to plant), and nutrition of plants.

1.5 Now turn your attention to the stone: **Look at the stone now! Can the stone move? Can it breathe? Can it eat? Can it drink? Can it grow? Can it have babies? A stone can't move; a stone can't drink, etc.**

GROWING • Living or not living?

2. POSTER: LIVING AND NOT LIVING

Time: 15 minutes
Materials: 4 copies of **Worksheet L-1**

2.1 PREPARATION

Make four enlarged sets of the pictures from **Worksheet L-1** representing the main vital processes (breathing, eating, drinking, moving, reproduction, growing) and cross through the pictures of one set with a red felt pen ✘. Prepare a poster divided into four columns like the one below.

Living and not living

GOLDFISH	HUMANS	PLANT	STONE
It can:	They can:	It can:	It can't:

2.2 Hand out the Worksheet pictures to the children and explain that they have to stick them in the correct column on the poster by following your instructions: ***A goldfish can breathe*** (a child who has a picture of the lungs has to go and stick it in the right column); ***A stone can't breathe*** (a child who has a picture of the lungs with a red cross ✘ on it can go and stick it in the appropriate column); and so on until all the columns have been completed. Then draw the children's attention to the poster: ***The goldfish, the plant, and humans can move, breathe, drink, eat, grow, and have babies. The stone can't move, breathe, drink, eat, grow, or have babies. The goldfish, the plant, and humans are LIVING things. The stone is NOT a LIVING thing.***

2.3 FURTHER DEVELOPMENT

Prepare some cards with the words corresponding to the **Worksheet L-1** pictures (move, breathe, eat, drink, grow, have babies); hand out the cards to the children and ask them to take turns to stick the words on the poster next to the appropriate pictures.

GROWING • Living or not living?

3. REINFORCEMENT AND CONSOLIDATION GAMES

Time: from 15-30 minutes for each activity listed
Materials: Worksheets L-2 to L-5

3.1 Split the class up into teams of three or four children. Give each team a pack of 18 picture cards [Worksheet L-2] which they have to sort into 'living things' and 'non-living things' (the pictures may be enlarged if you wish). The team that finishes first is the winner.

3.2 SIMON SAYS: stone ... plant ... duck ... tree!
Play the game 'Simon says'. When you say the name of a living thing, the children have to move and when you say the name of a non-living thing they keep still. You could use the words from Worksheet L-2.

3.3 SORT THE PICTURES INTO THE CORRECT BOX [Worksheet L-3].
Explain to the children that they have to cut the pictures out and stick them in the appropriate box. When the activity has been completed, you could ask the children to draw other living or not living things in the appropriate boxes.

3.4 BOOKLET: 'All living things ...'.
Give each child copies of Worksheets L-4 and L-5 and explain that they are going to make a booklet about the seven processes that characterize living beings (ALL LIVING THINGS ... breathe, eat, move, use senses, excrete, have babies, grow). Ask the children to colour in the pictures on Worksheet L-4, cut them out, and stick them next to the appropriate captions on Worksheet L-5. When the activity has been completed, ask the children to make a cover for the book and staple it together with the two pages of Worksheet L-5. If children have a Portfolio, you could ask them to include this booklet in the Portfolio Dossier together with a description form (Appendix 4).

4. Extension activity: ICT

Time: 15 minutes

4.1 PREPARATION

- scan in the pictures of living and non-living things from **Worksheet L-3**;
- save them in the My Pictures folder;
- open the drawing tool PAINT (you can find this in All Programs − Accessories on a standard PC with Microsoft Office software);
- insert the scanned pictures (Edit − Paste) at the top of a blank screen;

- draw two empty shapes using the Ellipse tool;
- write 'Living things' above one shape and 'Not living things' above the other;
- save the document in a folder.

4.2 Show the children where the document is and ask them to open the document, select the pictures with the Selection tool, and drag them into the appropriate ellipse.

When children have finished, save the work of each child and print it out.

5. Extension activity: ART

Time: 20 minutes
Materials: Worksheet L-6 or a coloured copy of the work of art *Gli scolari* by Felice Casorati, 1927–28, Galleria Civica d'Arte Moderna, Palermo.

5.1 Show the children the painting *Gli scolari* (*The pupils*) by Felice Casorati, [Worksheet L-6]. Ask the children first to guess the title of the painting and then to list in English all the elements they can recognize: ***What can you see in this picture?*** (*I can see a blackboard, a teacher, a globe, a table, a ruler; there are five pupils/children, two books, two sheets of paper.*) Then invite each child to add new elements to their copy of the picture, both 'living' (plants, animals, pupils ...) and 'not living' (school objects, furnishing ...).

6. ASSESSMENT

- Progress indicators: **Worksheets L-2/L-3**
- Informal evaluation: Any notes made on the observation sheet (Appendix 1)
- Skills children should have acquired (these can be recorded on the children's ability record (Appendix 2), downloadable from the website):
  - **Content skills:** the child can distinguish living things from non-living ones; can identify the characteristics of living things; can sort and classify according to chosen criteria; can describe a work of art.
  - **Linguistic skills:** the child can say what a living thing can do and what a non-living thing cannot do; can recognize simple words and match them with pictures; can describe and complete a picture according to given instructions.
- Self evaluation: Appendix 3. The following statements can be written into the 'What I can do' column:
  I can distinguish between a living and a non-living thing.
  I can say what a living thing can do and a non-living thing cannot do.
  I can read simple phrases in English and match them to pictures.
  I can describe a picture in English and complete one according to instructions.

GROWING • Living or not living?

L-1 WORKSHEET

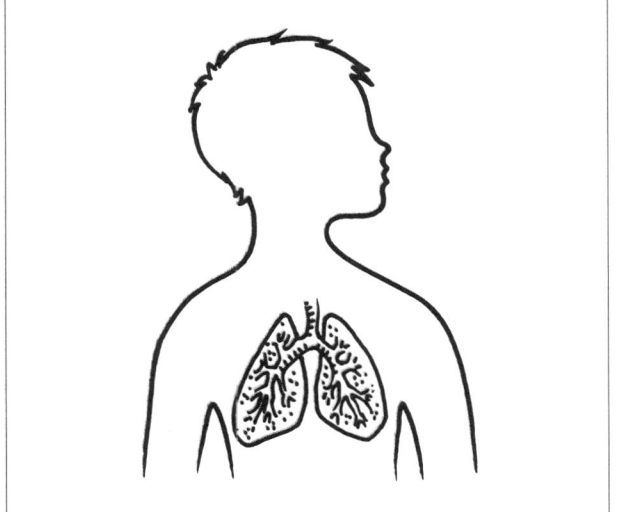

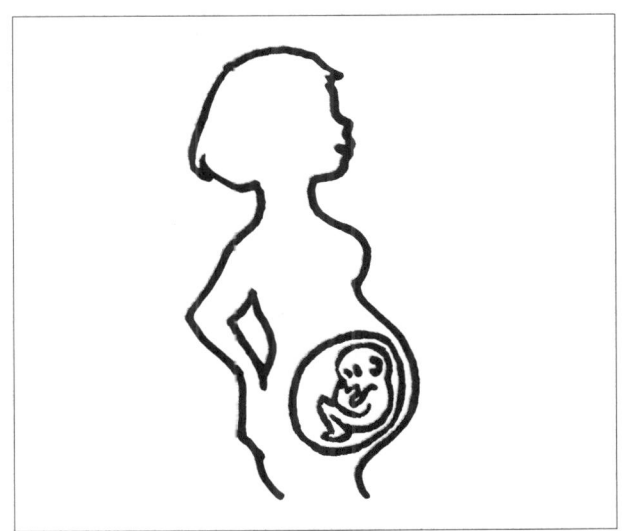

GROWING • Living or not living?

L-2 WORKSHEET

GROWING • Living or not living?

L-3 WORKSHEET

Living and not Living

Sort the pictures into the correct box.
Add other living and not living things.

not Living

Living

Photocopiable © Oxford University Press

 **GROWING** • Living or not living?

L-4 WORKSHEET

All living things ...

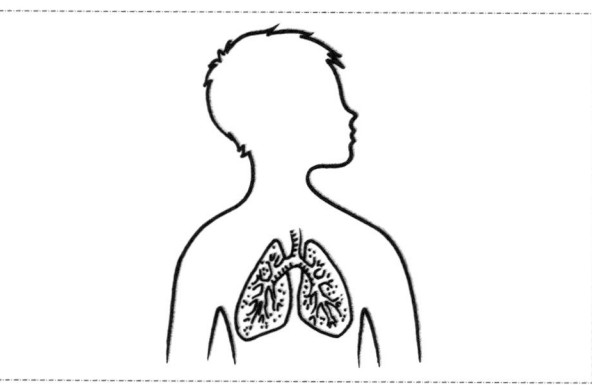
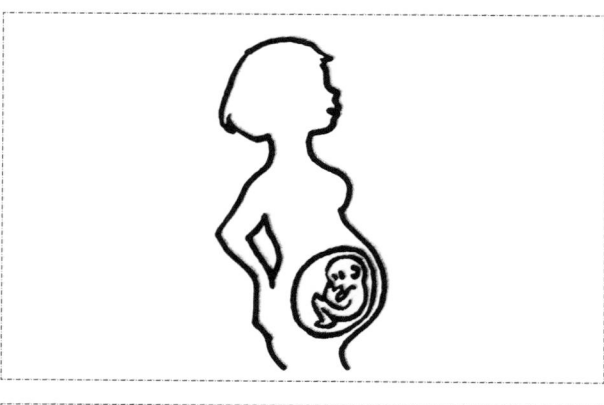

Cut out the pictures and glue them onto **WORKSHEET L-5**.

GROWING • Living or not living?

L-5 WORKSHEET

All living things ...

BREATHE	glue
EAT	glue
MOVE	glue

Cut out the pictures from **WORKSHEET L-4** and glue them in the right place.

GROWING • Living or not living?

L5-1

USE SENSES	glue
EXCRETE	glue
HAVE BABIES	glue
GROW	glue

Cut out the pictures from **WORKSHEET L-4** and glue them in the right place.

GROWING • Living or not living?

L-6 WORKSHEET

Gli scolari (The pupils)
Felice Casorati
(1927–28)

Add 'living' and 'not living' things to the picture. Colour the picture.

CONTENT AREA: GROWING

	TOPIC	Plants
	AIMS	• to do experiments, predict, make a record of observations, and interpret the results • to identify the factors that influence the growth of plants • to identify the different parts of a plant and their functions • to describe the growth process of a plant • to use ICT to present information in a bar chart
	LANGUAGE	• to use appropriate vocabulary • to talk about the conditions a plant needs to survive and grow healthily • to describe the different parts of a plant and their functions • to follow simple instructions • to make comparisons • to act out a simple story
	VOCABULARY AND STRUCTURES	Use words and phrases relating to: plants (*roots, stem, trunk, leaf, flower, branch*); growth (*seed, roots, shoot, no/little/good growth, water, light, air, good soil*); instructions on how to do experiments (*fill, make, put, cover, place, cut out, add, match*); adjectives (*big, small, tall, short*); affirmative and negative questions and answers (*What will happen? I think ...; How tall? Has it got ...? Is it ...? It is/isn't; It has/hasn't got. He is ... How many ...?*)
	WHAT CHILDREN NEED TO KNOW ALREADY	• how to do an experiment (predict, observe, record data ...) • the life-cycle of a plant • how to take simple measurements
	MATERIALS	• flower pots, compost, sand, sunflower seeds, beans, water, a small clear plastic bag, a paper plate, a hyacinth bulb, cotton wool • **Worksheets P-1–P-5**
	**CROSS-CURRICULAR ACTIVITIES**	1. *Discovering plants* 2. *What plants need to grow* 3. *Measuring growth* 4. Story: *Jack and the beanstalk* 5. ICT (Information Technology) 6. Art 7. Assessment

GROWING • Plants

1. DISCOVERING PLANTS

Time: 2 hours
Materials: food colouring, celery, a transparent container, **Worksheets P-1 to P-2.1**

1.1 PREPARATION
Organize a 'Plant Hunt' in the school garden or in the neighbourhood; ask the children to observe the plants and ask them questions to help them identify them: ***Do you know this plant? Can you see any flowers? What colour are they? Can you show me the trunk of this plant?*** The children may answer either in mother tongue or in English.

1.2 PLANT PARTS
Back in the classroom, ask the children to draw one of the plants or flowers they saw out in the garden. Once the children have finished their drawings, show them the 'Tree and Flower Pictures' (**Worksheet P-1**, enlarged and cut out) in order to introduce the vocabulary for the different parts of a tree or flower; get the children to point them out in their drawings: ***Point to the branches; point to the trunk; point to the petals,*** etc. Depending on the age of the class, repeat the activity using the 'Tree and Flower Words' [**Worksheet P-1**]. Show the words only, the children have to point to the corresponding part of the plant on their drawings.

1.3 PLANT AND FLOWER PUZZLE
Make a copy of **Worksheet P-1** for each child. Explain to the children that they have to cut out the pictures along the dotted lines; make a tree and a flower; stick them in their exercise books and glue the labels next to the right part of each plant.

1.4 EACH PART OF A PLANT IS IMPORTANT
Discuss the functions of the different parts of a plant with the children and help them with vocabulary as necessary (for example, ***the roots fix it to the ground and suck water and nutrients from the soil; the stem allows water and minerals to rise from the roots to the rest of the plant, gives the plant support, and enables it to turn towards the light***). Carry out a simple experiment to demonstrate how the stem and roots work: ***The roots take in water and minerals. The stem carries water and minerals from the roots to the rest of the plant.***

WHAT TO DO

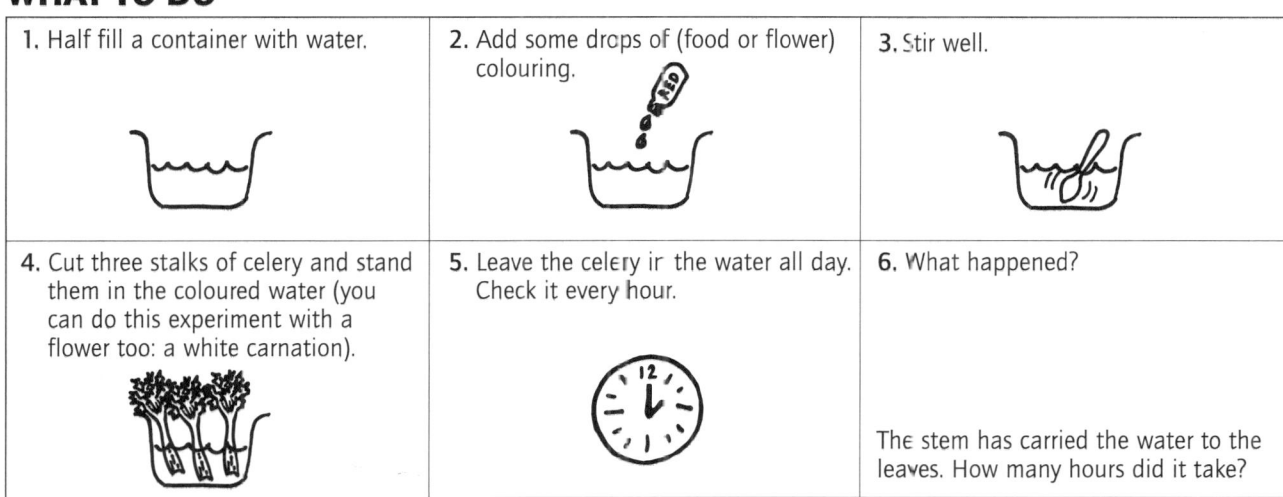

1. Half fill a container with water.	2. Add some drops of (food or flower) colouring.	3. Stir well.
4. Cut three stalks of celery and stand them in the coloured water (you can do this experiment with a flower too: a white carnation).	5. Leave the celery in the water all day. Check it every hour.	6. What happened? The stem has carried the water to the leaves. How many hours did it take?

The pictures can be photocopied, enlarged, and used to record the steps of the experiment.

GROWING • Plants

Depending on the age and language level of the children, you could investigate other plant functions, for example, ***Roots anchor plants into the soil. Stems hold the plant and move it towards the sun. Leaves use sunlight to make food for the plant (photosynthesis). Petals are usually coloured to attract bees and insects.***

1.5 ZIG-ZAG BOOK

Give each child a copy of **Worksheets P-2/P-2.1** Explain that they are going to make a zig-zag book. They have to fold the two Worksheets in half lengthwise along the black line; cut the flaps along the dotted lines; read the captions and fill in the gaps above the captions with the missing words. Under the flap they should draw the part of the plant that matches the description.

2. WHAT PLANTS NEED TO GROW

Time: 1 hour 30 minutes; (+ 20 days for the experiment)
Materials: 5 pots, sunflower seeds, soil, sand, water, plastic bag, poster (optional)

2.1 PREPARATION

The aim of the experiment is to observe and discover the factors that influence a plant's growth. The pictures that describe the experiment can be enlarged and used as flashcards either during the experiment, to make it easier to understand, or later, as a record of the different stages.

WHAT YOU NEED

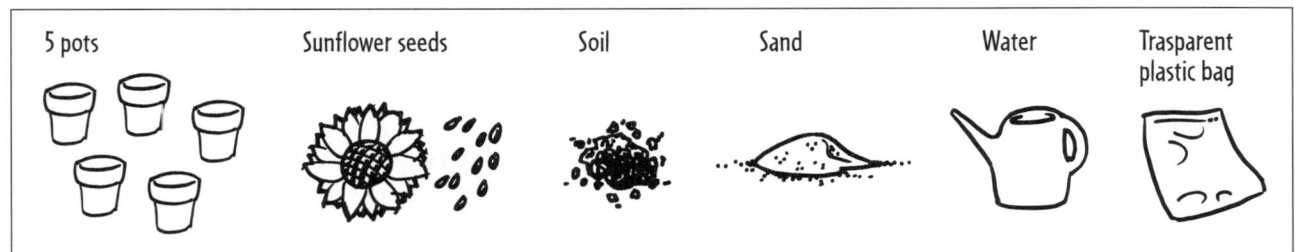

2.2 EXPERIMENT

Organize the class into five groups; give a pot and some sunflower seeds to each group; four groups should fill their pot with soil and one group with sand. Tell the children to follow your instructions for preparing the pots:

Fill a pot with soil (sand).

Make two small holes in the soil (sand).

Put a seed in each hole.

Cover the seeds with some soil (sand).

GROWING • Plants

2.3 When all the pots are ready, tell each group to label its pot by following your instructions: **Write number X on the label and stick it on the pot; then place it ...** The pots should be numbered 1–5 with the pot containing sand being number 5. Get the children to place the pots in various locations according to the instructions below:

Place pot 1 in a sunny place (window sill) and water it.

Place pot 2 in a sunny place but don't water it.

Place pot 3 in a dark place and water it.

Place pot 4 in a sunny place, water it, and close it in the plastic bag.

Place pot 5 (with sand) in a sunny place and water it.

2.4 Ask the children to predict what will happen to the seeds in the different pots and to record their predictions on a grid by using the following symbols:

| No growth | Little growth | Good growth |

Help the children to formulate hypotheses about how the seeds will grow: **The seeds in pot 1 will receive light, air, and water. What do you think will happen to these seeds: no growth, little growth, or good growth? The seeds in pot 2 will receive light, air but no water. What do you think ...? The seeds in pot 3 will receive air and water but no light. What do you think ...? The seeds in pot 4 will receive light and water but no air. What do you think ...? The seeds in pot 5 will receive light, water, and air but they are in sand. What do you think will happen?** They should write their predictions in a grid (see below).

At the end of the experiment (after about 20 days), get the children to record the results in the grid and compare them with their starting predictions: **What do you notice? What colour are the stems and leaves?** (possible results: pale leaves; short, yellow stems; tall, green stems; short, green stems; tall, yellow stems ...) **Did the seeds in the sand grow well? Can a plant grow without air/water/light/nutrients from the soil?**

GROWING • Plants

The results of the experiment will lead to the conclusion that the seed which has grown best is the one in pot number 1; it can therefore be stated that in order to grow healthily plants need water, light, air, and nutrients: ***The seeds grew best in pot 1. This is because plants need water, light, air, and good soil to grow well.***

	Date: .... What I think	Date: .... What happened
Soil + light / no water (2)		
Soil + light + water (1)	*Good growth*	*Tall and green stems*
Sand + light + water (5)		
Soil + water / no light (3)		
Soil + water + light / no air (4)		

2.5 WHAT PLANTS NEED TO GROW

Split the class into four groups; give each group a big, square sheet of paper and the name of one of the four elements necessary for the growth of a plant (water, light, air, soil). Explain that each group has to illustrate the assigned element by choosing a favourite technique (water colours, paint, collage, etc.).

3. MEASURING GROWTH

Time: 1 hour; (+ about 20 days for the experiment)
Materials: paper plate, beans, cotton wool, water, **Worksheet P-3**

3.1 PREPARATION

The aim of this experiment is to observe and record the growth of a broad bean plant.

WHAT YOU NEED

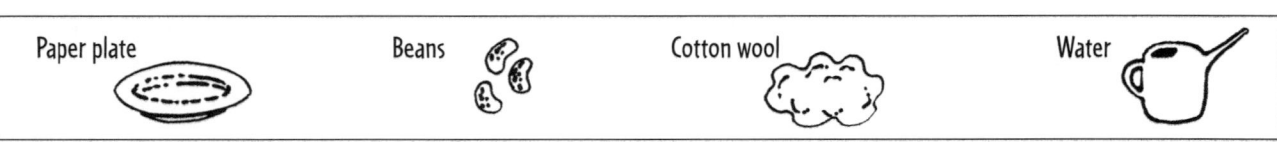

GROWING • Plants

3.2 EXPERIMENT

Follow the instructions to run the experiment (please note that cotton is used instead of soil so that the bean growth can be easily observed).

| 1. Dampen the cotton wool. | 2. Put the cotton wool on the paper plate. |
| 3. Put the beans on the cotton wool. | 4. Place the plate on the windowsill and water it every day. |

Get the children to draw a graph on which the time, in days, is recorded on the X axis and the height of the plant above the soil, in centimetres, is recorded on the Y axis.

Children have to write on the graph the date of sowing, the date when the first root appears, the date when the first shoot appears, the date when the first leaf appears, and the date of the last day of the experiment. From when the first shoot appears, children have to measure and record the height of the plant and the number of leaves on it. In this way it will be possible to establish how many days passed between the time of sowing and the appearance of the first root; between the appearance of the root and that of the first shoot, and between the appearance of the first shoot and the development of the whole plant. The information from the graph will enable children to establish the total duration of the growth and the increase in height of the plant up to the end of the experiment: ***How many days before the seed splits and a root grows? How many days between the first root and the growing of the shoot? How long is the stem after 8 days/12 days? How many leaves after 10 days?***

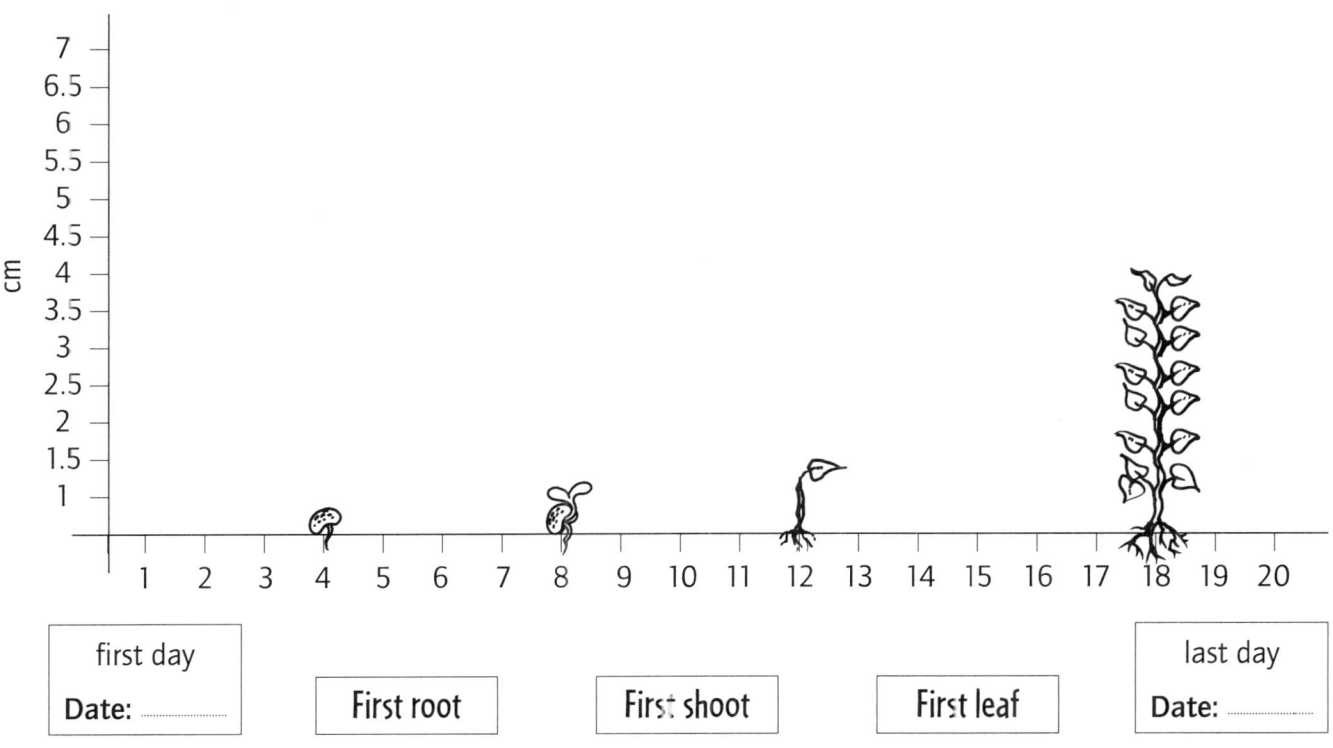

GROWING • Plants

3.3 WE WANT TO GROW A PLANT
Teach the actions that go with the song (to the tune of the traditional song 'The Farmer's in his Den') and get the children to join in.

We want to grow a plant, we want to grow a plant E, I, A, U, O, we want to grow a plant.	(pretend to sow a seed in a pot)
We sow a little seed, we sow a little seed E, I, A, U, O, we sow a little seed.	(dance in a ring holding hands)
The seed is in the soil, the seed is in the soil E, I, A, U, O, the seed is in the soil.	(crouch down and curl up as if you are the seed in the soil)
The seed grows a root, the seed grows a root E, I, A, U, O, the seed grows a root.	(still crouching, put one of your legs out to represent the root)
The seed grows a sprout, the seed grows a sprout E, I, A, U, O, the seed grows a sprout.	(still crouching, raise one of your arms to represent the stalk)
The sprout grows a plant, the sprout grows a plant E, I, A, U, O, the sprout grows a plant.	(stand up)
The plant grows a flower, the plant grows a flower E, I, A, U, O, the plant grows a flower.	(put your hands together above your head)
A bee is on the flower, a bee is on the flower E, I, A, U, O, a bee is on the flower.	(act out the flight and buzzing of a bee)
We all dance together, we all dance together E, I, A, U, O, we all dance together	(dance in a ring holding hands)

3.4 THIS IS HOW A BEAN GROWS
Using enlarged pictures from **Worksheet P-3**, help the children to sequence the stages of a broad bean's growth. Make a copy of **Worksheet P-3** for each child and help them to complete the captions with the data from the growth graph; then tell the children to match the pictures to each sentence: ***Match the drawings to the sentences. What happens first? What happens after ... days?***

4. JACK AND THE BEANSTALK
Time: 1 hour 40 minutes
Materials: Worksheets P-4 and P-5

4.1 STORY
Enlarge the 'story card dominoes' [**Worksheets P-4/P-5**] and use them to tell the story to the class.

GROWING • Plants

- This is a little boy. His name is Jack. He lives with his mother and they are very poor. They live in an old house and they only have one cow.
- One day Jack sells the cow to an old man for five magic beans.
- Jack's mother is very angry. 'Five beans for a cow!' she cries and throws the beans out of the window.
- During the night, a beanstalk grows ... and grows ...
- Jack climbs to the top of the beanstalk and sees a giant castle.
- Jack goes into the castle.
- Jack is in the kitchen. He can hear a thumping and a banging and a stamping and a crashing!
- 'Quick,' says the Giantess. 'Hide inside the oven! My husband is hungry!'
- A Giant comes into the kitchen with a magic hen and three bags of golden eggs.
- The Giant puts the hen on the table and shouts: 'Lay little hen, lay!' and the hen lays some golden eggs.
- The Giant has lunch and goes to sleep. Jack jumps out of the oven and takes the hen and the bag of golden eggs.
- Jack runs out of the castle. The Giant wakes up and runs after him.
- Jack climbs down the beanstalk.
- Jack picks up an axe and chops down the beanstalk. 'Help!' cries the Giant and he falls to the ground. This is the end of the Giant.
- Now Jack and his mother are rich and very happy.

4.2 Tell the story again and ask the children to act it out: *Jack is going to the market with his cow; Jack sells the cow; Jack is climbing to the top of the beanstalk; the Giant is very angry and runs after Jack,* etc. Get the children to think about and compare the growth of the imaginary beanstalk in the fairytale with the real growth recorded during the experiment.

4.3 JACK AND THE BEANSTALK DOMINOES

Give out copies of **Worksheets P-4/P-5** to each child. Explain to the children that they have to cut out the dominoes along the dotted lines and play the game (either at school or at home). The rules are the same as traditional dominoes: shuffle the cards, put the one with START on the table, and deal the others to the players; the player who has got the card with the caption that matches the picture of Jack and the cow, puts the card on the table matching the caption with the picture of the previous card. The aim of the game is to tell the story by matching pictures and captions; the winner is the first player left without cards.

4.4 Make a poster by dividing a piece of paper in half. Draw Jack on one half and the Giant on the other. Ask the children questions in order to get them to describe some features of the two characters. Record their answers on the poster.

- *How tall is the Giant?*
- *Has the Giant got a big nose?*
- *Are the Giant's hands big or small?*
- *What does the Giant eat?*
- *Is the Giant fat?*
- *Is Jack tall or short?*
- *What colour is Jack's hair?*

GROWING • Plants

5. Extension activity: ICT

Time: 30 minutes
Materials: PC

Use a Microsoft Word table or Excel graph to record the data from the experiments that have been carried out (for example, the duration of the growth process of a bean and its increase in height).

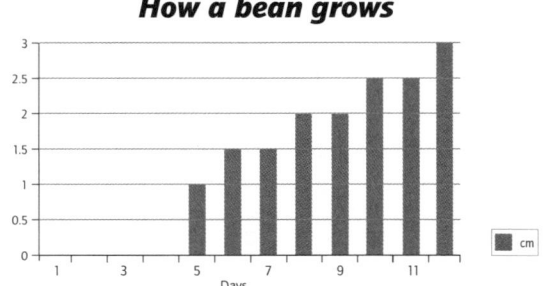

6. Extension activity: ART

Time: 1 hour
Materials: paintings by various artists depicting plants or flowers, paint, coloured paper, glue

6.1 PREPARATION

Get the children to look at and describe paintings by various artists, mentioning their colours, forms, lines, and painting techniques (e.g. *Sunflowers* or *Cypresses* by Vincent Van Gogh; *Big Flower* by Andy Warhol ...).

6.2 Explain to the children that they are going to make pictures of a flower and a plant by using parts of their bodies (hand, arm) and following your instructions.

Flower: dip the palm of one hand in a bowl filled with non-toxic paint; make a hand-print on a blank sheet of paper (this represents the flower); paint the stalk, the leaves, and the roots.

Tree: put your forearm and hand on a blank sheet of paper and draw round them with a pencil; colour the resulting silhouette brown (the arm is the trunk of the tree and the fingers are its branches); complete the picture by sticking leaves and flowers on to it. These should be made by roughly tearing coloured paper (children should tear the paper with their hands rather than cutting it with scissors to give the leaves a more irregular shape).

7. ASSESSMENT

- Progress indicators: **Worksheets P-1/P-2/P-3**
- Informal evaluation: Notes on the children's abilities in recording, organizing and analysing data, speaking and acting (Appendix 1)
- Skills children should have acquired (these can be recorded on the children's ability record (Appendix 2), downloadable from the website):
  - **Content skills:** the child can say which factors influence a plant's growth; can identify the different parts of a plant and their functions; can sequence the stages in the growth of a plant.
  - **Linguistic skills:** the child can talk about the conditions a plant needs in order to survive and grow healthily; can name the parts of a plant; can follow simple instructions; can tell a simple story by putting the scenes in the right order.
- Self evaluation: Appendix 3. The following statements can be written into the 'What I can do' column:
  I can identify the parts of a plant and talk about their function.
  I can observe, record, and describe the growth of a plant.
  I can name the parts of a plant in English and say what a plant needs to survive and grow healthily.
  I can follow simple instructions.
  I can read simple phrases and match them to pictures.

GROWING • Plants

 WORKSHEET

Plant and flower puzzle

Cut out the pictures along the dotted lines. Make a tree and a flower. Glue the labels next to the right part.

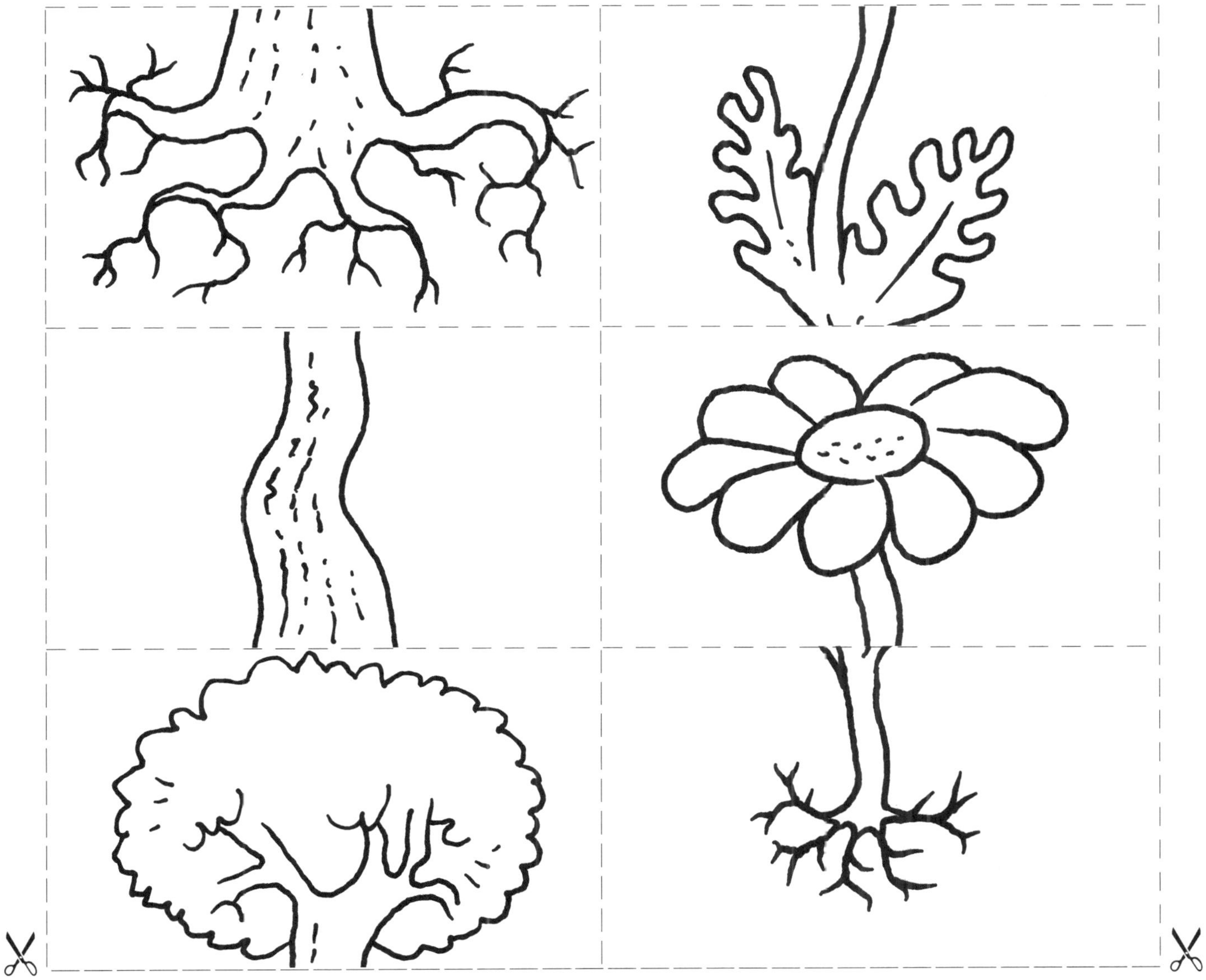

| Flower | Leaf | Trunk | Root |

| Stem | Root | Branch | Petal | Leaf |

GROWING • Plants

P-2 WORKSHEET

_____
anchor the plant into the soil.
They take in water and minerals.

(fold)

_____
attracts bees and insects.
It produces seeds.

Photocopiable © Oxford University Press

GROWING • Plants

P-2.1 WORKSHEET

(fold)

_____ use sunlight to make food for the plant (photosynthesis).

_____ holds the plant and carries water from the roots to the plant.

Photocopiable © Oxford University Press

GROWING • Plants

P-3 WORKSHEET

This is how a bean grows

The bean is in a jar with wet cotton. It takes in water.

↓

After .... days, the bean cracks and a root grows.

↓

After .... days, a shoot comes out and grows.

↓

After .... days, green leaves grow.

Match the drawings to the words.

GROWING • Plants

P-4 WORKSHEET

Jack and the beanstalk dominoes

START

Jack and his mother are very poor. They only have one cow.

Jacks sells the cow for 5 magic beans.

Jack's mother throws the beans out of the window.

During the night a beanstalk grows and grows...

Jack climbs to the top of the beanstalk.

Jack is in the kitchen with a Giantess.

A Giant is coming. Jack hides in the oven.

CUT ALONG THE DOTTED LINES

GROWING • Plants

P-5 WORKSHEET

CUT ALONG THE DOTTED LINES

GROWING • Animals

 CONTENT AREA **GROWING**

 TOPIC	**Animals**
 AIMS	• to group living things into animals and plants • to make comparisons based on differences and similarities • to classify animals according to chosen criteria (body type, movement, nutrition) • to learn about animal life-cycles • to solve simple mathematical problems • to plan a simple multimedia product
 LANGUAGE	• to mime and describe the way animals move • to talk about food animals eat • to describe animals' bodies (skin, feathers, scales, shell) • to talk about animals and their young • to talk about life-cycles (for example, frog/butterfly)
 VOCABULARY AND STRUCTURES	Use words and phrases relating to: the physical characteristics of animals: (*vertebrate, invertebrate, mammal, insect, fish, reptile, bird*); animal bodies: (*spots, stripes, wool, shell, scales, feathers, fur, 2/4/6 legs*); and animal movement: (*swim, jump, fly ...*); nutrition (*carnivore, herbivore, meat, fish, plants*); numbers 1–10; the life-cycle of a frog or a butterfly; affirmative and negative questions and answers (*Can it ...? It can/can't; What is it? Is it ...? It is/isn't; How many ...? It has got/hasn't got; What does ... eat/like? They like/don't like ...*)
 WHAT CHILDREN NEED TO KNOW ALREADY	• how to classify and interpret data • how to record data on double-entry tables • how to use ICT to search for/present information • how to use Word and PowerPoint programmes • how to use basic vocabulary related to living and non-living things
 MATERIALS	• pictures of plants and animals; magazines, encyclopedias, non-fiction books, the Internet • **Worksheets A-1–A-18**
 CROSS-CURRICULAR ACTIVITIES	1. *Plant or animal?* 6. *Life-cycles* 2. *The animal kingdom* 7. *Funny maths* 3. *Animal bodies* 8. *Art* 4. *What do they eat?* 9. *ICT* 5. *Adults and young* 10. *Assessment*

GROWING • Animals

1. PLANT OR ANIMAL?

Time: 1 hour 20 minutes
Materials: pictures of plants and animals, **Worksheets A-1 to A-4**, glue, paper, crayons

1.1 PREPARATION

Stick two pictures, one of a plant and one of an animal, on the board. Point to the picture of the plant and ask the children: *Is it a plant or an animal? Can it run? Can it hear? Can it see? Does it have leaves? Does it have roots? Does it have babies? Can it make noises? Can it move? Can it eat? Does it need water?* (you can use gestures to help the children understand). The children should be able to reply in English since the questions are related to language already dealt with in the previous activities. If they find anything difficult, you can accept answers in mother tongue and reformulate them in English. Children should be able to explain that plants move towards the light, produce seeds, and feed on minerals taken from the soil. They also produce food autonomously by photosynthesis. Then, point to the picture of the animal and ask: *What is it? Can it run? Can it hear? Can it see? Does it have babies? Can it make a noise? Does it have legs? Can it eat? Does it need water?* Help the children with vocabulary to answer the questions, if necessary.

1.2 PLANT OR ANIMAL GAME

Organize the class into teams of three or four children and give each team two pictures, one of a plant and one of an animal. Name one feature of an animal or a plant (for example, *It can run; it has roots; it has babies; it eats plants; it can move towards the light; it grows*); the team that raises the picture corresponding to the description first (either animal or plant, or animal and plant if they share the same feature) gets a point. The team that has collected most points by the end of the game is the winner.

1.3 FUNNY CREATURES

Make at least four enlarged photocopies of **Worksheets A-1/A-2/A-3**. Cut them along the dotted lines and place the parts in three different boxes: box 1 (heads), box 2 (bodies), box 3 (legs). Split the class into groups of three. Explain to each group that they have to pick a card out of each box, stick the different parts on a sheet of paper in the correct order to make a creature, and then colour it: *Pick up a card from the heads box, one from the bodies box and one from the legs box. Now make your funny creature.* Collect all the funny creatures in a class book.

1.4 PLANTS OR ANIMALS?

Tell the children to read the sentences on **Worksheet A-4** and write the group (plants/animals/animals and plants) they refer to in the appropriate space.

GROWING • Animals

2. THE ANIMAL KINGDOM
Time: 2 hours
Materials: Worksheets A-5 and A-6, animal pictures

2.1 PREPARATION
Ask the children to look through magazines for pictures of animals for homework. At school tell the children to stick the pictures on cardboard to make flashcards. Alternatively, enlarge the pictures of **Worksheets A-5 and A-6**.

2.2 SORTING ANIMALS
Divide the children into small groups, give a set of pictures from **Worksheets A-5/A-6** to each group and ask them to sort the animals according to the features they have in common. Then, get each group to compare and discuss the criteria they used for grouping the animals (for example, colour, habitat, food, skin, movement, number of legs).

2.3 ANIMAL GROUPS
a) Tell the children that all animals are sorted into groups. The groups are determined by characteristics that the animals share. This grouping (called classification) makes it easier to find, identify, and study animals. The table below can be used in different ways: as a stimulus for

ALL THE ANIMALS IN THE WORLD CAN BE PUT INTO TWO GROUPS: VERTEBRATES OR INVERTEBRATES

	VERTEBRATES are animals with a backbone			**INVERTEBRATES** are animals with no backbone
FISH	Breathe with gills	Lay eggs in water	Have fins and scales	**INSECTS:** 3 body parts – 6 legs
AMPHIBIANS	Develop gills into lungs	Lay eggs in water	Damp skin	
REPTILES	Breathe with lungs on land	Lay eggs	Dry scaly skin	**ARACHNIDS:** 2 body parts – 8 legs
BIRDS	Breathe with lungs	Lay eggs with hard shell	Have feathers	
MAMMALS	Breathe with lungs	Have babies	Body hair or fur / Feed babies with milk	**MOLLUSCS:** no legs – some have a shell – slimy body

31

scientific discussion in mother tongue or as a model for making a class poster on which children stick pictures of animals in the appropriate column.

b) Draw two ellipses on the board or make a shape with string on the floor; then write **Vertebrates** (animals with a backbone) in one of the ellipses and **Invertebrates** (animals without a backbone) in the other one. Give each child a picture of an animal to be placed in the appropriate group. Ask children to identify, within the two big groups (**Vertebrates and Invertebrates**), the animals that belong to the various sub-categories: ***Fish, Amphibians, Reptiles, Birds, Mammals.***

c) Discuss the characteristics of mammals with the children and ask them to compare a whale/dolphin (mammals) with a shark (fish). The first two, like all mammals, give birth to live young and have to go up to the surface of the sea to breathe; many kinds of shark lay eggs, and they breathe through their gills in water. After the discussion, fill in the table below with the children.

WHALE AND DOLPHIN	What they have in common	SHARK
Have babies	• Live in the sea • No legs • Have fins • Carnivores	Lays eggs

3. ANIMAL BODIES

Time: 1 hour 30 minutes
Materials: Worksheets A-7 to A-11, animal pictures

3.1 PREPARATION
Revise or introduce vocabulary related to animal names and action verbs.

3.2 HOW MANY LEGS?
Give each child a picture of an animal and ask them to count how many legs it has got: ***Look at your animal! How many legs has it got?*** Tell the children they have to form groups according to the number of legs their animals have while you chant the magic spell: ***Salacabula, Mencicabula, bibidibobidibu, get together and what have you got?*** At the end of the chant ask each group: ***How many legs have your animals got? What animals have you got?***

- Give each child a copy of **Worksheet A-7**, ask them to cut out the animal pictures, and glue them into the right group. At the end of the activity, tell the children to stick the Worksheet in their exercise book.
- Make a copy of **Worksheet A-8** for each child and explain that the activity consists of reading the texts and adding other animals in each group.

3.3 HOW ANIMALS MOVE
a) **The magic box.** Tell the children to crouch on the ground to represent a closed box. Give instructions as to which animal is going to come out of the box: ***Open the boxes and ... rabbits jump out!***; children have to mime the hopping of a rabbit. When you say: ***Close the boxes!*** the children have to crouch down on the ground again and wait for new instructions: ***Open the boxes ... fish swim out/birds fly out/cheetahs run out/snails slide out/caterpillars crawl out/children walk out.*** At the beginning of the activity, to help the children understand the instructions, you can show a picture of the animal whose movement they have to mime.

GROWING • Animals

b) **Can a lion swim?** Ask the children questions about animal movement: *Can a lion swim? Can a rabbit jump? Can a panda climb trees? Can an elephant fly? Can a snail run?* If the answer is affirmative (*Yes, it can*) the children mime the movement of the animal; if it is negative (*No, it can't*) they remain still.

c) Tell the children to match each animal with the word describing its movement on **Worksheet A-9** and read the statements at the bottom of the page: *Did you know?*

3.4 BODY COVERINGS

a) Introduce and practise words related to body coverings by using pictures of animals. Ask the children to classify the animals according to the type of skin covering they have (hair, fur, wool/fleece, shell, scales, feathers) and search for more information in books or on websites of scientific interest.

b) Give out copies of **Worksheet A-10**. Explain to the children that they have to cross ✗ the square corresponding to the type of skin covering that each animal has: *Put a cross in the right square.* Discuss the data in the table with the children: *How many animals have a shell? Tell me their names! How many animals have feathers? Tell me their names!*

c) Tell the children to complete the animal pictures in **Worksheet A-11** by adding the pattern on their skin (spots or stripes): *Draw the type of skin pattern each animal has: spots or stripes?*

4. WHAT DO THEY EAT?

Time: 1 hour
Materials: animal pictures, colours, white paper

4.1 CARNIVORE OR HERBIVORE?

a) Brainstorm with the children what they know about the diet some animals have: *What do cows eat? Do rabbits eat fish or carrots? What do lions eat? Cows eat grass. They don't eat meat or fish. Giraffes eat grass and leaves. They don't eat meat or fish.* Children can look for relevant information to check their ideas and find out further information in books or on the Internet. Next discuss the terms **carnivore, herbivore, omnivore**: *What does a carnivore eat? A carnivore eats meat or fish. What does a herbivore eat? A herbivore eats plants. What does an omnivore eat? An omnivore eats plants and meat or fish.*

b) Draw a Venn diagram on the board; show pictures of animals and ask the children to classify them into carnivores, herbivores, and omnivores: *What is it? It's a cow./What do cows eat? They eat grass./Are they carnivores or herbivores? They are herbivores!* Children can then copy the diagram in their exercise books, using words instead of the pictures.

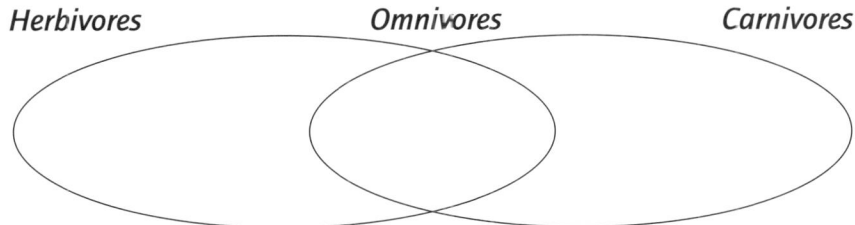

4.2 MY FANTASTIC ANIMAL

Invite the children to invent an animal by using the features they have analysed in the previous activities (for example, *This is a ...; It has got feathers, fur, spots, stripes; It has got ... number of legs, big/small body,* etc.; *It can jump, fly ...; It eats ... . It has babies/lays eggs,* etc.)

GROWING • Animals

5. ADULTS AND YOUNG

Time: 45 minutes
Materials: animal pictures (adults and young), **Worksheet A-12**

a) Using animal pictures, teach or revise the vocabulary for adult animals and their young (horse/foal, cow/calf, hen/chick, sheep/lamb, frog/tadpole, dog/puppy, etc.). Scatter the pictures on a table and ask children to say what kind of relationship these animals have to each other (mother-baby; adult-young).

b) Make enlarged photocopies of **Worksheet A-12**; fold them along the dotted lines and stand them on the table showing the children the side of the picture with the adult animal on it. Then ask the children: ***What animal is this? It's a horse!/What's the name of a young horse? Foal!*** (Turn the picture round to show the picture of the young animal.)

c) Divide the children into groups of three or four. Give each group a different musical instrument (drum, triangle, maracas, cymbals, flute, whistle), which has to be used as a 'buzzer' to indicate that they know the answer. Stand the pictures of **Worksheet A-12** on a table with the figure of the adult animal facing the groups. Say the name of an adult animal; the group that uses their 'buzzer' first gets to name the young animal. If the answer is correct they get a point.

Variation: use the cards with the pictures of the young animals facing the groups. Say the name of a young animal (e.g. calf); the group that claims the answer first by playing their instrument can name the adult, and if the answer is correct they get a point.

6. LIFE-CYCLES

Time: experiment (about 30 days); drama (30 minutes + preparation); other (1 hour)
Materials: tadpoles, glass bowl, water, caterpillars, information books, **Worksheets A-13 to A-16**

6.1 THE LIFE-CYCLE OF A FROG

a) Collect some tadpoles from a pond in the school area or ask the children to look for some with their parents. Place the tadpoles in a big glass bowl in the classroom and ask the children to feed them daily. Children can observe their evolution and record the stages of the tadpoles' transformation into frogs by taking photographs. NB This experiment may be replaced by videos or pictures taken from books or from websites about the frog life-cycle.

b) Ask the children to write or draw the main changes on a table like the one below: ***On what day did you see the back legs? On what day did you see the front legs? On what day did the tail disappear?***

Date: ...... **Day 1**	Date: ...... **Day 9**	Date: ...... **Day**	Date: ...... **Day**	Date: ...... **Day** ......

c) Help the children with the vocabulary to describe the various stages in the metamorphosis of a frog by using photographs or pictures:
  - ***Mother frog lays eggs in the water (frog spawn). The eggs are surrounded by jelly. She can lay as many as 4000 eggs.***
  - ***After 10–15 days hundreds of tadpoles hatch out. Tadpoles have a tail and gills to breathe.***

GROWING • Animals

- *After six weeks, tadpoles grow lungs and back legs.*
- *After nine weeks froglets are part tadpole and part frog. They have longer legs, the tail disappears and short front legs grow.*
- *After 14 weeks froglets are frogs at last.*

6.2 WHO AM I ?

a) Explain to the children that they are going to be involved in a play about the metamorphosis of a frog. Enlarge pictures from **Worksheets A-13/A-14** and use them to tell the story of the little tadpole.

Narrator	In the pond all is calm, all is quiet. Waterlilies and water plants are everywhere. The pondweeds shelter the new frogspawn.
1st pondweed	Be quiet! They are sleeping!
2nd pondweed	They are so small.
3rd pondweed	It's time to wake up. You must go!
Narrator	One by one, the tadpoles swim happily away.
1st tadpole	Quickly! It's time to go.
2nd tadpole	Hurry up! Let's go!
3rd tadpole	Oh, no! I'm afraid.
4th tadpole	Come on! Come with me!
5th tadpole	Bye, bye! See you later!
Narrator	All the tadpoles swim away except one. The others don't wait for it. The tadpole finally breaks out of its egg, but it is all alone.
Tommy	Oh, no! I'm all alone! Mummyyy! Is there anyone there? Please, help me!
Narrator	Tommy is confused and doesn't know what to do or where to go. A little fish is swimming by.
Tommy	Who are you?
Fish	I am a fish!
Tommy	Am I a fish too?
Fish	No, you are not!
Narrator	Tommy sees more little fish, but he knows he is not a fish.
1st fish	I can swim.
2nd fish	I can swim fast and slowly.
3rd fish	I can swim fast, too.
4th fish	Let's go and make new friends.
Narrator	A turtle swims by.
Tommy	Who are you?
Torty	I am a turtle.
Tommy	Am I a turtle too?
Torty	No, you are not!
Narrator	Tommy is all alone and still doesn't know who he is. Tommy notices that something is growing out from his body and that his tail is getting shorter. A few days later, the something grows into hands and legs and his tail is shorter still.
Tommy	Who are you?
Sally	I am a salamander.
Tommy	Am I a salamander too?
Sally	No you are not! Go away!
Tommy	I'm not a fish. I'm not a turtle. I'm not a salamander. Who or what am I?
Narrator	His tail is almost gone. Tommy wants to go on to the land to find out who or what he is. He swims up to the surface. The sun is shining, the sky is blue.
Sun	I'm hot, I'm shining!
1st cloud	Oh, how soft we are!
2nd cloud	You're right! We are very soft and light.
Narrator	Tommy sees a frog on a lily-pad. He is catching an insect to eat.
Tommy	Excuse me, who are you?
Fergy	I am Fergy. I am a frog.
Tommy	Am I a frog too?
Fergy	Yes, you are. We are the same.
Narrator	Tommy is so happy! Finally Tommy knows who he is.
Fergy	Let's go and meet Jumpy. He is on the land now.
Tommy	Oh, yes! I want to make new friends.
Jumpy	Nice to meet you. You won't be alone any more. We are your best friends!
Tommy	Thank you. Let's play and sing together!

Frogs jump
Frogs hop
Frogs leap
And never stop

b) Involve the children in making the scenery (a pond and aquatic plants) and simple costumes (hats or 'sandwich board' costumes) for the various characters of the play (reeds, tadpoles, fish, turtle, salamander, frogs, sun, and clouds).

c) Allocate a role to each child and tell them to act out their roles while you are telling the story. Repeat the acting-out activity more than once so that all the children can have a turn in interpreting a role.

d) Tell the children to cut out the pictures from **Worksheet A-13** and **A-14**; shuffle them and then put them back in the right sequence. Then, ask the children to stick the pictures on a strip of paper folded zigzag fashion, colour them in, and 'read' the story by themselves. Depending on the language level of the children you could ask them to add simple speech bubbles to the pictures *(Who am I? Am I a ...? No, you are not! ...)*.

GROWING • Animals

6.3 MY FROG BOOKLET

Give out copies of **Worksheets A-15** and **A-16**. Tell the children to colour the pictures in and number the stages in the life-cycle of a frog. Then, they can make a booklet by putting the two pages together. If they like they can also add other observations/pictures/photos. If you use a Portfolio, you can get the children to include all the work related to frogs in the Portfolio Dossier together with a description form (Appendix 4).

6.4 THE LIFE-CYCLE OF A BUTTERFLY

Follow the same procedure as for the life-cycle of a frog. You can collect caterpillars and observe stages in their metamorphosis.
(Suggested reading: E. Carle, *The Very Hungry Caterpillar*, London, Penguin, 1994)

 1. *The butterfly lays eggs on leaves.*

 2. *The egg hatches into a caterpillar.*

 3. *The caterpillar eats leaves and grows until it is ready to turn into a pupa/chrysalis.*

 4. *The body of a butterfly develops inside the pupa.*

 5. *The pupa cracks and a butterfly flies out.*

7. Extension activity: FUNNY MATHS

Time: 1 hour
Materials: Worksheets A-17 and A-18

7.1 TEN LITTLE TADPOLES SONG (to the tune of Ten green bottles)

Prepare, with the class, a boardgame with a green area representing a lawn and with a blue pond in the middle. Then make ten cards showing pictures of tadpoles and ten showing pictures of frogs. Place the tadpoles in the pond and the frogs on the table, out of the game. Sing the song with the children: during each verse, ask a child to take one tadpole out of the pond and place one frog on the grass, and ask: *How many tadpoles are left in the pond? How many frogs are there on the grass now?*

Ten little tadpoles
jumping in a pond
Ten little tadpoles
jumping in a pond

But if one little tadpole
should turn into a frog
there'll be nine little tadpoles
jumping in a pond.

GROWING • Animals

7.2 THREE JUMPS TO TEN
Ask the children to find different ways of making the number 10 using three numbers. Give out copies of **Worksheet A-17** and tell the children to mark, for each numbered line, three jumps that a frog has to make to get to number 10: ***How can the frog get to 10 in three jumps?***

7.3 HOW MANY?
Make copies of **Worksheet A-18**. Read the problems together with the children so that they understand what is being asked. Explain to the children that they have to follow the instructions and work out the solutions. According to the children's age, you can adapt them to the children's level in maths, add some more games, or ask them to make some more games of their own for their classmates to solve.

8. Extension activity: ART
Time: 1 hour
Materials: cardboard tubes, drawing paper, animal templates, felt-tip pens, **Worksheet A-19**

8.1 PREPARATION
Ask the children to collect cardboard tubes at home. If necessary, pre-teach vocabulary related to the parts of the body of different animals by using pictures or gestures (tail, whiskers, claws, paws, wings, beak, fins, gills).

8.2 CARDBOARD TUBE ANIMALS
This craft activity consists of making frogs using cardboard tubes. Children have to colour the frog body parts on **Worksheet A-19**; cover a cardboard tube in green paper; cut out the body parts and stick them on the tube in order to make a frog. You can ask the children to make other animals by drawing, colouring, and cutting out body parts of other animals and sticking them on cardboard tubes as for the frog. The animals can be used as puppets in simple dialogues, in stories (e.g. Noah's ark), and in role-plays.

Other language and art activities can be inspired by the use of the following works of art: *The Farm* by David Twining and *Noah's Ark* by Edward Hicks.

9. Extension activity: ICT
Time: it depends on how complex you make each activity
Materials: animal Clipart or pictures, PC, PowerPoint

Choose the activity that best suits your children's computing skills.
a) **Animal identity cards.** Get the children to use a word-processing programme to make animal identity cards. The ID cards can be printed out, put in a folder, and used to play guessing games: for example, ***Who am I?*** (a child chooses an ID card and reads out some of the characteristics of the animal to another child, who has to guess what animal it is, using as few clues as possible: ***It is a mammal; it is a herbivore, it has got four legs; it has got hair; it is grey with white stripes***, etc.).

GROWING • Animals

Animal group:	mammal
Food:	grass – herbivore
Colour:	black and white stripes
Body covering:	hair
Number of legs:	4
It can:	walk, run
It can't:	climb, fly, swim

Animal group:	
Food:	
Colour:	
Body covering:	
Number of legs:	
It can:	
It can't:	

b) **Who am I?** Create a simple game with children by using Word and hyperlinks.
Procedure:
- Create a folder in 'My Documents' entitled *Who am I?*
- Open a blank Word document and put the picture and the name of an animal in it.
- Save the file with the name of the animal, in the folder *Who am I?*
- Make and save other files in the same folder, one file for each animal that children want to use in the game.
- Open another Word document and create a table which has the same number of cells as the number of animal files previously saved in the *Who am I?* folder.
- Put the ID card of an animal in each cell but do not insert its name or its picture.
- Select a cell from the table containing the description of the animal, click Insert hyperlink – document (search for the folder *Who am I?* and for the document containing the picture of the animal that corresponds to the description).
- Click OK.
- Follow the same procedure to create a hyperlink between the ID cards of the other different animals and their pictures.
- Save the page containing the table in the folder *Who am I?* and give it the title *First page*.

In order to see the game the children have to open the folder *Who am I?* then open the 'First page' and read every ID card on it. When they have guessed what animal it is they click on the description to see if they are right. This opens the page containing the animal's picture. In order to go back they either click the 'Back' arrow on the Toolbar or click 'Close'. Example of a table:

Animal group:	mammal	**Animal group:**	**Animal group:**
Food:	grass – herbivore	**Food:**	**Food:**
Colour:	black and white stripes	**Colour:**	**Colour:**
Body covering:	hair	**Body covering:**	**Body covering:**
Number of legs:	4	**Number of legs:**	**Number of legs:**
It can:	walk, run	**It can:**	**It can:**
It can't:	climb, fly, swim	**It can't:**	**It can't:**

GROWING • Animals

c) Help the children to plan a PowerPoint presentation of the work they have done using photographs of animals and activities they have completed. Some possible themes are: animal groups; how animals move; carnivore or herbivore?; adults and young; life-cycles. If you use a Portfolio, you can ask the children to include a printout of the presentation in the Portfolio Dossier together with a description form (Appendix 4).

10. ASSESSMENT

- Progress indicators: **Worksheets A-4/A-5/A-7/A-8/A-16/A-17/A-18**
- Informal evaluation: Notes on children's performance in the song and drama activities (Appendix 1)
- Skills children should have acquired (these can be recorded on the children's ability record (Appendix 2) downloadable from the website):
  - **Content skills:** the child can group animals on the basis of the characteristics they share (the group they belong to, physical characteristics, diet); can identify changes in the life of an animal; can solve simple mathematical games; can use a Venn diagram and a double-entry table; can work with other children to design a simple multimedia project.
  - **Language skills:** the child can understand and follow simple instructions in English; can mime and describe the movement of some animals; can say what some animals eat; can describe the bodies of some animals; can say the names of some animals and their offspring; can describe the life-cycle of an animal (frog or butterfly).
- Self evaluation: Appendix 3. The following statements can be written into the 'What I can do' column:
  I can classify animals according to characteristics they have in common.
  I can identify similarities and differences between animals.
  I can describe some animals in English.
  I can say in English what animals eat.
  I can say the names of some animals and their young in English.
  I can put pictures in order to show the growth process of a frog or butterfly.
  I can solve simple mathematical problems.
  I can use a Venn diagram and a double-entry table.

GROWING • Animals

A-1 WORKSHEET

A-2 WORKSHEET

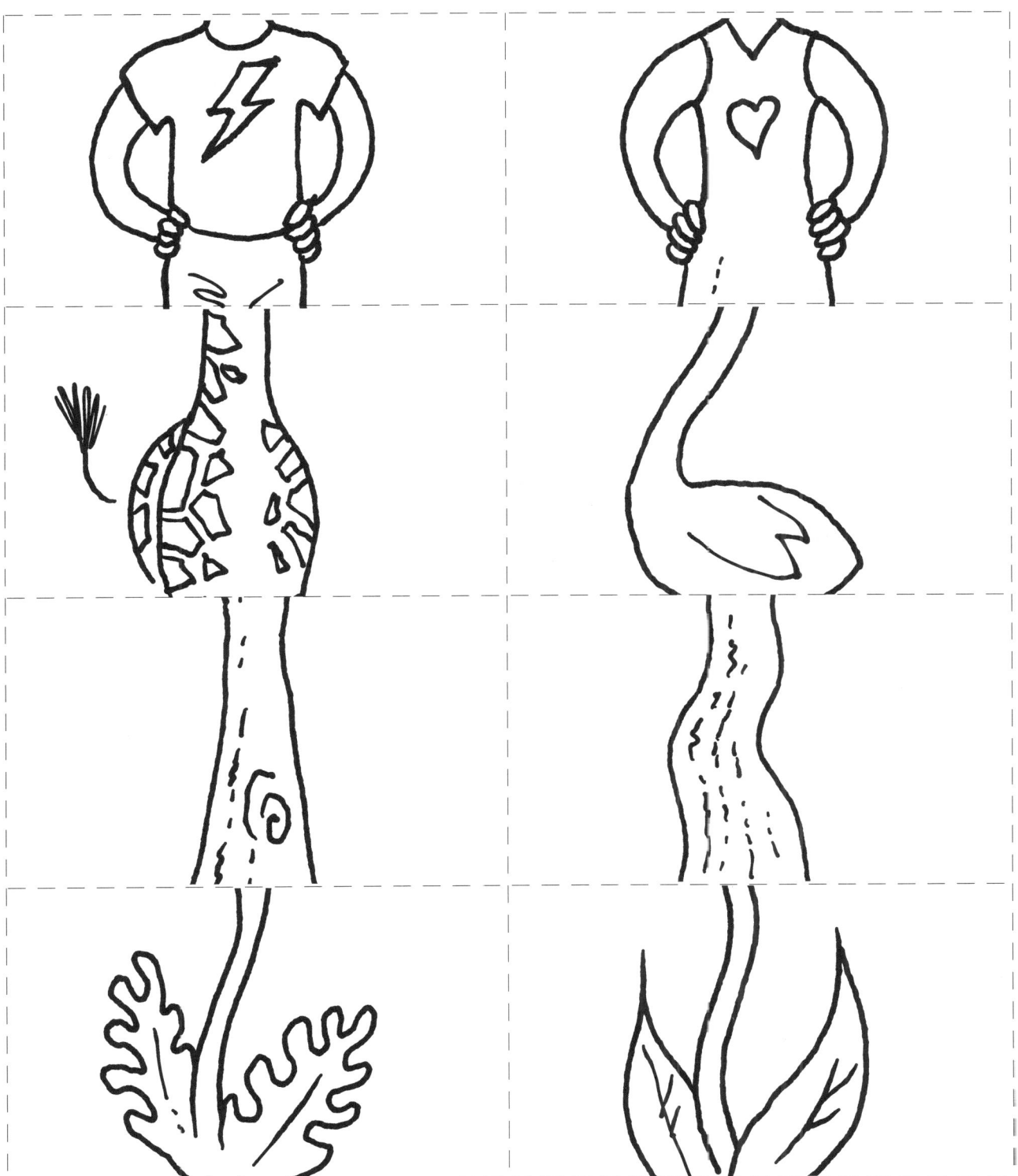

GROWING · Animals

A-3 WORKSHEET

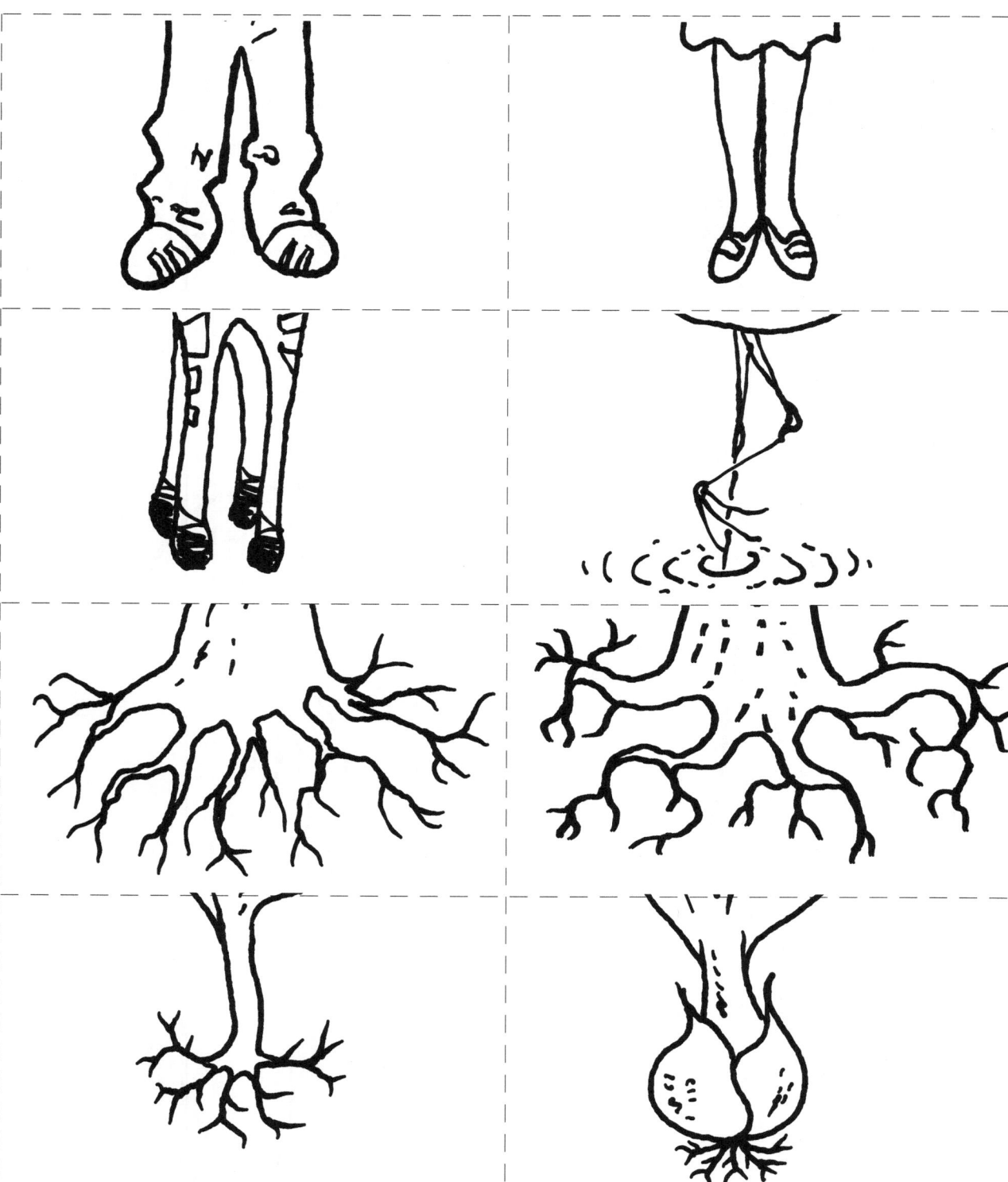

GROWING • Animals

 WORKSHEET

Plants or animals?

Box 1:
- can make their own food
- can produce seeds
- can't make a noise
- can move towards the light
- have leaves
- can't hear

Box 2:
- grow
- need food
- need water
- can move
- can reproduce

Box 3:
- can eat
- can run
- have babies or lay eggs
- can hear
- can make a noise
- have legs

Read and label each group.

| PLANTS | PLANTS and ANIMALS | ANIMALS |

GROWING • Animals

A-5 WORKSHEET

GROWING • Animals

A-6 WORKSHEET

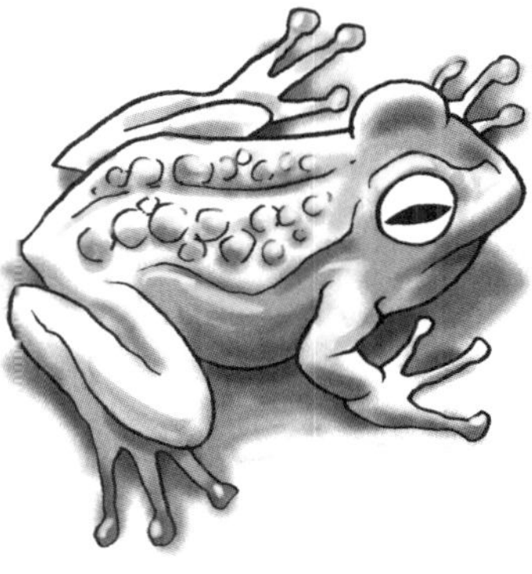

GROWING • Animals

A-7 WORKSHEET

Animal groups

Cut out the pictures and glue them into the right group.

mammals	insects

fish	
	reptiles
birds	

Cat	Eagle
Man	Crocodile	Butterfly	Parrot	Dolphin	Bee
Ladybird	Sole	Snake	Shark	Lizard	Goldfish

GROWING • Animals

A-8 WORKSHEET

How many legs?

Read and draw some animals in each group.

All these animals have **NO** LEGS	All these animals have **TWO** LEGS

All these animals have **FOUR** LEGS	All these animals have **SIX** LEGS

All these animals have **MORE THAN SIX** LEGS

 **GROWING** • Animals

A-9 WORKSHEET

How animals move

Match each animal to the word describing how it moves.

  run

 fly

  crawl

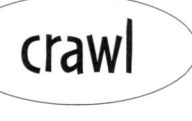 jump

  swim

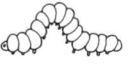  slide

DID YOU KNOW?

 The kangaroo is a big jumper.
Some jumps are as long as 12 metres. (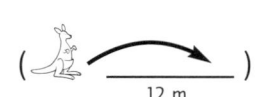)
12 m

 The cheetah is the fastest of all animals.
It can run as fast as a car. ( 96 km per hour)

The snail is the slowest of all animals.
It can move just a few metres in 1 hour. ()
9.00 am ⟶ 10.00 am

48

A-10 WORKSHEET

Body coverings

Animal	Hair/fur	Wool	Shell	Scales	Feathers
Dog					
Parrot					
Fish					
Bear					
Snail					
Fox					
Crocodile					
Crab					
Snake					
Cat					
Hen					
Squirrel					
Lizard					
Tortoise					
Flamingo					
Lion					
Duck					
Sheep					

Put a cross (x) in the right square.

GROWING • Animals

A-11 WORKSHEET

Spots or stripes?

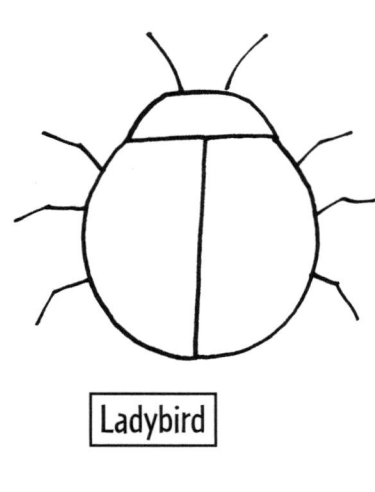
Ladybird

Zebra

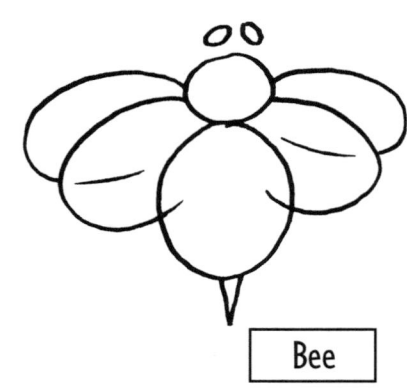
Bee

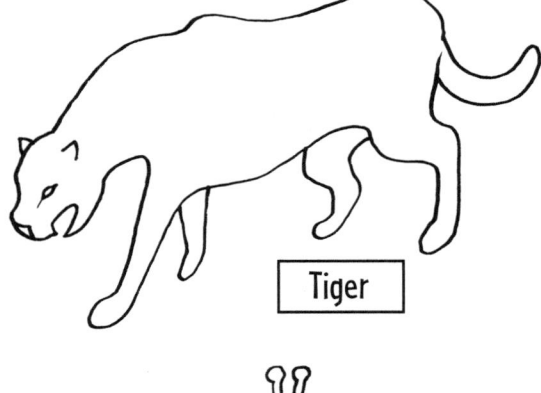
Tiger

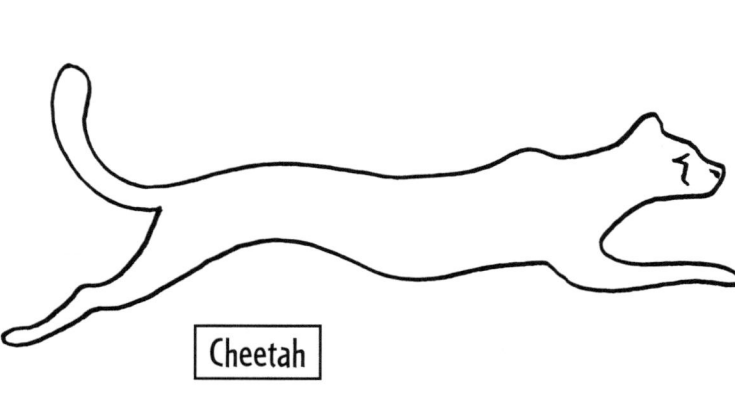
Cheetah

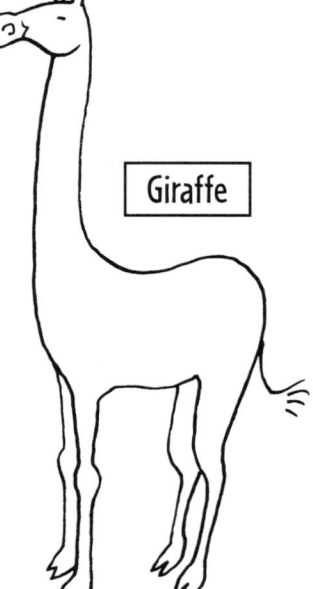
Giraffe

Draw the type of skin each animal has.

50

GROWING • Animals

A-12 WORKSHEET

Adults and young

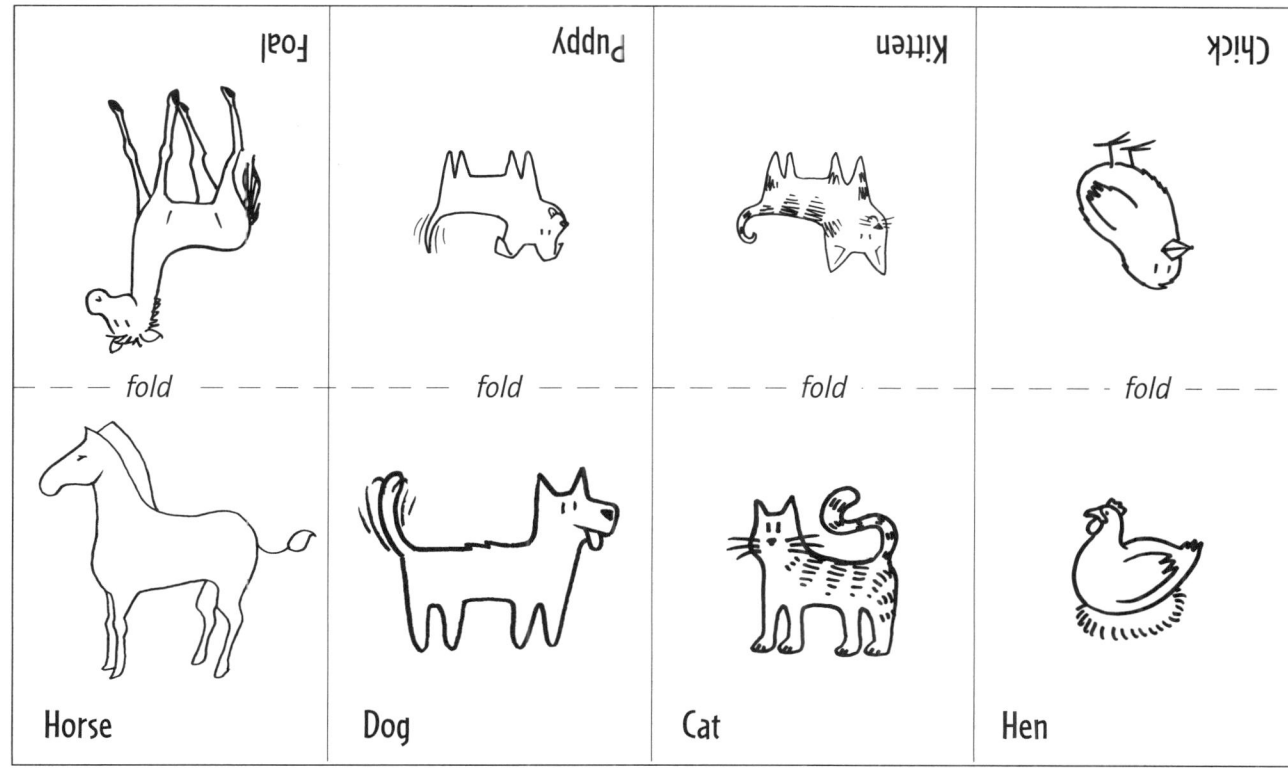

Foal	Puppy	Kitten	Chick
fold	*fold*	*fold*	*fold*
Horse	Dog	Cat	Hen

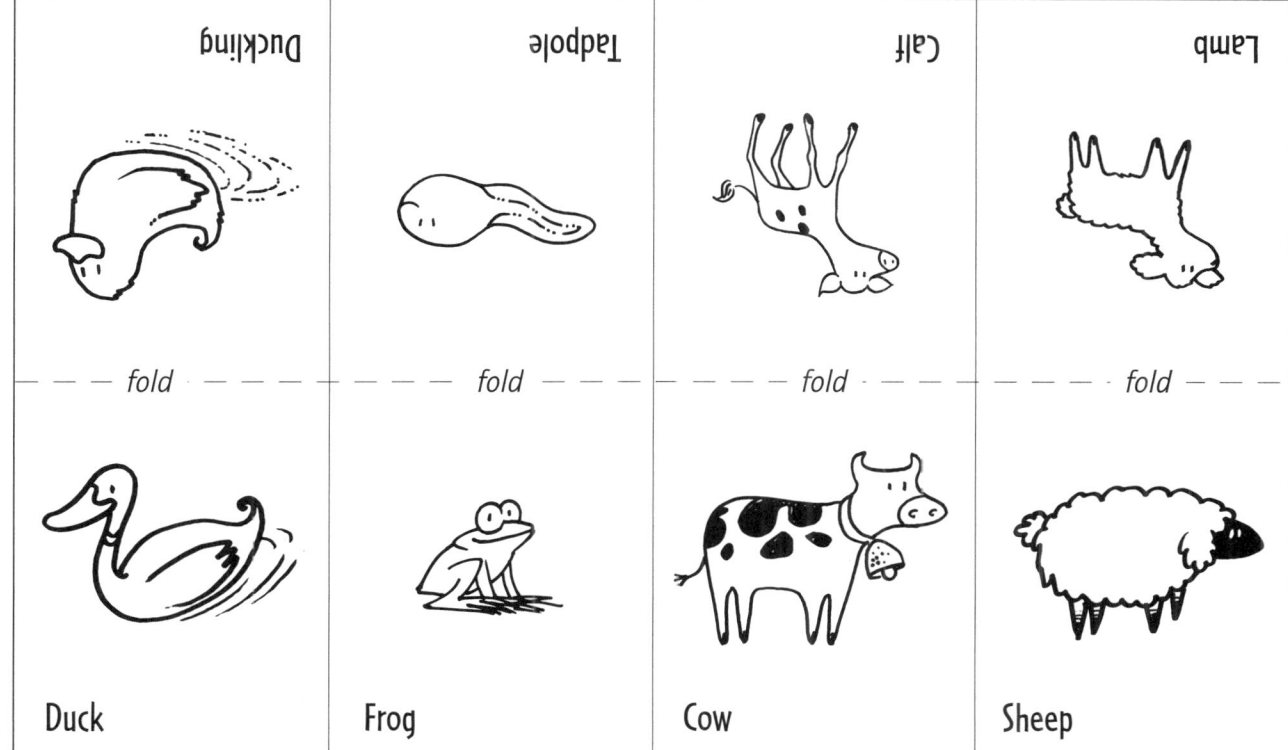

Duckling	Tadpole	Calf	Lamb
fold	*fold*	*fold*	*fold*
Duck	Frog	Cow	Sheep

A-13 WORKSHEET

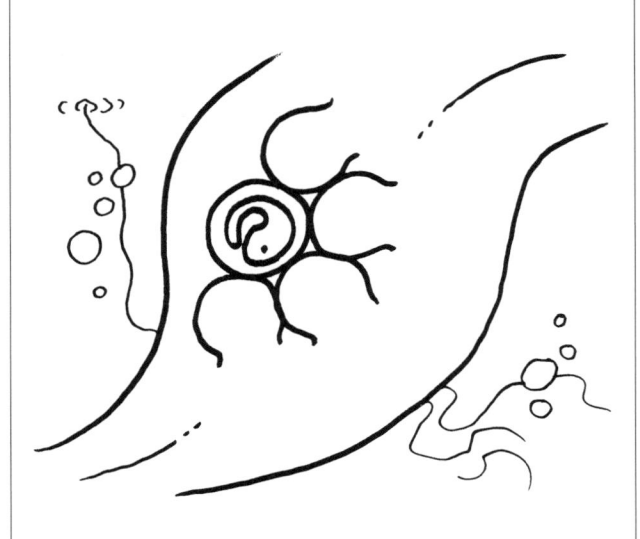

A-14 WORKSHEET

GROWING • Animals

GROWING • Animals

A-15 WORKSHEET

My FROG BOOKLET

by _____

GROWING • Animals

Life-cycle of a FROG

Number the pictures in the right order.

GROWING • Animals

A-17 WORKSHEET

Three jumps to ten

How can you get to 10 in three jumps?

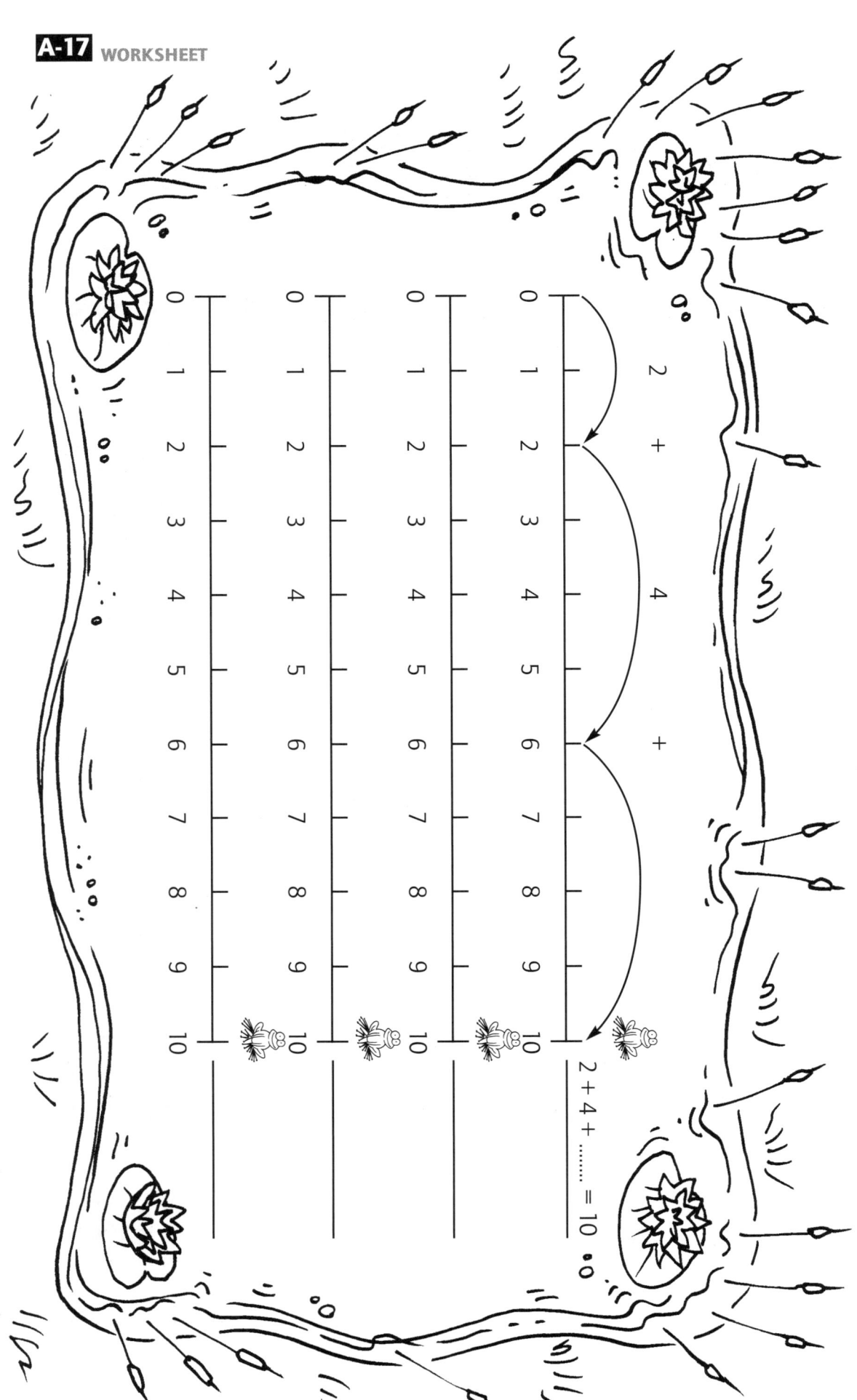

2 + 4 + ... = 10

GROWING • Animals

A-18 WORKSHEET

Funny maths

Draw 4 butterflies on a blue flower.
Draw 3 butterflies on a red flower.
How many butterflies in all? ....

A frog has 4 toes on a foot.
A frog has 4 feet.
There are 2 frogs.
How many feet in all? How many toes in all?
....

A frog family is sitting on a log in the pond.
It's very hot. Mummy frog and daddy frog jump into the pond.
How many frogs are there in the pond, now? ......
How many frogs on the log, now? ....

Draw 8 butterflies over the pond.
A frog is very hungry.
The frog likes butterflies very much (a lot).
The frog eats 5 butterflies.
How many butterflies are left? ....

GROWING • Animals

A-19 WORKSHEET

Frog

1. Cover the tube with green paper.
2. Colour the frog.
3. Cut out the frog body pieces and glue them on to the tube.

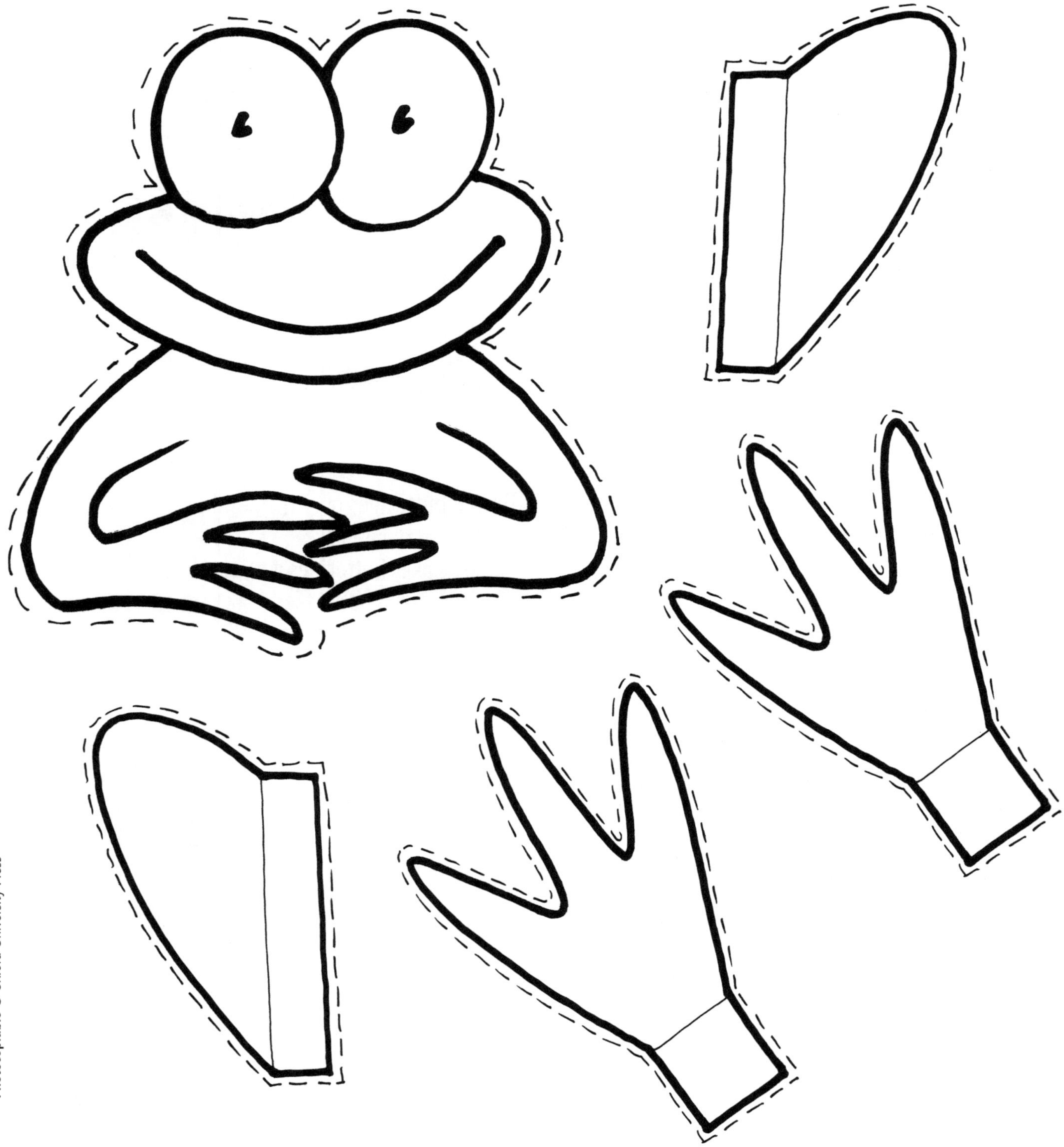

GROWING • Humans

CONTENT AREA: GROWING

	TOPIC	Humans
	AIMS	• to know how we grow from birth • to know there are different stages in the human life-cycle and the changes that happen between stages • to develop sequencing skills • to describe changes in human growth • to measure with non-conventional/conventional tools
	LANGUAGE	• to compare and express opinions • to identify and describe toys, clothes, food • to ask and answer about birthdays • to talk about the main stages in human life • to use can/can't to speak about abilities • to read and interpret data • to sequence works of art representing stages in human life
	VOCABULARY AND STRUCTURES	Use words and phrases relating to: human growth: (*baby, toddler, infant, teenager, adult, old*); toys; clothes; hand/foot size; birthdays; months of the year; measurements (*kilos, height, metres, centimetres*); abilities (*a baby can/can't crawl, laugh, cry, read, ride a bike, eat with a spoon, walk ...*); Questions and answers (*What's different? Who is ...? I'm growing; A baby needs ...; This is ...*)
	WHAT CHILDREN NEED TO KNOW ALREADY	• how to sort and classify according to chosen criteria • the names of some parts of the human body in English • some adjectives (*big, small, old, young, tall, short*) • to be able to place events on a timeline • to use ICT to present information
	MATERIALS	• Photos of children as babies; a baby layette (toys, clothes, food, dishes) • **Worksheets H-1–H-4**
	CROSS-CURRICULAR ACTIVITIES	1. *Who's who* 2. *What babies need* 3. *Watch me grow from head to toes* 4. *My personal history* 5. Art 6. ICT 7. Assessment

GROWING • Humans

1. WHO'S WHO
Time: 45 minutes
Materials: photos of some stages of the teacher's growth, photos of the children both recent and as babies

1.1 PREPARATION: MY TEACHER'S HISTORY
Show the children some photos of some stages of your growth (e.g. when you were a little baby, a toddler, a schoolchild, a young woman/man, an adult woman/man); ask them to guess who is the person depicted in the photos and to sequence the photos by sticking them on a strip of paper.

1.2 THIS IS ME AS A BABY
a) Discuss with the children how they have changed since they were babies. Help them with vocabulary and structures to describe changes, similarities, and differences.

b) Tell the children to bring in two photos: one recent and one of them as babies. Stick all the recent photos on a big poster leaving a space next to them to stick the photos as babies and write down children's comments. Shuffle the baby photos, ask each child to pick one and match it to the 'now' photo of the classmate they think it portrays. Help the children with vocabulary to describe how the classmate has changed since s/he was a baby. Write down their observations and opinions on the poster.

This is me as a baby	This is me now	What's different?
PHOTO Name:	PHOTO	HAIR, SIZE, CLOTHES

c) Ask the children to make individual fact-files about changes in their habits over time using pictures or drawings: *These are my toys as a baby/my toys now; this is my food as a baby/my food now; these are my clothes as a baby/my clothes now; other things as a baby/other things now.*

2. WHAT BABIES NEED
Time: 1 hour
Materials: baby clothes and objects

2.1 PREPARATION
Ask parents to help collect clothes and objects the children used when they were babies. Sit the children in a circle so that they can all look at the objects and help them with the vocabulary to describe and classify the objects (toys, clothes, food, other things). Get the children to speak about a baby's life and habits. It could be very useful to invite a mother to school with her small baby to talk about babies' needs.

GROWING • Humans

2.2 Ask the children to think about what activities babies can or can't do and when they need the help of adults. Babies need a lot of special care and affection. ***Babies tell us what they need by crying (or making faces, babbling, etc.). Babies suck milk at the breast or at a bottle. Babies need to have nappies. Babies need to play and be with other people.***

2.3 Collect all the information in a table using pictures, photos, or children's drawings related to when they were babies and now. (The headings can be: ***different food, different toys, bigger shoes, longer trousers,*** etc.)

I'M GROWING: WHAT'S DIFFERENT?

Food		Clothes		Toys		Other things	
As a baby	Now	As a baby	Now	As a baby	Now	As a baby	Now
🍼	🍽️	👕	👟	🪀	🎮		

3. WATCH ME GROW FROM HEAD TO TOES

Time: 2 hours
Materials: Worksheets H-1 and H-2, paper strips, metre sticks

3.1 PREPARATION

Tell the children to interview their mothers, in mother tongue, to find out how much the children weighed and how long they were at birth, when they had their first tooth, when they said their first word, when they started walking, eating, and going to the toilet by themselves: ***Ask your mummy to remember when you had your first tooth ... when you said your first word and what it was, when you started walking by yourself ... when you started eating with a spoon ... when you started going to the toilet by yourself. Colour the timeline according to the information you have.*** Children have to record the information, in English or mother tongue, and bring it to school.

3.2 I'M GROWING

In class, give out a copy of **Worksheet H-1** and show the children where to write the information they collected and how to fill in the timeline. Here is an example:

MY FIRST...

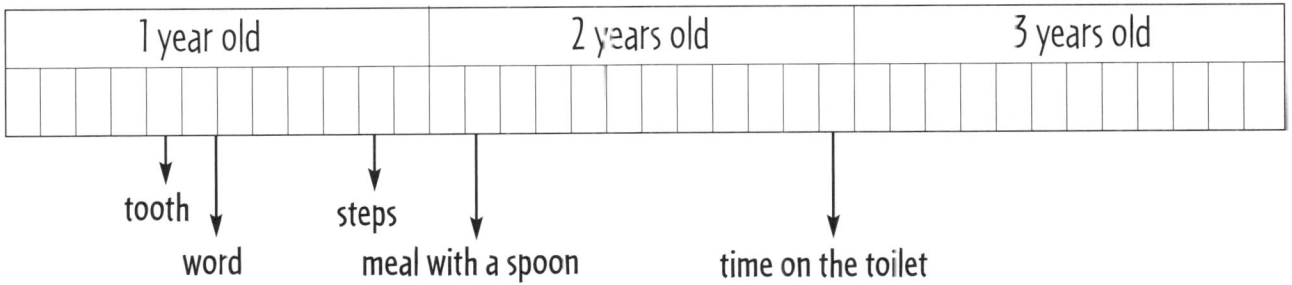

GROWING • Humans

3.3 HEIGHT AND WEIGHT

a) Ask the children to read **Worksheet H-1** through and compare data. Explain that they have to record their body length as babies on a strip of paper by cutting the strip to the right length and then fixing it to the wall with string: **When I was a baby I was ... cm long.**

b) Next, measure how tall each child is now and ask the children to cut out another strip of paper as long as their current height. They should stick this next to the previous one (showing their length as babies). Now get each child to calculate the difference in height between the two strips and fill in **Worksheet H-2**: *I've grown ... centimetres!* (You can follow a similar procedure to compare weight as babies and now.)

c) Repeat the measurement activity more than once during the school year and over the following years so that children can register their personal growth and make simple comparisons: *I was shorter, I've grown 10 cm!*

d) Another interesting measurement activity consists of outlining a hand and a foot and observing how they become bigger over time.

3.4 WHAT CAN THEY DO?

Explain to the children that they have to draw a table (2 x 3 squares) and write, in each space, the following headings: A baby can ...; A baby can't ...; A toddler can ...; A toddler can't ...; A schoolchild can ...; A schoolchild can't ... (see model below). Then they have to draw the actions a baby, a toddler, and a schoolchild can or can't do: *a baby can cry, laugh, crawl, suck milk from a bottle, wear a nappy. A toddler can cry, laugh, walk, eat with a spoon, take himself to the toilet, talk. A schoolchild can cry, laugh, ride a bike, eat with a knife and fork, read, write.*

A baby can ...	A baby can't ...
A toddler can ...	A toddler can't ...
A schoolchild can ...	A schoolchild can't ...

4. MY PERSONAL HISTORY

Time: 20 minutes
Materials: all materials produced so far

Explain to the children that they have to collect and staple together all the materials they have produced (worksheets, drawings, photos, timelines, etc.) in a book called: **My Personal History**. They can add a cover to the book on which they can draw themselves inside their mother's womb. If you use a Portfolio, you can ask the children to include the book in the Portfolio Dossier together with a description form (Appendix 4).

5. Extension activity: ART

Time: 30 minutes
Materials: Worksheet H-3, works of art depicting people of different ages, drawing paper, crayons

GROWING • Humans

5.1 PREPARATION

Look for the works of art from **Worksheet H-3** in art books or on the Internet. You can use other pieces of art if you prefer, such as: *The cradle* by B. Morisot; *Playing child* by T. Eakins; *Jean* by A. Renoir; *Self-portrait* by Louise Elisabeth Vigée-Lebrun; *Portrait of Dirck Tybis* by H. Holbens; *Portrait of Jan Rijcksen* by R. Rembrandt.

Depending on the language level of the class and the children's co-operative skills, you can choose either the first or the second option below.

a) Option 1. Give out copies of **Worksheet H-3** and explain to the children that they have to cut the pictures out and stick them on a strip of paper from the youngest to the oldest person. Then ask questions to promote speaking: **Look at this boy! How old do you think he is? Where is he? What is he doing? What is he wearing?** etc.

Baby	Toddler	Schoolchild	Young woman	Adult man	Old man

b) Option 2. (This could also be done in addition to option 1.) Split the class into groups of three or four. Give a copy of **Worksheet H-3** to each group. Explain to the children that they have to cut the pictures out; think of a scene appropriate for the pictures; draw and colour the scene on a sheet of drawing paper, and stick the pictures on it.

6. Extension activity: ICT

Time: 30 minutes
Materials: PC, drawings, photos, work produced during the previous activities

a) **When is your birthday?**
Ask the children to line up according to their birthday month, starting from January. **Is there a connection between the month of birth and height? Are the oldest of the class the tallest?** Tell the children to make a graph of the class's heights and birthdays using Excel.

b) This activity can be a good starting point to discuss personal differences and to introduce the next topic about the human body.

c) Depending on the level of computer literacy of the children, you could ask them to organize all the materials produced during the project on human growth in hypertext.
The homepage could look like this:

Each area could have links to other pages where children have stored examples of their work. Here are some ideas of materials that could be included in the hypertext:

This is our class (list of the children's names with links on each name to open single pages with two photos of the child: This is Jessica as a baby. This is Jessica now!);

It all started in our mum's womb (children's drawings about how they imagine themselves inside their mum's womb; or ultrasound scan images ...);

Our birth (birth certificates; birthdays bar chart; interviews with mums about how they felt when they had the baby ...);

We are growing (children's time lines related to their first tooth, word, steps; pictures of their baby objects; weight and height graphs);

At pre-school (photos of experiences; drawings gallery; measurements ...);

At primary school (first day of school photos and impressions; school activities and experiences ...)

7. ASSESSMENT

- Progress indicators: **Worksheets H-1–H-4**
- Informal evaluation: Notes on children's comprehension, speech, and interaction during the activities.
- Skills children should have acquired (these can be recorded on the children's ability record (Appendix 2), downloadable from the website):
  - **Content skills:** the child can describe changes in human growth; can sequence events on a timeline; can measure with non-conventional/conventional tools; can collect and interpret data and present it on a graph.
  - **Language skills:** the child can name the main stages of the human life-cycle; can make simple comparisons; can describe objects; can speak about human abilities at different stages of growth; can ask about and say the date of their birthday.
  - **What do all living things need?** At the end of all the activities related to growing (animals, plants, humans) you can use **Worksheet H-4** to test children's knowledge. Tell the children that they have to read the table and fill it in by putting a cross in the squares that show what animals/plants/humans need to live.
- Self evaluation: Appendix 3. The following statements can be written into the 'What I can do' column:

  I can describe changes in my growth (toys used, clothes, foods eaten as well as physical changes).
  I can put pictures of people in order from youngest to oldest.
  I can measure and present data in a graph or table.
  I can place events on a timeline.
  I can name stages of human growth in English and say what a baby, a 3-year-old and a 6-year-old can and can't do.
  I can describe a person using simple adjectives.
  I can say when my birthday is in English.

GROWING • Humans

H-1 WORKSHEET

I'm growing ...

This is me as a baby

(Stick in your photo as a baby)

My first...

1 YEAR OLD	2 YEARS OLD	3 YEARS OLD
months	months	months

tooth: ....

word: ....

steps: ....

time on the toilet: ....

meal with a spoon: ....

 I was .... cm long    I weighed .... kilos

GROWING • Humans

H-2 WORKSHEET

I'm growing ...

This is me now

(Stick a picture of you now here)

Date: _____   I'm _____ years old

I'm _____ cm high    I weigh _____ kilos

LOOK! I'VE GROWN _____ cm and _____ kilos!

GROWING • Humans

H-3 WORKSHEET

How old are they?

Look at the pictures. How old do you think the people are?
Cut out the pictures. Glue the pictures on a string of paper from the youngest to the oldest.

Blanche Pontillon as a baby,
B. Morisot, 1872

Portrait of Baldassare Castiglione,
Raffaello Sanzio, 1514

Altarpiece of the Church Fathers,
Michael Pacher, 1483

Louise de Broglie, Contesse d'Haussonville, Jean-Auguste-Dominique Ingres, 1845

Portrait of a Venetian senator, Jacopo Tintoretto, 1580

Bellelli Family, Edgar Degas, 1858

GROWING • Humans

H-4 WORKSHEET

What do all living things need?

	ANIMALS	PLANTS	HUMANS
Air			
Sunlight			
Water			
Soil			
Food			
Home			
Friends			
Sleep			
Books			
Exercise			
Transport			

Put a cross (✗) in the right square.

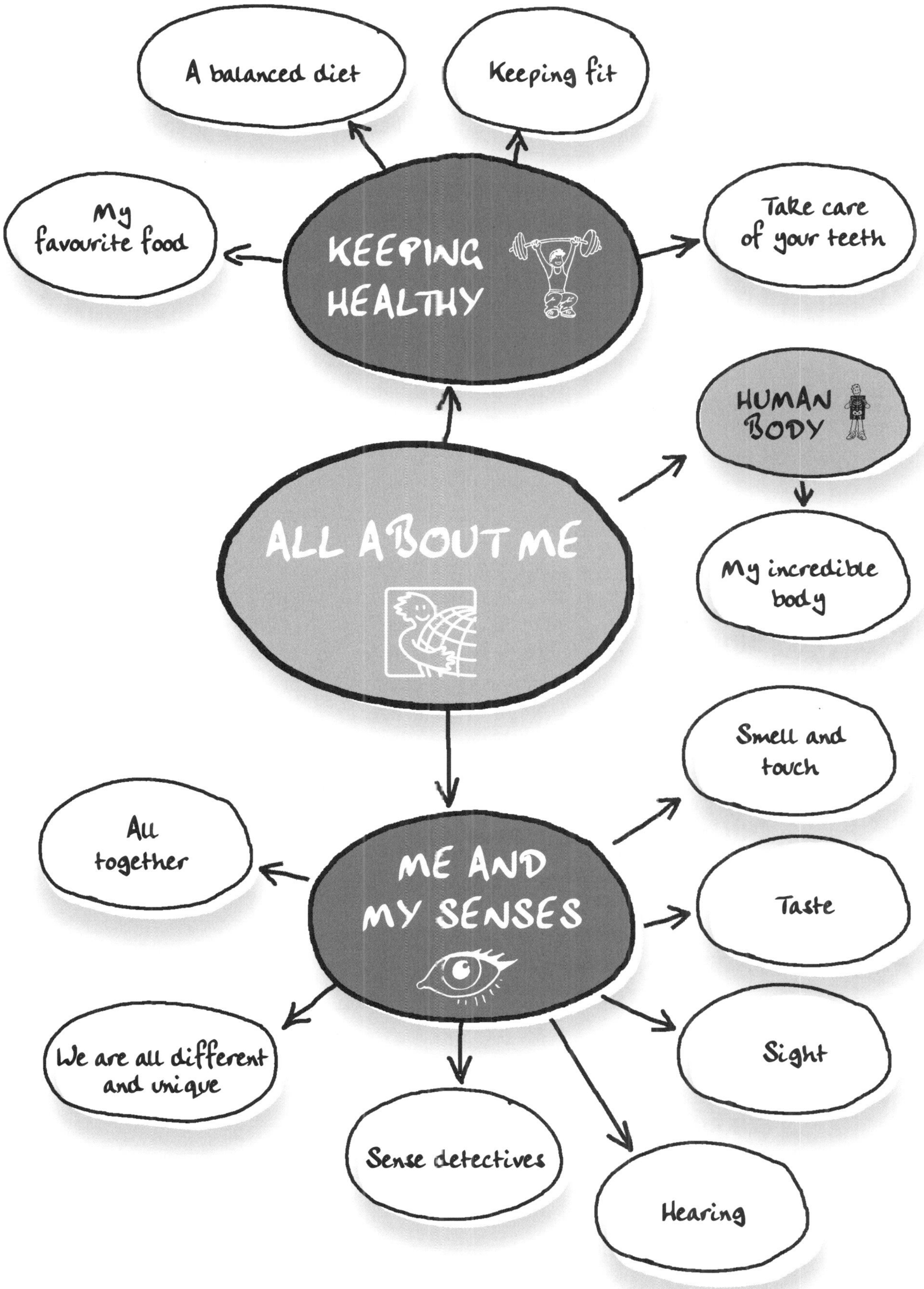

ALL ABOUT ME

- **KEEPING HEALTHY**
  - A balanced diet
  - Keeping fit
  - My favourite food
  - Take care of your teeth

- **ALL ABOUT ME**

- **HUMAN BODY**
  - My incredible body

- **ME AND MY SENSES**
  - Smell and touch
  - Taste
  - Sight
  - Hearing
  - Sense detectives
  - We are all different and unique
  - All together

	**CONTENT AREA**	# ALL ABOUT ME
	TOPIC	Keeping healthy
	**AIMS**	• to know that a balanced diet, good sleep, and regular physical exercise help to keep our bodies healthy • to be aware of the importance of personal hygiene and taking care of our bodies • to know the food groups and their functions • to know how to make a balanced meal
	**LANGUAGE**	• to elicit information about other people's tastes and habits and talk about our own tastes and habits • to identify and name foods, drinks, and main meals in English • to match captions with pictures or situations • to talk about likes and dislikes relating to food • to talk about the main rules for correct hygiene
	**VOCABULARY AND STRUCTURES**	Use words and phrases relating to: meals (*breakfast, snack, lunch, dinner*); food (*cereals, fruit, vegetables, milk, meat, raw, cooked*); nutrients (*carbohydrates, proteins, minerals, fibre, vitamins, fats*); adverbs of frequency (*never, sometimes, often, always*); dental care (*incisor, canine, molar, dentist, toothpaste, toothbrush*); affirmative and negative questions and answers (*What do you have for …? I usually have …; How often do you …? How do …? I like/I don't like …*).
	**WHAT CHILDREN NEED TO KNOW ALREADY**	• the names of some foods and parts of the body • how to use: *I like/I don't like* • the names of the meals • how to record data on a pie chart
	**MATERIALS**	• model of a food pyramid, fruit, and vegetables • **Worksheets K-1–K-17**
	**CROSS-CURRICULAR ACTIVITIES**	1. *My favourite food* 2. *A balanced diet* 3. *Keeping fit* 4. *Take care of your teeth* 5. ICT 6. Art 7. Assessment

ALL ABOUT ME • Keeping healthy

1. MY FAVOURITE FOOD

Time: 1 hour
Materials: board, chalk, exercise books, food flashcards

1.1 PREPARATION
Revise or introduce the names of the meals and new food vocabulary using flashcards.

1.2 WHAT DO YOU HAVE FOR BREAKFAST?
Ask the children to talk about the food they usually eat during the day and the meals they have: *What do you usually have for breakfast/lunch/snack/dinner?* Record the answers on the board using a table like the one given below (use a cross ✘ or some other symbol to indicate how often the same food is mentioned by the children). At the end of the interview, add the kind of food you usually eat, taking particular care to include the food that the children tend to lack in their diet (e.g. fruit and vegetables).

Breakfast	Snack	Lunch	Snack	Dinner
Milk ✘✘✘✘	Chocolate ✘✘✘	Pasta	Pizza ✘✘✘✘✘✘✘	Soup
Tea ✘✘	Sandwich ✘	Rice	Apple ✘	Fish
Biscuits ✘✘✘✘✘✘	Crisps ✘✘✘✘	Meat	Cakes ✘✘✘✘	Cheese
....	Fruit juice ✘✘✘✘	Carrots	Buns ✘✘	Eggs
	....	....	....	....

1.3 Help the children to analyse the data from the table with questions: *How many children have milk/tea/biscuits for breakfast? How many children have pasta/rice/meat for lunch? Which is the most popular food for lunch? Which is the least popular food?*

1.4 Tell the children to copy the table in their exercise books replacing crosses with total numbers for each food, or to show the same data in bar or pie charts (one for each meal).

2. A BALANCED DIET

Time: 3 hours
Materials: paper, crayons, food pictures, **Worksheets K-1 to K-5**

2.1 PREPARATION
Collect pictures of food or use food flashcards; make a poster divided into four columns corresponding to the four main food groups and introduce new vocabulary if necessary: bread and cereals group; fruit and vegetables group; meat/fish, dairy products, and eggs group; fats and sweets group.

2.2 FOOD GROUPS
Give out a food card to each child and explain that, in turn, they have to say the name of the food depicted on the card and stick it in one of the four groups.

ALL ABOUT ME • Keeping healthy

Bread and cereals	Fruit and vegetables	Meat/fish, dairy products, and eggs	Fats and sweets
pasta ………	carrots	steak	*crisps*

2.3 IS IT HEALTHY?

Ask the children if they think some foods are 'good' for them and others 'bad': **Can a food be good or bad for you?** Discuss the fact that there are no 'good' or 'bad' foods, but while some should be consumed in large quantities others must be consumed in moderation. Draw an empty food pyramid on the board (see the model) and explain to the children that the internal subdivision represents the percentage of each food that should be eaten for a well-balanced diet. Tell them that the food at the

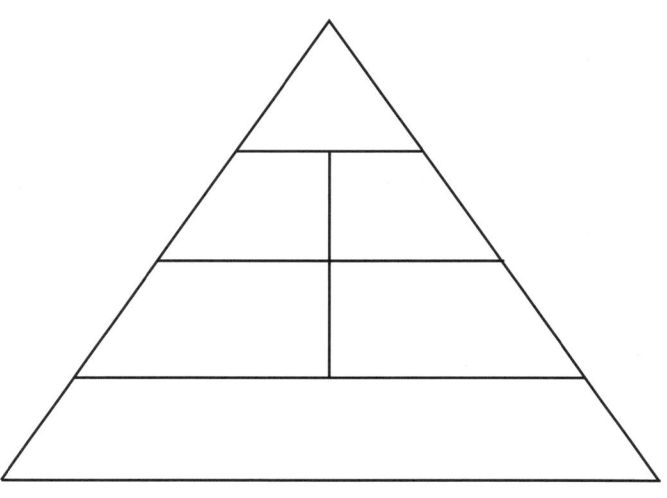

bottom of the pyramid has to be eaten in larger quantities and that the further you move towards the top, the less food should be eaten. Pointing to the different sections of the pyramid, ask the children to predict which kind of food should be put where and write their hypotheses on the pyramid: **What's at the bottom of the pyramid? What's above that? What's at the top?** (starting from the bottom the order should be: pasta, rice, potatoes, bread; fruit and vegetables; dairy products and eggs/meat/fish/nuts; fats and sweets.

2.4 THE FOOD PYRAMID

Ask the children to compare the pyramid drawn on the board with the one on **Worksheet K-1** and to discuss the results: **What's at the bottom of the pyramid? What's above that? What's at the top? We need to eat a lot of cereals, fruit, and vegetables; not too much meat/fish/eggs/dairy products; not too many sweets and fats**. Then children have to fill in the pyramid by inserting the names of the food groups in the right places: bread and cereals; fruit and vegetables; dairy products, meat, eggs, and fish; fats and sweets. Point out that water is an important part of our diet.

2.5 MY BODY NEEDS …

Illustrate the table of nutrients on **Worksheet K-2** and organize some games to help the children learn their functions and the foods they can find them in.

a) **Jump in.** Scatter six hoops on the floor and stick labels with the name of nutrients inside them: carbohydrates – fats – proteins – minerals – vitamins – fibre. Read the functions of the nutrients, one at a time, and explain to the children they have to jump into the hoop with the label of the nutrient you have read the function of. You can help comprehension by using body gestures: **They provide energy to your body, what are they? (carbohydrates). They give energy to your body and help keep it warm, what are they? (fats). They help your body grow and**

ALL ABOUT ME • Keeping healthy

repair injuries, what are they? (proteins). They help build strong bones, teeth, and soft tissues, what are they? (minerals). They help to fight germs, what are they? (vitamins). They help to digest food and get rid of solid waste, what are they? (fibre).

b) **Where can you find them?** Give out food flashcards and tell the children to place them in the right hoop according to the kind of nutrients they give to our bodies. At the end of the activity, get the children to check if all the foods are in the right hoops and give reasons for foods that are in the wrong group.

c) Finally give out an enlarged copy of **Worksheet K-2** to each child and ask them to draw the foods in the column on the right.

2.6 DAILY MENU

a) Divide the class into groups of three or four and give a copy of **Worksheet K-3** to each group. Explain to the children that they have to agree and write a daily menu, including mid-morning and afternoon snacks, taking into account the table of nutrients and the food pyramid. Tell the children they have to include both water and milk in their menu, the latter being an essential element for the strengthening of teeth and bones.

b) Ask the children to look at the list of foods on the chart they made in the first activity (My favourite food) and ask them to identify the foods that come from plants (e.g. ***jam: fruit, cornflakes: maize, bread: wheat, chocolate: cocoa, orange juice: oranges***). Write on the board the foods that the children have identified; help the children to find others and ask them to write a menu based only on foods coming from plants. Remind the children that pulses (beans, peas, lentils, chickpeas) are rich in protein.

2.7 HOW DO YOU EAT FRUIT AND VEGETABLES?

a) Bring in a basket of fruit and vegetables; discuss how children eat them: ***How do you eat fruit and vegetables? Do you wash them before eating? Do you peel them before eating? Do you eat them raw, cooked, or both?*** Get the children to find criteria to classify fruit and vegetables according to the way they eat them.

b) Give each child a copy of **Worksheet K-4** and ask them to write the letter **W** in the square next to the food they have to wash before eating or the letter **P** next to the food that needs to be peeled.

c) Venn diagram. Give out copies of **Worksheet K-5** and explain to the children that they have to trace a line from each vegetable to the appropriate section of the diagram according to the way in which vegetables can be eaten: ***raw, cooked,*** or ***both***.

3. KEEPING FIT

Time: 1 hour
Materials: Worksheet K-6 and K-7

3.1 PREPARATION

a) Brainstorm what the children think of the word 'health' in mother tongue. ***What does the word 'health' make you think of? What are the rules for keeping healthy? Why is good, regular sleep important? Why is adequate physical exercise important? How important is it to keep clean?***

At the end of the brainstorming, help the children to sum up the discussion by eliciting five basic rules for keeping healthy. ***Five golden rules: keeping clean; healthy eating; looking after my teeth; getting exercise; getting rest.***

b) Pre-teach adverbs of frequency: never, sometimes, often, always.

ALL ABOUT ME • Keeping healthy

3.2 HEALTHY LIFE QUIZ
Ask the children some questions related to their daily habits (*Do you clean your teeth after every meal? Do you sleep for 8–10 hours per night?*). Help the children to reply by using an adverb of frequency: *I always brush my teeth after every meal*. Make copies of **Worksheet K-6** and cut off the section describing how points are awarded (put these on one side to give back to the children at the end of the quiz). Give out the Worksheets and explain that the children have to read and answer the questions, work out their score, and draw conclusions about their personal habits. Start a discussion about any changes that might be introduced in order to achieve a better lifestyle.

3.3 I HAVE TO WASH MY HANDS
Talk about the importance of washing hands, especially in certain circumstances (before eating a meal, after playing outside or going to the toilet, after touching animals). Give out **Worksheet K-7**: ask children to match the captions with the appropriate pictures and to draw the missing one.

4. TAKE CARE OF YOUR TEETH
Time: 2 hours
Materials: Worksheets K-7 to K-13

4.1 Depending on the language level of the children, discuss in English or in mother tongue what children know about teeth, their functions, diseases, and dental care.

4.2 SMILE PLEASE!
Explain to the children that they are going to make a booklet about teeth and dental care by binding together the following pages with coloured string:
- [Worksheet K-8]. **Book cover.**
- [Worksheet K-9]. **Types of teeth.** Look for information about milk teeth and adult teeth in science books. Ask the children to read and complete the Worksheet by writing in the names of the teeth.
- [Worksheet K-10]. **Golden rules!** Discuss some basic rules for having healthy teeth with the children and ask them to draw a picture of each rule in the tooth shapes on the Worksheet.
- [Worksheet K-11]. **How often do you follow the rules?** Tell the children to read and understand the cartoons showing the results of bad oral hygiene.
- [Worksheet K-12]. **Shining teeth!** Read the poem with the children and help them to fill in the gaps using the missing words written along the sides of the tooth shape.
- [Worksheet K-13]. **The teeth maze!** In this game children have to find the best way out of the maze by choosing the snacks that are best suited to keep teeth healthy: find the exit by choosing healthy snacks. Colour the snacks on the healthy route!
- The finished booklet could be added to the children's Portfolio if they have one, along with a description form (Appendix 4).
- **My tooth brush.** Invite the children to write, in pairs, a simple song about dental care using the words they have learnt. Here is an example by Frank Dally based on the traditional tune of *Twinkle, Twinkle, Little Star*.

ALL ABOUT ME • Keeping healthy

Got my toothpaste, got my brush
I won't hurry, I won't rush.
Making sure my teeth are clean
Front and back and in between
When I brush for quite a while
I will have a happy smile!

5. Extension activity: ICT

Time: 3 hours
Materials: PC, Excel, and PowerPoint programmes

a) Get the children to transfer the data from activity 1 (My favourite food) into Excel in order to create a pie chart.

b) **Keeping fit.** Help the children to create a PowerPoint presentation which can be shown to other classes, parents, or published on the school website. Insert captions in each slide, illustrated by drawings or photographs.

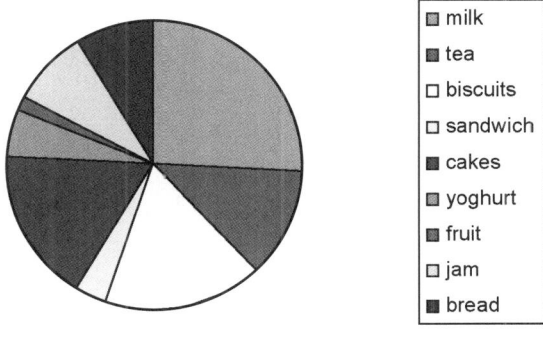

What do we have for breakfast?

- milk
- tea
- biscuits
- sandwich
- cakes
- yoghurt
- fruit
- jam
- bread

Slide 1	Slide 2	Slide 3	Slide 4	Slide 5
Eat a large amount of vegetables!	Brush your teeth regularly!	Wash your hands before eating!	Don't drink too many fizzy drinks	Don't eat too many sweets and fats!

Slide 6	Slide 7	Slide 8	Slide 9	Slide 10
Don't stay up till late at night!	Don't watch television for too many hours!	Do exercise every day!	Do take a shower or a bath regularly!	....

6. Extension activity: ART

Time: 1 hour
Materials: works of art depicting food, e.g. *Vertumnus* (*Autumn*) by Giuseppe Arcimboldo (see Worksheet K-14), fruit and vegetables, digital camera, printer

6.1 PREPARATION
Bring to school a basket containing different kinds of fruit and vegetables (e.g. lemons, grapes, strawberries, apples, fennel, lettuce, potatoes, tomatoes, celery, etc.).

6.2 FOOD IN ART
There is a big choice of paintings you can use to explore different ways of depicting food (e.g. works by artists such as Cezanne, Vermeer, Magritte, Warhol). Among the most famous is the series by

Arcimboldo which uses fruit to depict the four seasons. These paintings can be easily analysed or be used as a model for still-life work: **What can you see in the picture? Can you see any fruit? Can you see any vegetables? Can you see any flowers? What colour are they? How many pears can you see? How many flowers can you see?** Divide the children into small groups and ask them to create faces by using fruit and vegetables as Arcimboldo did. At the end of the activity take pictures of the 'collages' (if possible with a digital camera), print them, and ask the children to describe the picture and the materials they used: **It is a ....; we used the following fruit and vegetables: 2 yellow pears as ears, a red apple for the nose, 3 fennel as hair ...**

7. ASSESSMENT

- Progress indicators: The following extra Worksheets can be used to assess what children have learnt in this unit:

Worksheet K-15 Healthy food

The children colour the foods according to their food groups and how much of them they should eat – **green** = large amount; **yellow** = moderate amount; **red** = small amount.

Worksheet K-16 True or false?

The children have to read the sentences and write **T** if they are right and **F** if they are wrong (solutions: T, F, T, T, F, T, F, T).

Worksheet K-17 I'm healthy when I do this.

The children write a letter in each box – **A** = Always; **S** = Sometimes; or **N** = Never, according to how frequently the actions listed in the Worksheet should be carried out in order to have a healthy lifestyle. **Read the sentences and put an A, S, or N in the boxes to show the ideal frequency of each action for a healthy lifestyle** (solutions from left to right: A, N, S, A/S, S/A, A, A, A, S, N, A (except for allergies), A, A, N, S, N).

- Skills children should have acquired (these can be recorded on the children's ability record (Appendix 2) downloadable from the website):
  - **Content skills:** the child knows the basic hygiene rules for keeping healthy; can recognize the food groups and what nutrients they contain; can identify the kind of food necessary for a well-balanced diet; can describe the golden rules for good oral hygiene.
  - **Language skills:** the child can answer questions about hygienic and dietary habits; can express likes or dislikes about food; can elicit information about somebody else's tastes; can name food, drinks, and main meals; can match captions with pictures or situations; can speak about how to keep healthy teeth.
- Self evaluation: Appendix 3. The following statements can be written into the 'What I can do' column:

I can recognize what food groups foods belong to.
I know the fundamental guidelines for staying healthy.
I can identify which nutrients are in foods.
I can talk about my personal hygiene and dietary habits.
I can say what foods I like or don't like.
I can name the main meals and some foods in English.
I can write a healthy, balanced menu.

K-1 WORKSHEET

The food pyramid

A healthy diet includes a variety of food.

| FRUIT | VEGETABLES |

| BREAD, CEREALS, POTATOES, PASTA, AND RICE |

| MEAT, FISH, POULTRY, DRIED BEANS, EGGS, AND NUTS |

| FATS, OILS, AND SWEETS |

| DAIRY PRODUCTS |

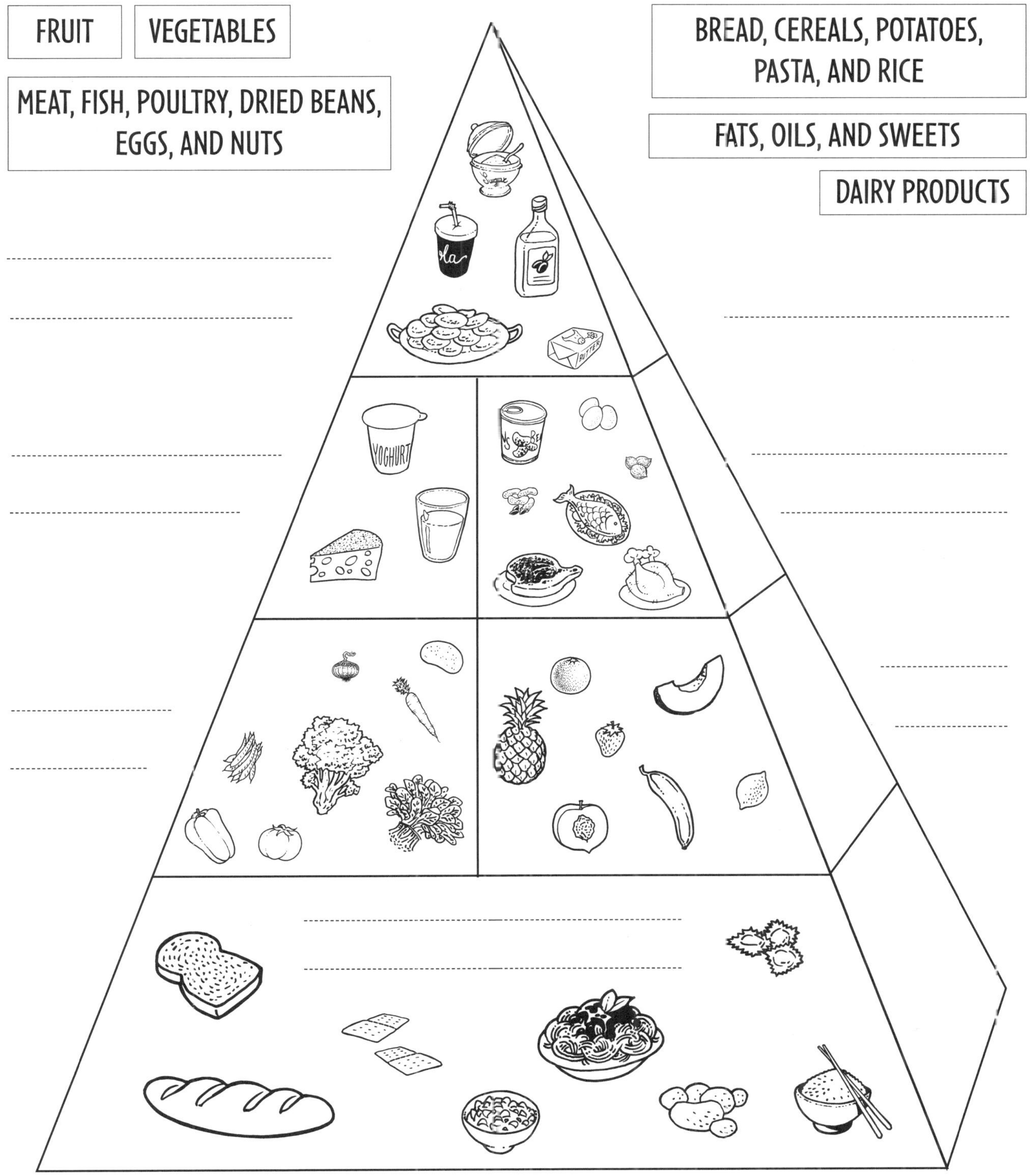

Write the names of the food in each group.

ALL ABOUT ME • Keeping healthy

K-2 WORKSHEET

MY BODY NEEDS...	I CAN FIND NUTRIENTS IN...
CARBOHYDRATES ... provide energy for our bodies.	pasta, rice, bread, potatoes, pizza, jam, biscuits
FATS ... give us energy and help keep the body warm.	butter, cheese, oil, cream
PROTEINS ... help the body grow and repair injuries.	meat, chicken, fish, eggs, beans, peas, milk, cheese
MINERALS ... help build strong bones, teeth, and soft tissues.	milk, cheese, yoghurt, fruit, vegetables
VITAMINS ... help to fight germs, to make energy from other foods, to keep skin, eyes, bones, nerves, and teeth healthy.	fruit, vegetables, liver, milk, cheese, yoghurt
FIBRE ... helps to digest our food and gets rid of solid waste.	cereals, vegetables, fruit

Read and draw the foods in the column on your right.

ALL ABOUT ME • Keeping healthy

3 WORKSHEET

A DAILY MENU

Breakfast ....

....

Snack ....

Lunch ....

....

....

Snack ....

Dinner ....

....

....

ALL ABOUT ME • Keeping healthy

K-4 WORKSHEET

How do you eat fruit and vegetables?

Do you wash [W] them before eating?   Do you peel [P] them before eating?

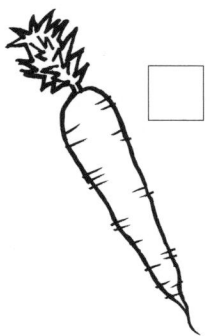

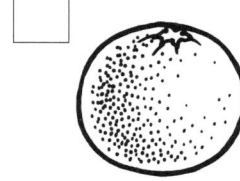

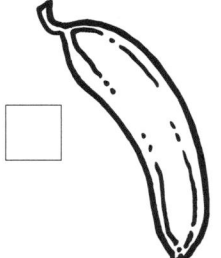

80

ALL ABOUT ME • Keeping healthy

K-5 WORKSHEET

Cooked or raw?

COOKED — **BOTH** — **RAW**

Vegetables: Lettuce, Spinach, Potatoes, Asparagus, Fennels, Peppers, Tomatoes, Pumpkin, Onions, Broccoli, Carrots, Beans, Peas

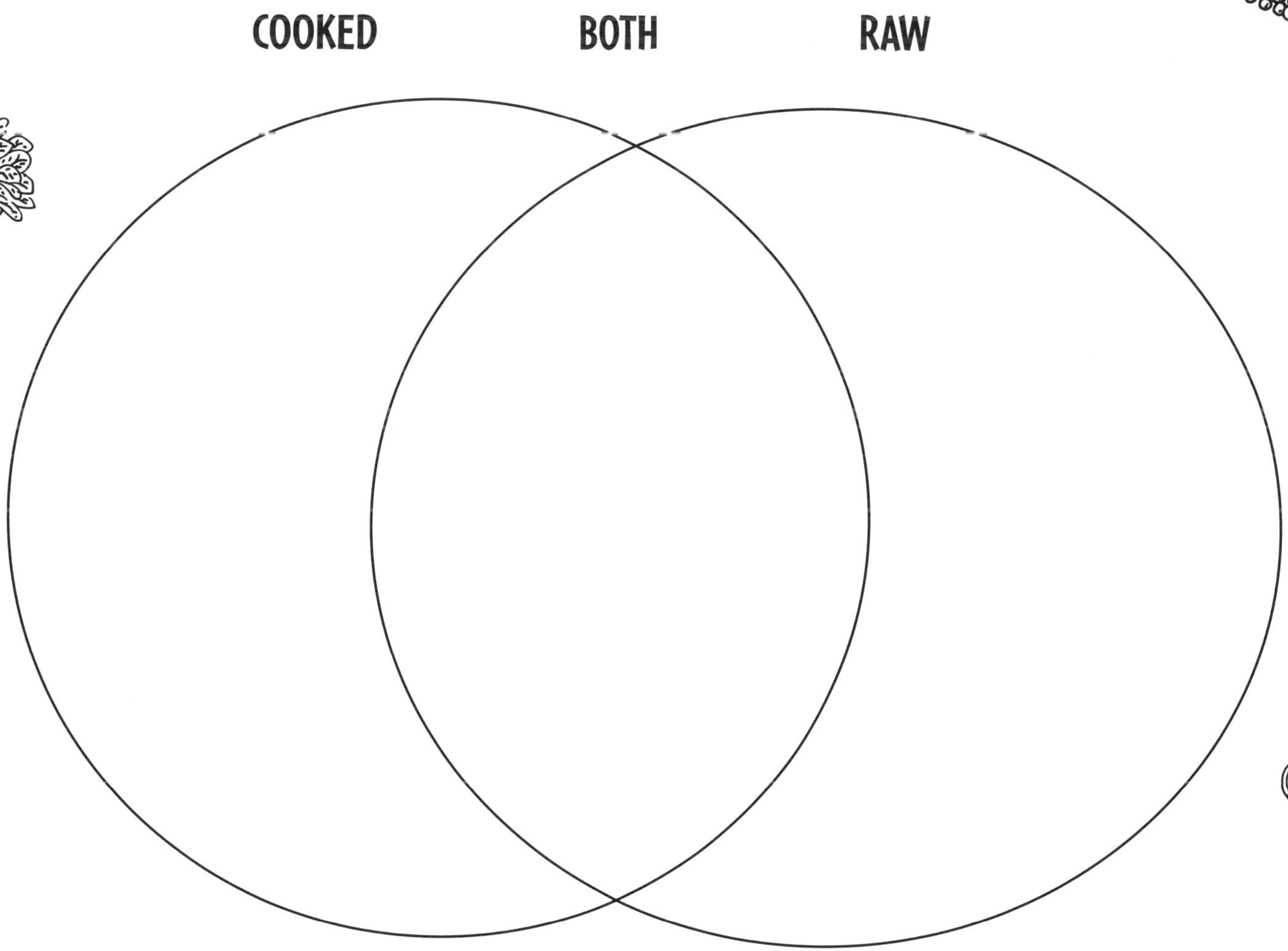

Write the names of the vegetables in the right places on the Venn Diagram.

Photocopiable © Oxford University Press

ALL ABOUT ME • Keeping healthy

K-6 WORKSHEET

Healthy life quiz

Read and answer the questions. See your score.

1. How often do you watch television?	A. never	B. sometimes	C. often	D. always
2. How often do you eat vegetables?	A. never	B. sometimes	C. often	D. always
3. How often do you eat fruit?	A. never	B. sometimes	C. often	D. always
4. Do you sleep 8–10 hours at night?	A. never	B. sometimes	C. often	D. always
5. How often do you play sports?	A. never	B. sometimes	C. often	D. always
6. Do you brush your teeth after a meal?	A. never	B. sometimes	C. often	D. always
7. Do you wash your hands before a meal?	A. never	B. sometimes	C. often	D. always
8. How often do you have a bath or a shower?	A. never	B. sometimes	C. often	D. always
9. How often do you have fizzy drinks?	A. never	B. sometimes	C. often	D. always
10. How often do you go to school on foot?	A. never	B. sometimes	C. often	D. always

Circle your score

1.	A. 4	B. 3	C. 2	D. 1	6.	A. 1	B. 2	C. 3	D. 4
2.	A. 1	B. 2	C. 3	D. 4	7.	A. 1	B. 2	C. 3	D. 4
3.	A. 1	B. 2	C. 3	D. 4	8.	A. 1	B. 2	C. 3	D. 4
4.	A. 1	B. 2	C. 3	D. 4	9.	A. 4	B. 3	C. 2	D. 1
5.	A. 1	B. 2	C. 3	D. 4	10.	A. 1	B. 2	C. 3	D. 4

32–40
Congratulations! You are a very healthy boy/girl.

23–31
Cheer up! You are a nearly healthy boy/girl.

14–22
You are not so healthy.

ALL ABOUT ME • Keeping healthy

K-7 WORKSHEET

I have to wash my hands

Dirty hands have germs on them. Soap and water keep my hands and my body clean.
Match the sentences and pictures.
Draw and colour the missing picture.

| before eating a meal | after playing outside |
| after touching animals | after going to the toilet |

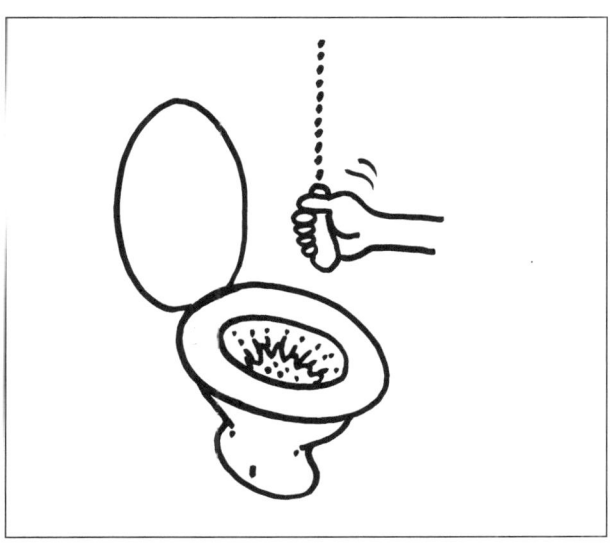

ALL ABOUT ME • Keeping healthy

K-8 WORKSHEET

SMILE, PLEASE!

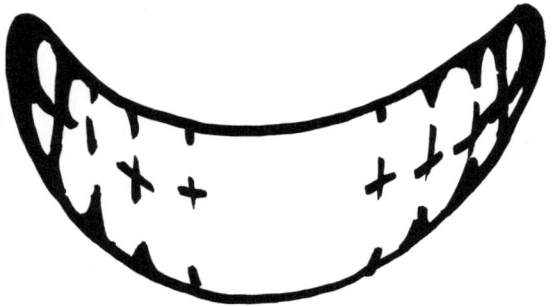

A book about my teeth

by

....

Photocopiable © Oxford University Press

K-9 WORKSHEET

TYPES OF TEETH

- **Milk teeth** grow when I am a baby. There are 20 of them.

- **Adult teeth** grow after the milk teeth when I am 6. There are 32 of them.

- I have teeth to break my food into small pieces.

Big teeth at the front: ....

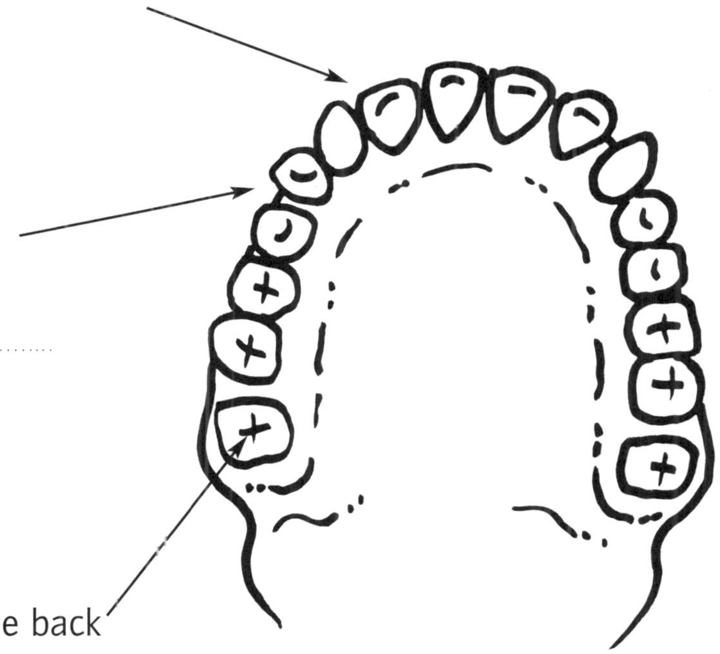

Pointy and sharp teeth at the sides of my mouth:
....

Big flat teeth at the back of my mouth: ....

Molars

Canines

Incisors

Fill in the gaps with the missing words.

ALL ABOUT ME • Keeping healthy

K-10 WORKSHEET

GOLDEN RULES!

Don't eat too many sweets, or sticky things.

Eat plenty of milk, cheese, yoghurt, fruit, and vegetables.

Brush your teeth properly after every meal.

Don't use your teeth for chewing pencils!

Visit the dentist every six months.

Draw a picture of each rule in the tooth shapes.

ALL ABOUT ME • Keeping healthy

K-11 WORKSHEET

HOW OFTEN DO YOU FOLLOW THE RULES?

ALWAYS

OFTEN

SOMETIMES

NEVER

Look at the pictures and colour how often you brush your teeth.

All About Me • Keeping healthy

K-12 WORKSHEET

MORNING   CLEAN

SHINING TEETH!

I use my 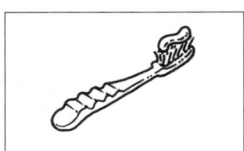 every day

to brush my 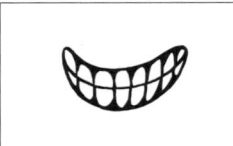 the healthy way.

I brush them each

I brush them each

'till every one is shining,  and white

NIGHT   TEETH   TOOTH BRUSH

Fill in the gaps with the missing words.

ALL ABOUT ME • Keeping healthy

K-13 WORKSHEET

THE TEETH MAZE!

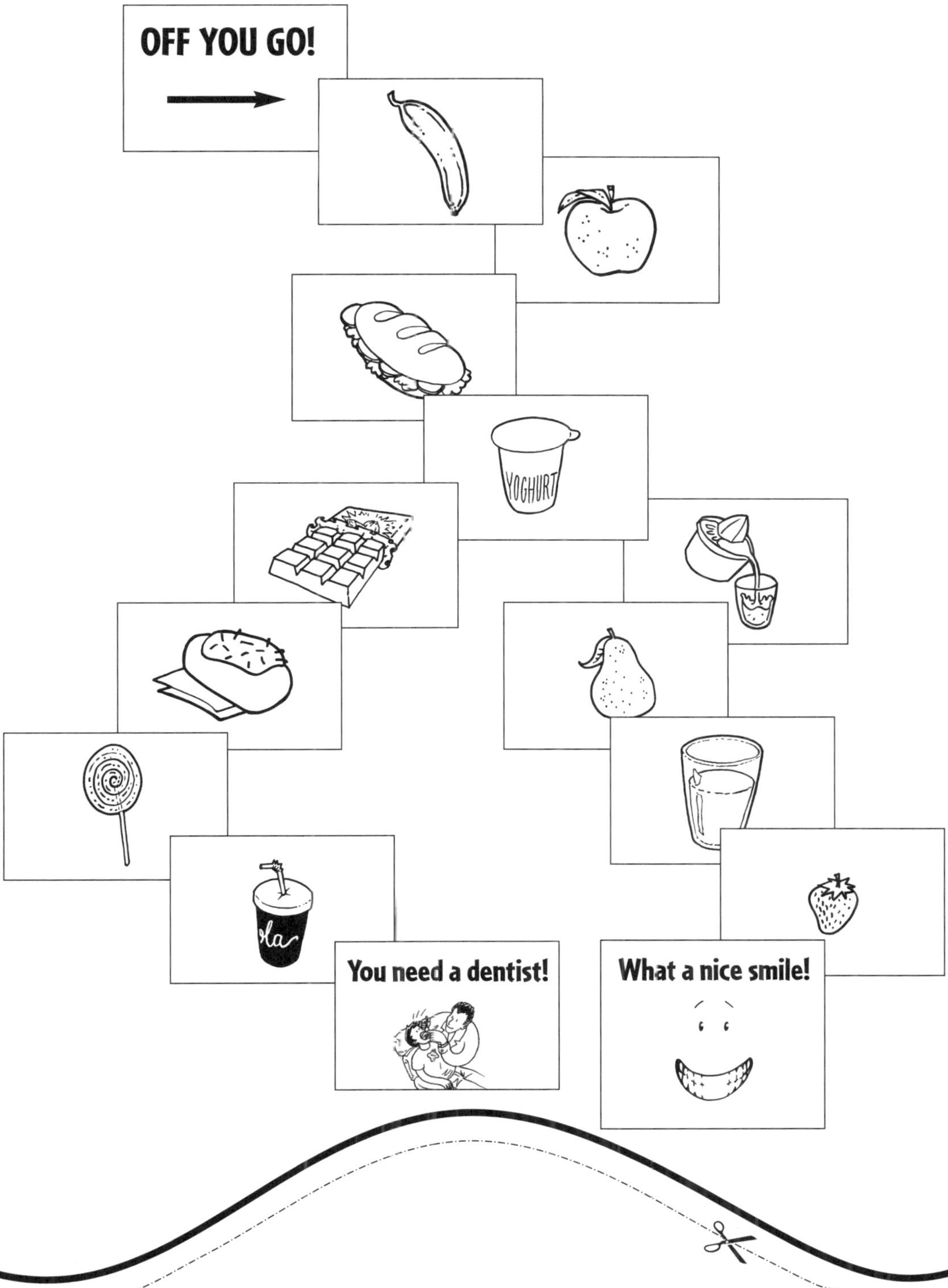

OFF YOU GO! →

Find the exit by choosing healthy snacks. Colour the snacks on the healthy route!

89

ALL ABOUT ME • Keeping healthy

K-14 WORKSHEET

MY FRUIT AND VEGETABLES PAINTING

inspired by *Vertumnus (Autumn)*
by Giuseppe Arcimboldo

Stick a photo of your painting here or draw it.

I used the following fruit and vegetables: ....
....
....

Photocopiable © Oxford University Press

ALL ABOUT ME • Keeping healthy

K-15 WORKSHEET

Healthy food

- Colour the foods green if you need to eat a large amount of them (carbohydrates-vitamins, minerals-fibre);
- Colour the foods yellow if you need to eat a moderate amount of them (dairy products-proteins);
- Colour the foods red if you need to eat a small amount of them (fats and sugars).

PASTA	TOMATO	YOGHURT	BEANS
BANANA	CHEESE	SPINACH	STEAK
BREAD	CRISPS	PEAR	CARROT
EGGS	STRAWBERRY	SWEETS	RICE
CEREALS	CAKES	HAM	FISH

ALL ABOUT ME • Keeping healthy

K-16 WORKSHEET

True or false?

Read the sentences; write a **T** if you think the sentence is true, or **F** if you think it's false.

🍰	• Fats and carbohydrates give my body energy.	☐
🥛	• Water is not important for my body.	☐
🍝	• I need carbohydrates, vitamins, proteins, fats, and fibre in my diet.	☐
🐟	• Meat, fish, cheese, and eggs give my body proteins.	☐
🍐	• I can't find vitamins in fruit and vegetables.	☐
🍗	• Proteins help me to grow.	☐
🥣	• Fibre is not in fruit, vegetables, and bread.	☐
🥛	• Milk, yoghurt, fruit and vegetables give my body minerals.	☐

ALL ABOUT ME • Keeping healthy

K-17 WORKSHEET

I'm healthy when I do this

A = ALWAYS   **S** = SOMETIMES   **N** = NEVER

	Sleep 8–10 hours a night.	**A**	
	Watch TV.		
	Go for walks.		
	Eat fruit.		
	Do exercise.		
	Drink milk and water.		
	Eat breakfast.		
	Travel by bus.		
	Eat too much.		
	Play outside in fresh air.		
	Keep my body clean.		
	Clean my teeth.		
	Eat sweets.		
	Wash my hands.		
	Eat chips.		
	Go to bed late.		

ALL ABOUT ME • Me and my senses

	**CONTENT AREA**	**ALL ABOUT ME**
	**TOPIC**	*Me and my senses*
	**AIMS**	• to identify similarities and differences between human beings • to understand how our five senses help us to know the world • to identify and describe object properties • to sort and classify according to chosen criteria
	**LANGUAGE**	• to read and understand instructions • to name the main external parts of the body • to talk about the use of the five senses • to classify sounds, smells, and tactile properties • to describe object properties • to identify and name the taste of some foods
	**VOCABULARY AND STRUCTURES**	Use words and phrases relating to: parts of the body; sense organs and their functions *(eyes: sight; nose: smell; skin: touch; ear: hearing; tongue: taste)*; it smells/tastes/looks/sounds/feels like ...; it is ...; a/an; adjectives for physical descriptions *(tall, brown, long ...)*; adjectives to describe food and object properties *(it's sweet, salty, sour, transparent, opaque, pleasant, unpleasant, bitter, hard, soft, rough, hot, cold, high, low, loud, fast, slow)*; action verbs *(shake, vibrate, bang, hit, rattle, pluck)*; structures *(I can/can't; there is/are; I think ...; Yes, it is/they are; No, it isn't/they aren't; We use ... to ...)*
	**WHAT CHILDREN NEED TO KNOW ALREADY**	• how to record data on tables and graphs • how to compare and interpret data • how to read a map of the school • indefinite articles • some words related to the human body, food, school • some adjectives (colours, sizes) • *I like/don't like; I can/can't*
	**MATERIALS**	• tape-recorder; musical instruments; food items; materials for games and activities concerning the five senses • **Worksheets S-1–S-11**
	**CROSS-CURRICULAR ACTIVITIES**	1. *We are all different and unique* 5. *Taste* 2. *Sense detectives* 6. *Smell and touch* 3. *Hearing* 7. *All together* 4. *Sight* 8. *Assessment*

ALL ABOUT ME • Me and my senses

1. WE ARE ALL DIFFERENT AND UNIQUE

Time: 2 hours
Materials: white paper, crayons, body labels, **Worksheet S-1**

1.1 PREPARATION
Revise known vocabulary and teach new words related to the parts of the body (e.g. chin, elbows, hips, knees ...). Trace the outline of a child on a large sheet of paper and ask children to label the various parts of the silhouette.

1.2 TOUCH YOUR NOSE!
Play a game to help children remember the body vocabulary. Explain to the children that they have to close their eyes and touch parts of their bodies according to your instructions: **Touch your knees ... touch your head ... touch your elbows.**

1.3 HOW ARE WE DIFFERENT?
Ask a couple of children to stand, one beside the other, in front of the class. Ask questions to establish which characteristics they have in common and in which ways they differ: **How are Marco and Sara the same? (They have a head, a body, legs, arms, a nose.); How are they different? (He is a boy/She is a girl/He has got blue eyes/She has got green eyes/He is ... metres tall/She has got long brown hair ... .)** Repeat the activity with other couples in order to help children become aware that certain physical characteristics are peculiar to each of us and make us unique: **Everyone has a head, a body, legs, and arms but there are some things that make everyone look different: colour of eyes, colour of hair, height, size of feet,** etc.

1.4 I'M THINKING OF A PERSON
Describe a member of the class and ask the children to look for a child who corresponds to your description: **I'm thinking of someone with brown hair.** All the children with brown hair have to stand up. Then add **I'm thinking of someone with brown hair and light-blue eyes.** Only those with brown hair and light-blue eyes remain standing. Keep on adding other details gradually reducing the number of people until there is only one person left standing who has all the characteristics described. **I'm thinking of someone who has brown hair and light-blue eyes and who is a girl.**

1.5 WHAT'S YOUR FOOT SIZE?
Draw a shoe on the board and ask the children what size shoes they wear. Get them to record the results of the survey on a bar graph (for example: 8 pupils have size 32; 7 pupils have size 30; etc.).

1.6 PORTRAIT OF A FRIEND
Divide the children into pairs; ask them to draw a picture of their classmate and describe his or her physical characteristics (e.g. **This is a picture of ...; hair colour: brown; hair style: straight; colour of eyes: green; shape of face: oval; other ...**). If necessary, introduce new words to support the description.

ALL ABOUT ME • Me and my senses

> **Eyes:** close – distant – long – wide – expressive – light – dark
> **Nose:** long – short – big – small – hook – snub – straight
> **Mouth:** big – small – wide – thin – thick – prominent lips
> **Teeth:** white – yellow – straight – crooked
> **Ears:** small – big – dirty – protruding
> **Hair:** short – long – straight – curly – fair – dark – wavy – frizzy – thick – thin
> **Face:** oval – square – round

1.7 HOW MANY FACES CAN YOU MAKE?

Give out **Worksheet S-1** and explain to the children that they have to find out how many combinations can be made with three different haircuts, three types of noses, and three kinds of mouths. *You can only use: 3 hairstyles, 3 noses, and 3 mouths.* **(They can make 18 faces.)**

2. SENSE DETECTIVES

Time: 1 hour
Materials: food items (orange, carrot, celery, onion, potato, apple, pear, banana, liquorice), knife, aluminium foil, blindfolds, **Worksheet S-2**

2.1 PREPARATION

Before starting the activity, peel the foods, cut them into pieces, and prepare 15 parcels by wrapping each piece in aluminium foil. Make a set of cards showing the names and pictures of the foods and another set showing the symbols of the five senses (nose, mouth, ears, eyes, hands – **Worksheet S-2**). Depending on the language level of the children you could add, below each sense symbol, the structure they have to use to talk about the senses: *it smells/tastes/feels/looks/sounds like ...*

2.2 Elicit the names of the food items and senses by showing the children the ready-made cards: *Today we are going to find out what the five senses are! Here are some food cards (What is it? It's a/an ...) and these are the five senses cards (sight, smell, taste, touch, hearing).* Organize the class into five groups and give instructions to each group explaining that they have to wait for your sign before starting the experiment:

a) Give three parcels to the first group (for example, apple, onion, orange) and show the picture of the nose to indicate that they will have to guess what the food in the parcels is by smell only. Blindfold the children and ask them to smell the parcels: *Here you have three wrapped pieces of food. You have to open the parcels and identify the foods by smell only! (It smells like ... .)*

b) Give three parcels to the second group (for example, banana, carrot, pear) and show the picture of the hands to indicate that they will have to guess what the food in the parcels is by touch only. Blindfold the children and ask them to touch the parcels: *Here you have three wrapped pieces of food. You have to open the parcels and identify the foods by touch only! (It feels like ... .)*

c) Give three other parcels to the third group and show the picture of the mouth to indicate that they will have to guess what the food in the parcels is by taste only. Blindfold the children and ask them to taste the food: *Here you have three wrapped pieces of food. You have to open the parcels and identify the foods by taste only! (It tastes like ... .)*

d) Give three parcels to the fourth group and show the picture of the ears to indicate that they will have to guess what the food in the parcels is by hearing only. Blindfold the children and ask them to listen for any noises made by the food when they shake the parcels: *Here you have three wrapped pieces of food. You have to shake the parcels and identify the foods by hearing only! (It sounds like ... .)*

ALL ABOUT ME • Me and my senses

e) The children of the last group are not blindfolded and have to use their senses of smell, touch, taste, hearing, and sight, one after the other, to identify the food: **Identify the foods by smell, touch, taste, hearing, and sight.**

f) Tell the children not to take off the blindfolds until you have closed all the parcels again. Then they can take the blindfolds off and pick out the cards with the names of the foods they think they have identified. Lastly they can open the parcels to check whether they were right or not: **Pick out the cards with the names of the foods you identified, open the parcels, and check their content.**

g) Get the children to sit in a circle and discuss the results. **Which group found it most difficult to guess the foods? Why? Which sense did group one use? Was it difficult for group one to identify the food? Which sense was the most helpful? What kind of conclusions can be drawn from this experiment? (We have five senses. All the senses are important. Our senses help us to know the world.)** Depending on the language level of the children, you could ask them to show the results of the experiment either by drawing pictures or writing short sentences.

Variation

Instead of organizing the class into groups, you could ask the children to sit at their desks and keep their eyes shut while you go around asking each of them to identify foods. First, place the set of cards showing the pictures of the foods up on the board or on the walls and elicit their names. Then show a sense card (see preparation) and elicit the name of the sense children have to use to identify the food (e.g. smell). Get the children to shut their eyes, smell (or taste, touch, listen for any noises, look at) the food you are passing around and identify what it is.

3. HEARING

We can hear with our ears. We hear many different sounds each day. People who can't hear can communicate by lip-reading or sign language.

Time: 2 hours
Materials: ground plan of the school, blank sheets of paper, tape-recorder, empty plastic pots, rice, potato, coins, flour, buttons, sugar, corks, beans, **Worksheet S-3**

3.1 PREPARATION

Make copies of the school plan. Collect six plastic pots, number each pot (1-6), and put one of the following materials inside each of them: rice, potato, coins, flour, buttons, sugar, corks, beans. Prepare some cards showing the pictures and the names of the materials that are inside the pots. Using pictures, pre-teach or revise the words: sound, hearing, listen, write, draw, drum, maracas, trumpet.

3.2 A LISTENING WALK

a) Divide the children into pairs and give each pair a pen and a plan of the school building (including the external area). If the children do not know how to use a map, give them a blank sheet of paper. Explain to the children that they are going to go for a walk round the school, both inside and outside, listening for sounds. Each pair has to write down on the plan or sheet of paper the sounds they hear during their walk: **I can hear ...** (if the children cannot yet write they can draw what they hear). While taking the children around, record sounds on a tape-recorder.

b) Back in the classroom, each pair tells the rest of the class the sounds they have heard and recognized; they then listen to the tape, identify the sounds, and compare them with those they recorded on their map or sheet of paper.

c) Write all the sounds identified by the children up on the board or on a poster by using a double-

ALL ABOUT ME • Me and my senses

entry table. The children can then copy the table into their exercise books and fill it in by writing words or drawing pictures.

SOUNDS WE CAN HEAR AT SCHOOL

	Classroom	Computer Lab	Library	Hall	Street	Garden
Telephone					X	
Teacher		X				
Cat						X
Footsteps						
Cars						
Children						
Birds						

3.3 WHAT'S IN THE POT?

Put the numbered plastic pots on a table and scatter the cards in random order around and between the pots (see preparation).

a) Divide the children into groups of three and tell them to take turns in shaking the pots in order to guess what is inside them.

b) Explain to the children that they have to match each pot with the card bearing the name of the material they think is inside it and record their predictions on **Worksheet S-3** (*I think there is/are ... in pot number 1*). When all the children have finished the activity, you can open the pots and let them check whether they were right or not. Ask the children to check their predictions on **Worksheet S-3**: they have to write YES next to the prediction if they guessed the material correctly or write NO and the right material if they were wrong.

3.4 WE HEAR DIFFERENT KINDS OF SOUNDS

Discuss with the children the sounds they hear every day and the importance of hearing for safety (e.g. ears help to keep us safe when we cross the road). Depending on their language level, introduce words or structures necessary to talk about sound sources by showing pictures or getting them to recognize recorded sounds. Then ask them to look for criteria by which sounds might be classified: e.g. *sounds you make yourself (talking, clapping, stamping, whistling, singing, screaming ...); sounds other things make (doorbell, siren, bee, violin, telephone, radio, washing machine ...); pleasant sounds (radio, bells, birds ...) and unpleasant sounds (siren, children screaming ...).* Depending on the language level of the children, you can ask them to illustrate the results of the discussion individually in their exercise books or in groups by making four posters: *Sounds we make ourselves – Sounds other things make – Pleasant sounds – Unpleasant sounds.*

3.5 LET'S PLAY SOME MUSIC

Get the children to move to the rhythm of a tambourine: *Move according to the beat: fast or slow.* Ask the children to shut their eyes and listen to a sequence of sounds you make by playing various musical instruments (drum, maracas, trumpet). They have to identify the sounds and reproduce the sequence they have heard.

ALL ABOUT ME • Me and my senses

FOLLOW UP
Involve the children in making a sound bingo by recording different sounds in the school area and preparing several bingo cards with pictures of the sound sources. Ask the children to identify instrument sounds and explore how to play them in order to make sounds (bang, pluck, rattle, hit, scrape).

4. SIGHT

We see with our eyes. We can see colours, shapes, sizes, movement. Sight helps us in everything we do! Blind people need other help: guide dogs, canes. They can read using Braille by touching raised dots.

Time: 2 hours
Materials: small cardboard box, greaseproof paper, a piece of cloth, slide projector, black and coloured paper, glass of water, different coloured rulers, felt pens, and pencils, **Worksheet S-4**

4.1 PREPARATION
Take a box, paint the inside black, and make a small hole on one side. Make a long slit (about 2 cm wide) in the top of the box and cover the slit with greaseproof paper. Then cover it with a piece of cloth in order to keep all light out of the box and put a yellow pencil (or another yellow object) inside the box, directly under the slit. Revise known vocabulary and teach new words related to sight (e.g. light, reflect, see, shadow, silhouette).

4.2 WHAT'S IN THE BOX?
Ask the children to look into the box through the hole: *Can you see anything? (No, I can't)*. Move the piece of cloth slightly away from the opening and ask: *Can you see anything, now? (I can see an object but not the colour)*. Take the piece of cloth away from the box completely and ask: *What can you see now? (I can see a yellow pencil)*. Repeat the experiment with other objects which are all similar but different in colour (e.g. rulers of various colours) and ask the children which colour can be seen most clearly: *Which colour is the easiest to see?* Help the children to draw conclusions from the experiment: **We can only see things when there is light. We can see objects because light is reflected from them** (ask the science teacher to explain, in mother tongue, how reflection works and how images form inside the eye).

4.3 SHADOWS
On a nice sunny day take the children out into the playground and ask them to look at their shadows on the ground: *Can you all see your shadow?* Ask the children, in pairs, to jump on their partner's shadow and on their own: *Can you jump on your shadow or run away from it?* Get the children to stand with their backs to the sun and then ask them to say where their shadows appear: **Stand with your backs to the sun - where are your shadows? (in front)**. Get the children to stand facing the sun and say where the shadows appear now: **Stand facing the sun - where are your shadows? (behind)**. Discuss, in English or in mother tongue, how the shadows of their bodies form: **Why do we have a shadow? Because the sun's light cannot go through our bodies.** Get the children to look for other shadows in the school playground. **Shadows are formed when light is blocked by an opaque material.** Organize a treasure hunt within the school building to find out which materials are transparent or opaque. Ask the children to classify materials and make a poster about what they have found out.

ALL ABOUT ME • Me and my senses

4.4 SILHOUETTES
Get the children to put a light source (e.g. a slide projector), a child, and a sheet of paper in the right order to produce the shadow of the child's face profile on the paper: *In which order do we have to place the paper, the child, and the light to make a shadow on the paper?* Once it has been established that the child has to stand in profile between the sheet of paper and the light source, the children have to find the best position for bringing the profile into clear focus. They then trace the outline of the child's profile on the paper using a felt pen: *Draw around the shadow with a felt pen.* Each child traces his/her own outline, cuts it out and sticks it on a coloured background.

4.5 I CAN SEE THE COLOURS OF THE RAINBOW
a) Draw the outline of a rainbow on the board and ask the children if they can say how many colours a rainbow has: *How many colours are there in a rainbow?*

b) Write a list of numbers from 1-7 and ask the children to guess the colours and their order (starting from the lower arch): *What are the colours of the rainbow? Which is colour number 1?* Each child colours in the first rainbow on **Worksheet S-4** and tells the others what the colours are in his/her opinion: *I think number 1 is orange!*

c) The children can check their predictions by doing a simple experiment: they take a glass of water and go to one of the classroom windows; they then hold the glass above a blank sheet of paper and move it about until they find a position which will enable the sun's rays to filter through the glass onto the paper and produce a rainbow. In this way they can observe the sequence of colours, and check their predictions: *Let's find out the order of the colours in a rainbow. Hold up a glass of water over some white paper near a sunny window. Look at the colours of the rainbow on the paper. Compare the order of the colours with yours on Worksheet S-4.* Then write the correct order and ask the children to colour in the second rainbow. (The correct order is: red, orange, yellow, green, blue, indigo, violet.) The experiment is intended to demonstrate that although light seems to be white, it is really made up of a range of colours. If you have a science laboratory in your school, you can use an optical prism to show the spectrum of colours.

FOLLOW UP
Investigate primary/secondary colours; warm/cold colours; Braille code.

5. TASTE
We use little taste buds on our tongue to taste things.
Time: 1 hour 30 minutes
Materials: lemon juice, salted crisps, unsweetened coffee, cake, honey, grapefruit segments, pizza, bitter chocolate, **Worksheets S-5 and S-6**, food pictures

5.1 PREPARATION
Put some different kinds of food on a table and cover them with a cloth (e.g. lemon juice, crisps, unsweetened coffee, cake, honey, grapefruit segments). Make a set of pictures of salty/sweet/sour/bitter foods (e.g. lemon, chips, coffee, cake, honey, grapefruit, orange, yoghurt, vinegar, sweets, chocolate, cake, pizza, etc.).

ALL ABOUT ME • Me and my senses

5.2 THE TASTING TABLE

Ask the children to take turns to go to the table and, with their eyes shut, taste what you give them. They have to guess what it is (in English or in mother tongue) and say whether they like it or not: *Come to the tasting table, close your eyes. Are you ready? Open your mouth. Taste this food. What is it? That's right! Do you like it?*

5.3 TASTE BUDS

a) Explain to the children, by showing the tongue picture on **Worksheet S-5**, that we can taste things because of the taste buds on our tongues **(back of the tongue = bitter like some medicines and coffee; tip of the tongue = sweet like candies and ice-cream; front at the side = salty like chips and pizza; back at the side = sour like lemon juice and grapefruit).**

b) Repeat the tasting table activity, this time asking children to identify the tastes: *Does it taste sweet/sour/salty/bitter?*

c) Ask the children to colour in the different parts of the tongue on **Worksheet S-5** according to the instructions. Then, they have to cut out the different kinds of food and stick them on the part of the tongue that enables us to identify different tastes: *Colour the sweet place on the tongue yellow. Colour the sour places on the tongue grey. Colour the bitter place on the tongue brown. Colour the salty place on the tongue orange. Cut out the foods and glue them on the right place on the tongue. Colour the foods the same colour as the taste.*

5.4 SENSE OF TASTE

Check if the children can identify different tastes by asking them to sort out pictures of food you prepared in advance (see preparation) into foods that taste salty, sweet, bitter, or sour. Ask the children to circle the correct taste for each food on **Worksheet S-6**.

6. SMELL AND TOUCH

We can smell with our nose. Don't taste things because they smell good: they can be dangerous! We use our skin to touch and feel.

Time: 1 hour 50 minutes
Materials: garlic, cinnamon, vinegar, orange, liquid soap, perfume, teddy bear, sandpaper, ball, bag, copies of **Worksheet S-7**

6.1 PREPARATION

a) Prepare sets of pairs of jars, each pair containing a particular substance (garlic, cinnamon, vinegar, orange, liquid soap, perfume ...). Seal the jars with a gauze and set them on a table in a jumbled order.

b) Make a poster divided into four columns, each for a different tactile property. Stick a picture of an object or a piece of material in each column and write its tactile property (for example, soft: teddy bear; hard: desk; smooth: ball; rough: sandpaper).

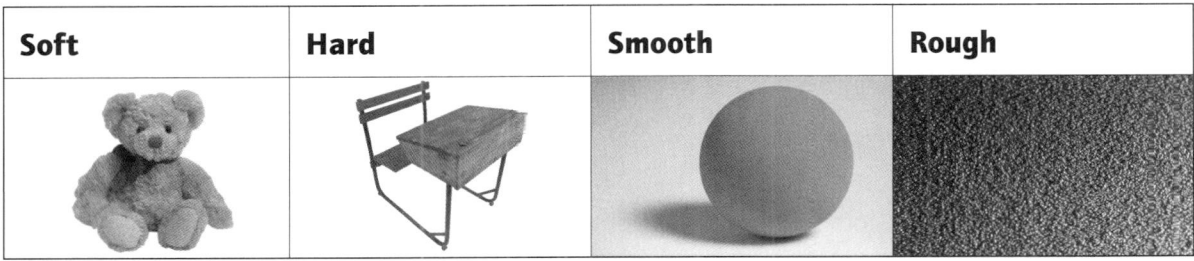

c) Prepare a feely bag containing objects that all feel different (hard, soft, smooth, rough).

ALL ABOUT ME • Me and my senses

6.2 SMELLING JARS
Explain to the children that they have to smell the jars and match those with the same smell: *Smell the jars. What can you smell? Does it smell good? Match the two jars that smell the same.*

6.3 HOW DOES IT SMELL?
Give out copies of **Worksheet S-7** and ask the children to identify pleasant and unpleasant smells and match them with the two faces: *Join the pictures to the faces. (It smells bad. It smells good.)*

6.4 FEELY BAG
a) Elicit the names of tactile properties by using real objects or the tactile poster (see preparation): *The teddy bear is very soft/The desk is hard/The ball is smooth/The sandpaper is rough.*

b) Sit the children in a circle and ask them to pass the feely bag around (see preparation) while some music plays. When you stop the music, the child who is holding the bag puts his/her hand in it, chooses an object, and describes its characteristics without taking it out of the bag (e.g. *What is it? What does it feel like? It's cotton, it's soft.*). The activity may be more entertaining if the children are blindfolded and use their feet rather than their hands.

c) Get the children to complete the tactile poster by drawing each object from the feely bag in the column corresponding to its tactile property.

6.5 FEELY BOOK
Ask the children to bring in materials with different textures (e.g. velvet, cotton, sand, salt, sandpaper, etc.). Tell them to use the materials to make collages representing different objects and to write captions for each of them (for example, *This is a ball. Touch it! It's soft; This is a sandcastle. Touch it! It's rough!*). The collages can then be made into a class book.

FOLLOW UP
Let the children experiment with other tactile properties: hot/warm/cold; wet/dry; sharp/blunt; prickly, etc.

7. ALL TOGETHER
Time: 1 hour 15 minutes
Materials: senses cards (see preparation in 'Sense detectives'), **Worksheets S-8–S-11**
(Activities suggested in this section revise and evaluate content and language covered within the whole 'five senses' content area.)

7.1 PREPARATION
Make some copies of the senses cards so that each child can have one.

7.2 I HAVE FIVE SENSES
Ask the children to complete **Worksheet S-8** by putting in the missing words and symbols: *Complete the sentences with symbols and words. Colour in the pictures.*

7.3 NONSENSE POEM
Explain to the children that they have to write a nonsense poem, in the space provided on **Worksheet S-9**, by combining the words in the three columns of the text in a bizarre way: *Write a nonsense poem matching words from the three columns (e.g. I see bells with my nose).*

ALL ABOUT ME • Me and my senses

7.4 FIVE SENSES QUIZ
Worksheet S-10 is a multiple-choice quiz on the five senses in which children have to complete each sentence with the right word.

7.5 GOLDILOCKS
The story of Goldilocks can be used to revise the five senses. Give each child a card showing the symbol of a sense (see preparation). Tell the story, supporting new vocabulary by miming. Each child has to raise his/her card whenever the action of a character in the story involves that particular sense (e.g. **Goldilocks tastes the porridge in the big bowl. Ouch! It's too hot!**). All the children with the symbol of the tongue on their card have to raise it and show it to the others. At the end of the story, give out copies of **Worksheet S-9** with multiple-choice questions about the story: *Read and circle the right answer.*

> Here are three bears: Mummy Bear, Daddy Bear, and Baby Bear. Mummy Bear makes some porridge.
> Mummy Bear pours the porridge into three bowls: a big bowl - a medium bowl - a small bowl.
> 'What a delicious **smell**!' Daddy Bear tastes the porridge. 'Oh! This porridge is too **hot**.'
> Mummy Bear **tastes** the porridge. 'Oh! This porridge is too **hot**.'
> Baby Bear **tastes** the porridge. 'Oh! This porridge is too **hot**.'
> 'Let's go for a walk and pick blueberries!'
> Here are a small bear's footsteps. Can you **hear** him? (tip tip tip)... a medium bear's footsteps.
> Can you **hear** him? (tip tap tip tap) ... a big bear's footsteps. Can you **hear** him? (tiiiiiip taaaaaap!)
> Here is Goldilocks! Knock! Knock! Goldilocks opens the door and smells: 'Yum Yum, porridge! I like porridge!'
> Goldilocks **sees** three bowls. 'Oh! Three bowls!'
> 'A **big** bowl! Yuck! I don't like this porridge, it's too **hot**!'
> 'A **medium** bowl! Yuck! I don't like this porridge, it's too **cold**!'
> 'A **small** bowl! Yum Yum! This is good. I like it.' Goldilocks sees three chairs. 'Oh! Three chairs!'
> 'A big chair! Ouch! I don't like this chair, it's too **hard**!'
> 'A medium chair! Ouch! I don't like this chair, it's too **soft**!'
> 'A small chair! I like this... Oh no!' Goldilocks sees three beds. 'Oh! Three beds!'
> 'A big bed! Ouch! I don't like this bed, it's too **hard**!'
> 'A medium bed! Ouch! I don't like this bed, it's too **soft**!'
> 'A **small** bed! I like this bed. Zzzzzzzzz!'
> The bears come back. Can you hear them? A small bear's footsteps, a medium bear's footsteps, a big bear's footsteps!
> Daddy Bear: '**Look** at my porridge!'; Mummy Bear: '**Look**! My porridge!'; Baby Bear: '**Look**! Boo! Boo! My porridge!'
> Daddy Bear: '**Look** at my chair!'; Mummy Bear: '**Look**! My chair!'; Baby Bear: '**Look**! Boo! Boo! My chair is broken!'
> Daddy Bear: '**Look** at my bed!'; Mummy Bear: '**Look** at my bed!'; Baby Bear: '**Look**! There is a girl in my bed!'
> Goldilocks wakes up and **sees** the bears. 'Aaagh! Three bears!!!'
> Goldilocks runs and runs as fast as she can!

8. ASSESSMENT

- Progress indicators: **Worksheets S-5/S-6/S-8/S-10/S-11**
- Informal observations on children's comprehension and performance in class (Appendix 1).
- Skills children should have acquired (these can be recorded on the children's ability record (Appendix 2) downloadable from the website):
  - **Content skills:** the child can identify similarities and differences between human beings; understand how the five senses help to know the world; can identify and describe object properties; can sort and classify according to chosen criteria
  - **Language skills:** the child can read and understand instructions; can describe himself and his classmates; can name the main external parts of the body; can talk about the use of the five senses; can classify sounds, smells and tactile properties; can describe object properties; can identify and name the taste of some foods
- Self evaluation: Appendix 3. The following statements can be written into the 'What I can do' column:

  I can identify and describe similarities and differences between humans.
  I can describe myself and a friend in English.
  I can identify the tastes of some foods.
  I can describe the functions of the sense organs.
  I can describe an object by its properties (colour, sound, smell, what it's like to touch).

ALL ABOUT ME • Me and my senses

S-1 WORKSHEET

How many faces can you make?

YOU CAN ONLY USE:

- 3 hairstyles ⟶

  curly   straight   long

- 3 noses ⟶ ○   △   ▢

  circle   triangle   square

- 3 mouths ⟶ ‿   ⌒   ~

  happy   sad   angry

LET'S TRY!

○ ○ ○ ○ ○ ○

○ ○ ○ ○ ○ ○

○ ○ ○ ○ ○ ○

ALL ABOUT ME • Me and my senses

S-2 WORKSHEET

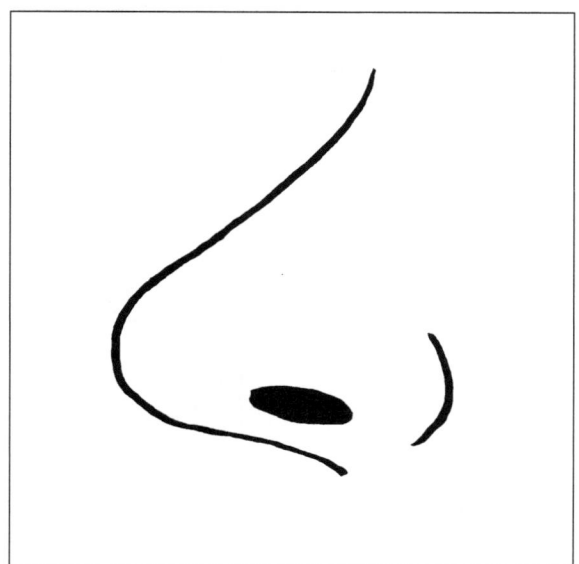
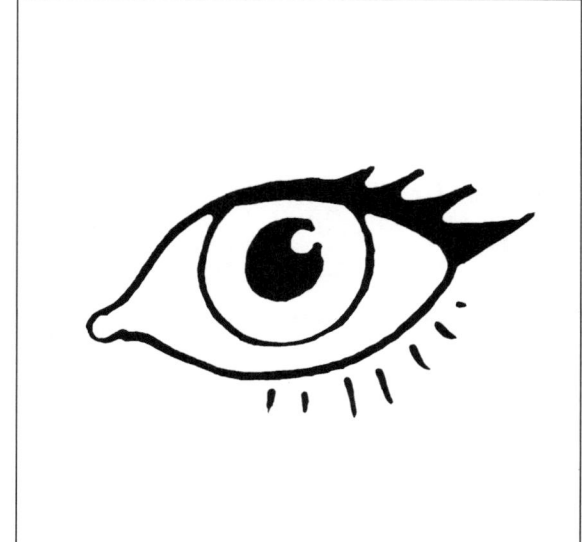

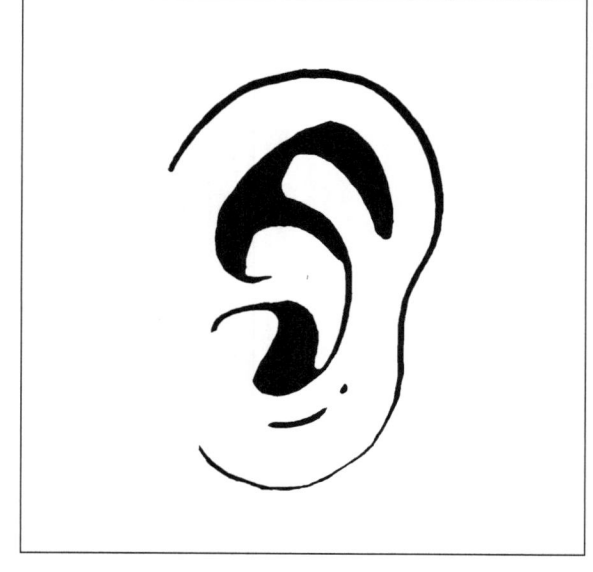
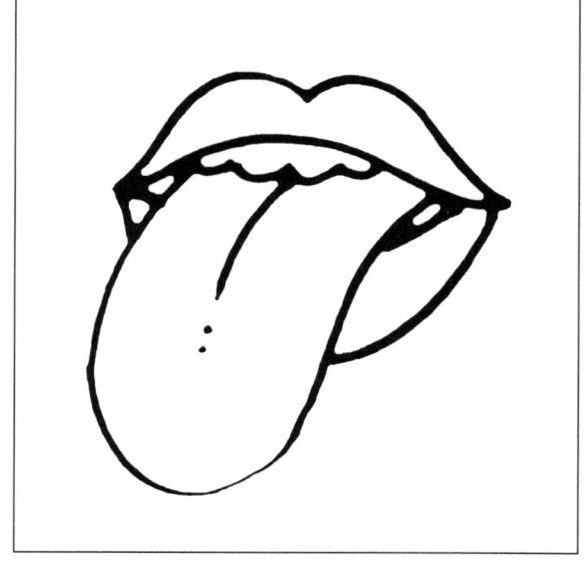

ALL ABOUT ME • Me and my senses

S-3 WORKSHEET

What's in the pot?

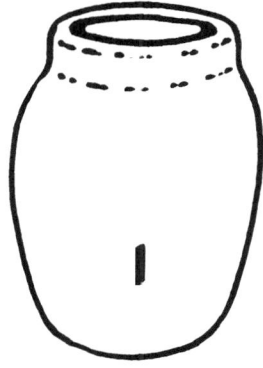

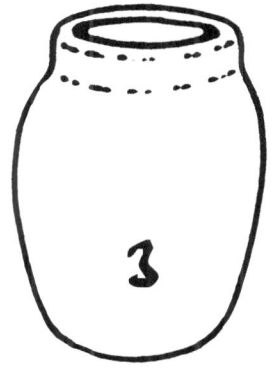

I think it's _____

☐ YES

☐ No, it's _____

I think it's _____

☐ YES

☐ No, it's _____

I think it's _____

☐ YES

☐ No, it's _____

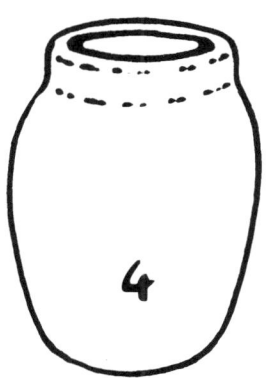

I think they are _____

☐ YES

☐ No, they are _____

I think they are _____

☐ YES

☐ No, they are _____

I think they are _____

☐ YES

☐ No, they are _____

ALL ABOUT ME • Me and my senses

S-4 WORKSHEET

I can see the colours of the rainbow

I THINK THEY ARE...

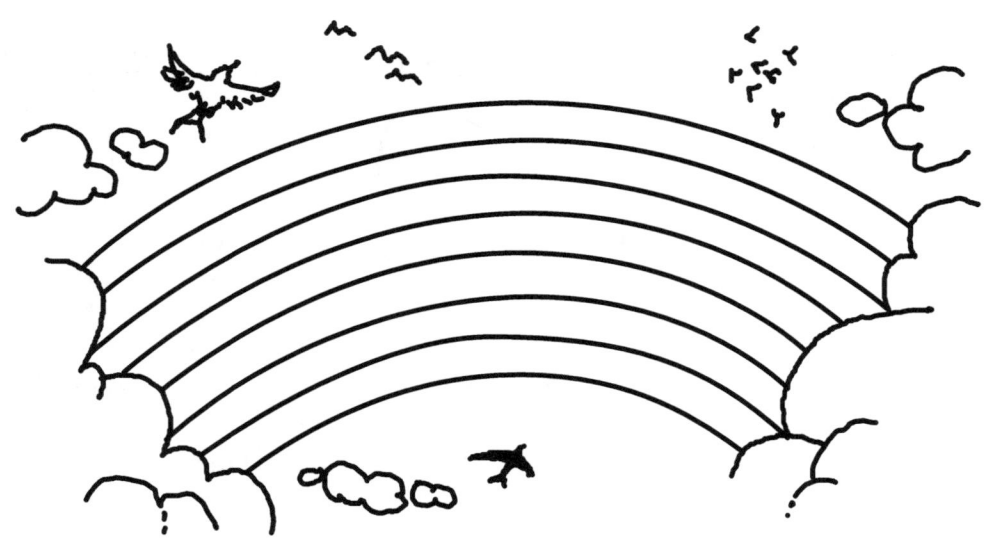

LET'S EXPERIMENT!
THERE ARE ... COLOURS IN A RAINBOW IN THIS ORDER:

1 .... 2 .... 3 .... 4 ....

5 .... 6 .... 7 ....

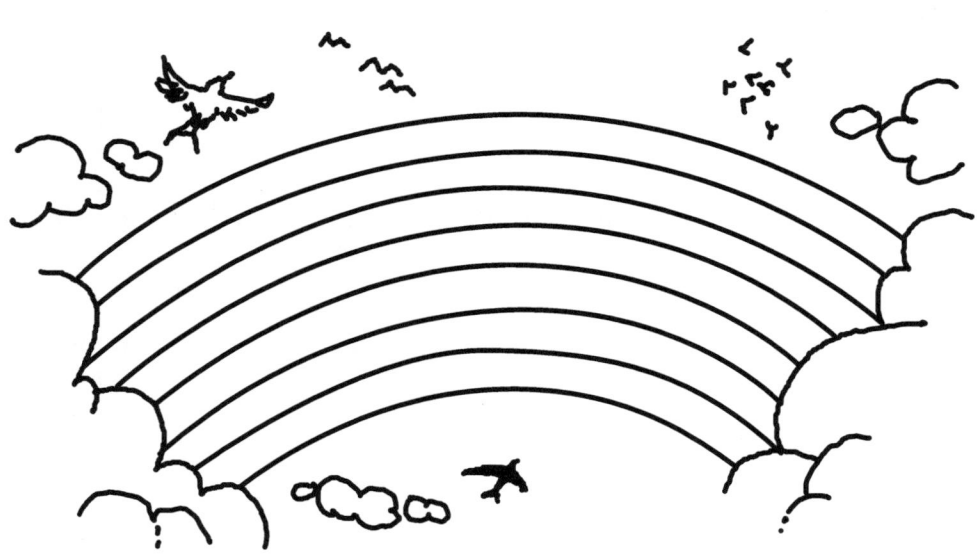

S-5 WORKSHEET

Taste buds

- Colour the **sweet** place on the tongue **yellow**.
- Colour the **sour** places on the tongue **grey**
- Colour the **bitter** place on the tongue **brown**.
- Colour the **salty** place on the tongue **orange**.

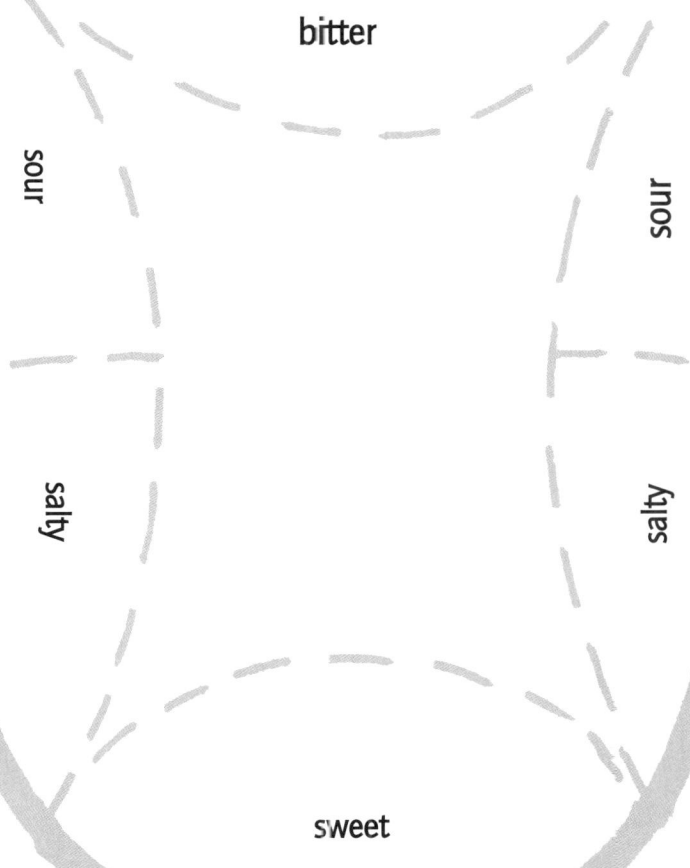

Cut out the foods and glue them in the right places on the tongue.
Colour the foods the same colour as the taste.

Sense of taste

Circle the correct taste for each food.

sweet　　salty　　sour　　bitter

sweet　　salty　　sour　　bitter

sweet　　salty　　sour　　bitter

sweet　　salty　　sour　　bitter

sweet　　salty　　sour　　bitter

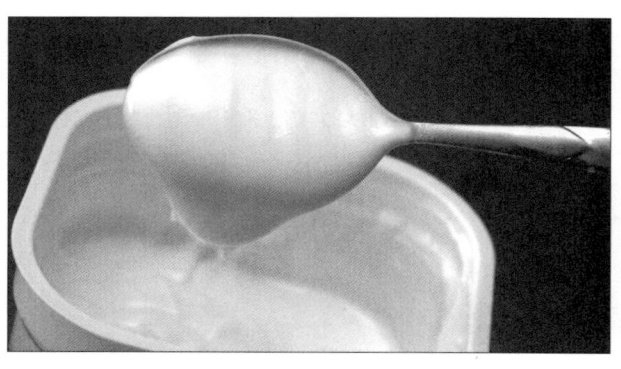

sweet　　salty　　sour　　bitter

How does it smell?

Join the pictures to the faces.

I have five senses

Colour in the pictures. Complete the sentences with the symbols and the words.

I can _____

with my tongue

I can _____

with my nose

I can _____

with my eyes

I can _____

with my ears

I can _____

with my hands

    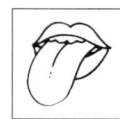   hear   taste   touch   see   smell

ALL ABOUT ME • Me and my senses

S-9 WORKSHEET

Nonsense poem

Write a nonsense poem matching words from the three columns.

My nonsense poem

ALL ABOUT ME • Me and my senses

S-10 WORKSHEET

Five senses quiz

Choose the right answer for each question.

I use my .... to see colours and shapes	I use my .... to hear a cat miaow
a) hand b) eyes c) tongue	a) nose b) eyes c) ears
I use my .... to taste chocolate	I use my nose to ....
a) ears b) eyes c) tongue	a) touch b) smell c) taste
I use my hands to	Cotton wool feels ....
a) taste b) smell c) touch	a) cold b) hard c) soft
A lemon tastes	An ice-cream tastes ....
a) sweet b) sour c) salty	a) cold b) salty c) sweet

All ABOUT ME • Me and my senses

S-11 WORKSHEET

Goldilocks

Read and circle the right picture.

What did Goldilocks see?

a school	a cottage	a tent

What did Goldilocks smell?

sausages	a cake	porridge

What did Goldilocks taste?

hot porridge	hot milk	ice-cream

What did Goldilocks touch?

a sofa	a bed	a cat

What did Goldilocks hear?

three birds	three dogs	three bears

   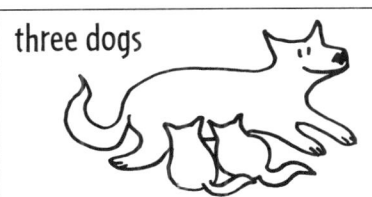  

Photocopiable © Oxford University Press

ALL ABOUT ME • Human body

	**CONTENT AREA**	**ALL ABOUT ME**
	**TOPIC**	Human body
	**AIMS**	• to identify the various parts of the human body • to recognize how some organs and internal systems work
	**LANGUAGE**	• to read and understand simple texts • to name the main organs of the body • to talk about the function of the main organs of the body • to speak about what we can do with our body • to describe a work of art
	**VOCABULARY AND STRUCTURES**	Use words and phrases relating to: organs and internal systems of the human body (*heart/brain/skeleton/intestine/nerves/spinal cord/brain/bones/blood/lungs/muscles/skin/tendons/chest/artery/vein/carbon dioxide/windpipe/liver/kidneys/stomach; break/mix/breathe/contract/relax/pull up/take in/remove*); adjectives (*fat, thin, long, short ...*); verbs of motion (*skip, roll, hop, crawl*); maths (*How many arms in all? plus/equals*); structures (*I can/can't; there is/are; It's made up of ...; Yes, I have/No, I haven't; I'm + ing; It's good at ...; it protects ...; the biggest/the smallest; shorter/longer; it makes me ...*)
	**WHAT CHILDREN NEED TO KNOW ALREADY**	• how to carry out an experiment and interpret the results • some words related to the human body • some adjectives (*curly/straight/long/short/young*) • superlatives/comparatives • *I can/can't* • *I'm + ing*
	**MATERIALS**	• **Worksheets B-1–B-12**
	**CROSS-CURRICULAR ACTIVITIES**	1. *My incredible body* 2. *Funny maths* 3. ICT 4. Art 5. Assessment

ALL ABOUT ME • Human body

1. MY INCREDIBLE BODY

Time: over many lessons
Materials: pictures of the human body, Worksheets B-1 to B-9

1.1 PREPARATION

This is a topic that, due to its difficult content, should be well integrated with the science curriculum. If the teacher of English is not the class science teacher, it's very important he/she plans the activities with the subject teacher in order to facilitate the acquisition of the content through a range of different activities both in English and mother tongue.
Check the children's knowledge about the human body and its functions. Use pictures of the human body to start a simple discussion in English: *Look at the human body. It's made up of different parts. It's like a complicated machine always working to keep you alive. Each part has a special job to do. All these parts need energy to work. Can you show me where the brain is in the body? Where is the heart?*

1.2 MY INCREDIBLE BODY BOOK

Use Worksheets B-1–B-8 to find out some basic information and curious facts about the internal systems and organs of the human body. Cut out the worksheets along the dotted lines, put them together in ascending order of size and staple them together to form a personal book entitled 'My incredible body'. If you use a Portfolio, you can get the children to include the completed book in the Portfolio Dossier together with a description form (Appendix 4).
The use of the Worksheets should be supported by other activities as suggested in the following steps:

a) **Skin covers and protects my body** [Worksheet B-1]

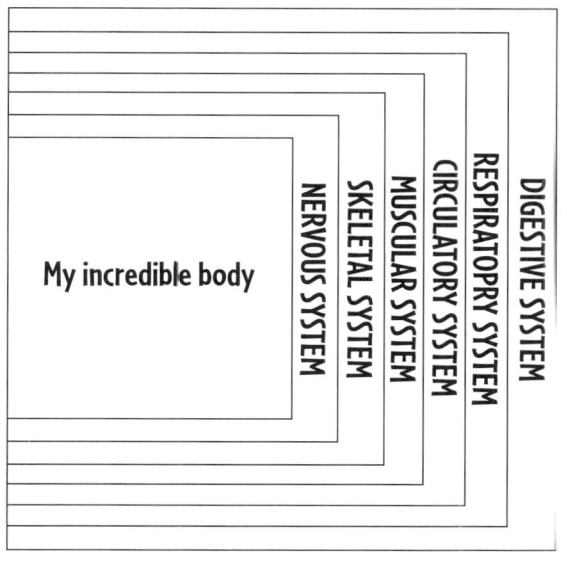

- Discuss with children about skin and its functions: *Why is skin important? What can you feel with your skin? Skin holds your body and protects you from the outside world. It is only about 2 mm thick. Some people's skin is darker than others' because it has more melanin. Dark skin is better protected from the sun.*
- Ask the children to touch different objects and describe what they feel (*it's hot/cold/smooth/rough/prickly/etc.*) (see the five senses topic for more activities).
- Give each child a copy of Worksheet B-1. Explain to the children that this Worksheet will become the front cover of their book about the human body and they should colour it in.

b) **Nervous system** [Worksheet B-2]
- Create a mind map with children. Write: *The brain is my body's control centre* in the centre of the board and ask children to give examples of how the brain controls our bodies.
- Play a game to revise or introduce new vocabulary where the children have to mime words linked to the different parts of the brain breathe (breathe deeply); balance (stand on one foot with arms out); sight (touch eyes); hearing (touch ears); touch (clap hands); action (turn around); speech (repeat a word); memory (point to a temple); thought (point to the forehead).

ALL ABOUT ME • Human body

- Split the class into teams of three or four. Explain to the children that they have to read through the information about the brain on **Worksheet B-2** and answer your questions. The first team to give a correct answer gets a point: *Which part of the brain is good at maths? (left); Does the brain work when you sleep? (yes); Which part of the brain is good at art (right); How is the brain linked to the rest of the body? (by nerves); What does the body send to the brain? (messages); What takes messages to and from the body (spinal cord and nerves); What is the nervous system? (it consists of nerves, spinal cord, and brain).*
- Get the children to test their memory by playing a memory game. In pairs, they have to look carefully for one minute at eight objects placed on a tray; then cover the tray with a cloth and ask each pair to draw or write the names of all the objects they can remember.

c) **Skeletal system** [Worksheet B-3]
- Bring in a poster or a model of a skeleton and ask children: *What is it? Why is it important? Do you know the name of any bone?* Teach the name of some bones of the skeletal system by labelling them and asking the children to practise reading and saying the new words. Help the children to remember the new words by giving out labels and asking them to put them next to the correct bones.
- Tell the children to read **Worksheet B-3**, match the names with the bones of the human skeleton, and answer the questions: *Why is the skeleton important? (because it holds my body and protects important organs); What does the skull protect? (the brain); What's the name of the bone that protects the spinal cord? (backbone); How many bones are there in you skeleton? (about 206); What's the biggest bone? (femur); How many bones are there in each hand? (27).*
- Highlight the function of the joints that let us bend and twist by making a jointed skeleton which can be hung up and used as a mobile. For a model and instructions see **Worksheet B-9** (to be photocopied and enlarged).

d) **Muscular system** [Worksheet B-4]
- Get the children to read the information on **Worksheet B-4**, identify and colour in the muscles in the picture. Check comprehension by asking: *How many muscles are there in your body? (about 620); How many muscles do you use for a single step? (about 200); Which muscles work automatically? (chest and stomach muscles; heart); How are muscles attached to the bones? (by tendons); How do muscles work? (in pairs; when one contracts the other one relaxes).*
- Play a game in which children have to mime different movements according to your directions: *We can move in different ways; we can walk, we can jump, we can skip, we can crawl ... roll ... bend ... stretch ... twirl ... hop, etc.*
- **My hands can ... /My legs can ...** Split the class into two groups. Explain that each group has 30 minutes to make a poster about actions hands and legs can perform (one group makes a poster about hands and the other one about legs). Children can choose to draw, or find pictures in magazines to illustrate the actions. At the end of the activity, hang the posters up in the classroom and ask each group to give a presentation of their work.

e) **Circulatory system** [Worksheet B-5]
- Start by asking the children what they know about the circulatory system. Get the children to read, in pairs, the information given on **Worksheet B-5** and report what they understood in mother tongue. Then help children to ask each other questions by writing some examples on the board: *How many ...? What colour is ...?* Tell the children to look at **Worksheet B-5**, identify and colour the heart and arteries red and the veins purple.

ALL ABOUT ME • Human body

- Get the children to measure their heartbeat when at rest and after a run: *Sitting still, count how many times your heart beats in one minute; now run on the spot for a minute; count your heart beats again. What's different? When does your heart beat fastest?*

f) **Respiratory system** [Worksheet B-6]
- Start by playing some games involving respiration.
  Blow football: make a miniature football pitch on a table, putting wooden bricks all round it to stop the ball getting out, (but leaving two openings for the goals). Put a table tennis ball on the pitch. Divide the children into two teams of three or four that have to stand at either end. Each player takes a straw with which s/he must try to blow the ball into the other goal: *Has everyone got a straw? Are you ready? At the first whistle you have to blow the ball into your opponent's goal! How many goals do you think you can score in five minutes?*
  Blow a candle out: place a candle on the table; in turn, the children try to find out how far away they can stand from the candle and still be able to blow it out: *From how far away can you blow the candle out?*
- Give out **Worksheet B-6** to each child. Introduce new words and explain how the respiratory system works. Ask the children to match the organ names to the parts of the respiratory system and to ask each other questions in pairs: *What are the lungs? How many times a minute do we breathe? What's 'windpipe' in ...* (mother tongue)?

g) **Digestive system** [Worksheet B-7]
  Explain to the children that our body needs food to keep it going. Before our body can use the food we eat, it has to be broken down into tiny pieces so that it can be carried all around our body by blood. This is called digestion. Introduce new words: stomach – oesophagus – intestine. Ask the children to match the different parts of the digestive system to the correct position on the outline of the human body on **Worksheet B-7** and fill in the text about the digestive process with the missing words (mouth, oesophagus, stomach, intestine). Tell them they can use the words twice.

1.3 LOOK AT MY BODY!
[Worksheet B-8]. This worksheet can be used for assessment. Give each child a copy of **Worksheet B-8** and ask them to identify the internal organs of the human body and colour them in according to the given instructions.

1.4 MR SKELETON
[Worksheet B-9]. Ask the children to glue the skeleton parts on to cardboard; cut out the bones, punch holes on the circle marks; connect the bones using brass paper fasteners and attach a short piece of string to the skeleton's skull.

2. Extension activity: FUNNY MATHS
Time: 20 minutes
Materials: Worksheet B-10
Give out **Worksheet B-10** and explain to the children that they have to do simple addition sums involving body parts: *Two feet, how many toes in all? Two dogs, how many legs in all? Three elephants, how many ears in all? Two monsters, how many noses in all? Four hands, how many fingers in all? Six boys and four girls, how many arms in all? Three dogs and four ducks, how many legs in all?*

3. Extension activity: ICT
Time: 30 minutes
Materials: computer, digital photos of each child

3.1 PREPARATION
Take a close-up photograph of each child with a digital camera. Correct the photographs, if necessary, with an imaging programme and save them in My Pictures folder.

3.2 THIS IS ME
Explain to the children that they have to open the Paint programme, insert their photo (Edit – Paste from – My Pictures) and place it in the centre of the page. They then have to draw the rest of the body following the teacher's instructions: ***Draw your neck, draw your body, draw your arms ...*** Depending on the language level of the children, you can ask them to add clothes and describe the way they are dressed: ***This is me. I'm wearing ...***

4. Extension activity: ART
Time: 1 hour 30 minutes; 20 minutes
Materials: Worksheets B-11 and B-12

- [Worksheet B-11]. Tell the children to cut out the parts of the body of Mr Man and put them together on a sheet of coloured paper to represent the actions that you say: ***he can jump; he can run; he can play football; he can swim.*** At the end of the activity children have to look for pictures in magazines and use them as backgrounds on which to stick Mr Man performing the different actions (e.g. a picture of the sea and Mr Man swimming; a picture of a stadium and Mr Man playing football).
- [Worksheet B-12]. **Bodies in art.** Bring in a selection of pieces of work by famous artists; analyse and discuss with the children how the artists represent the human body. Have the children look at the pictures by Modigliani, Botero, Giacometti, and Degas on Worksheet B-12, read the captions, and circle the words that match the description of the characters.

5. ASSESSMENT
- Progress indicators: **Worksheets B-8/B-10**
- Skills children should have acquired (these can be recorded on the children's ability record (Appendix 2) downloadable from the website)
  - **Content skills:** the child can identify and name the various parts of the body; knows how some organs and internal systems work; can find information in a simple text in English.
  - **Language skills:** the child can locate and name different parts of the body; can describe some characteristics of the organs and internal systems of the human body; can describe a picture or a portrait of the human body; can solve simple mathematical problems.
- Self evaluation: Appendix 3. The following statements can be written into the 'What I can do' column:
  I can name and talk about some internal organs and body systems and their functions.
  I can describe the human body in English.

B-1 WORKSHEET

ALL ABOUT ME • Human body

B-2 WORKSHEET

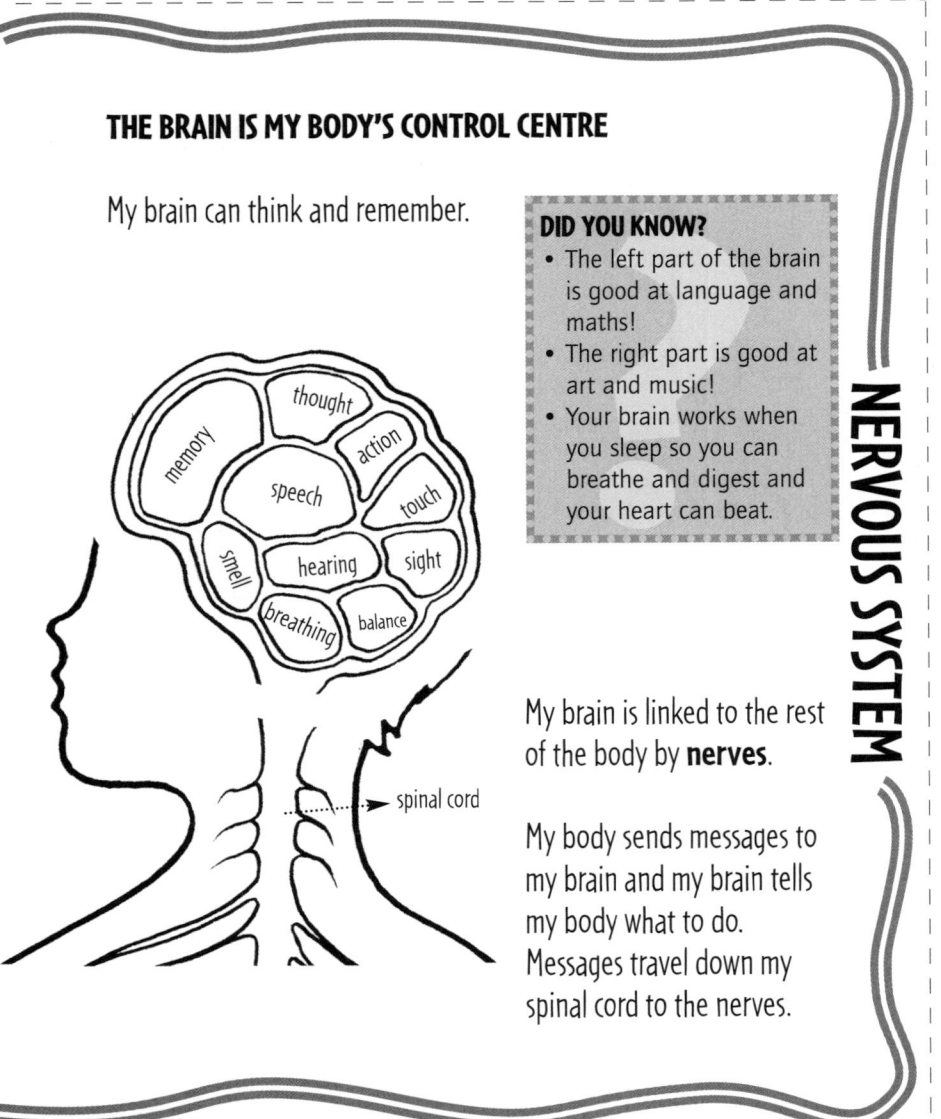

THE BRAIN IS MY BODY'S CONTROL CENTRE

My brain can think and remember.

DID YOU KNOW?
- The left part of the brain is good at language and maths!
- The right part is good at art and music!
- Your brain works when you sleep so you can breathe and digest and your heart can beat.

Brain parts: memory, thought, action, speech, touch, smell, hearing, sight, breathing, balance

spinal cord

NERVOUS SYSTEM

My brain is linked to the rest of the body by **nerves**.

My body sends messages to my brain and my brain tells my body what to do. Messages travel down my spinal cord to the nerves.

Colour the parts of the brain with different colours.

B-3 WORKSHEET

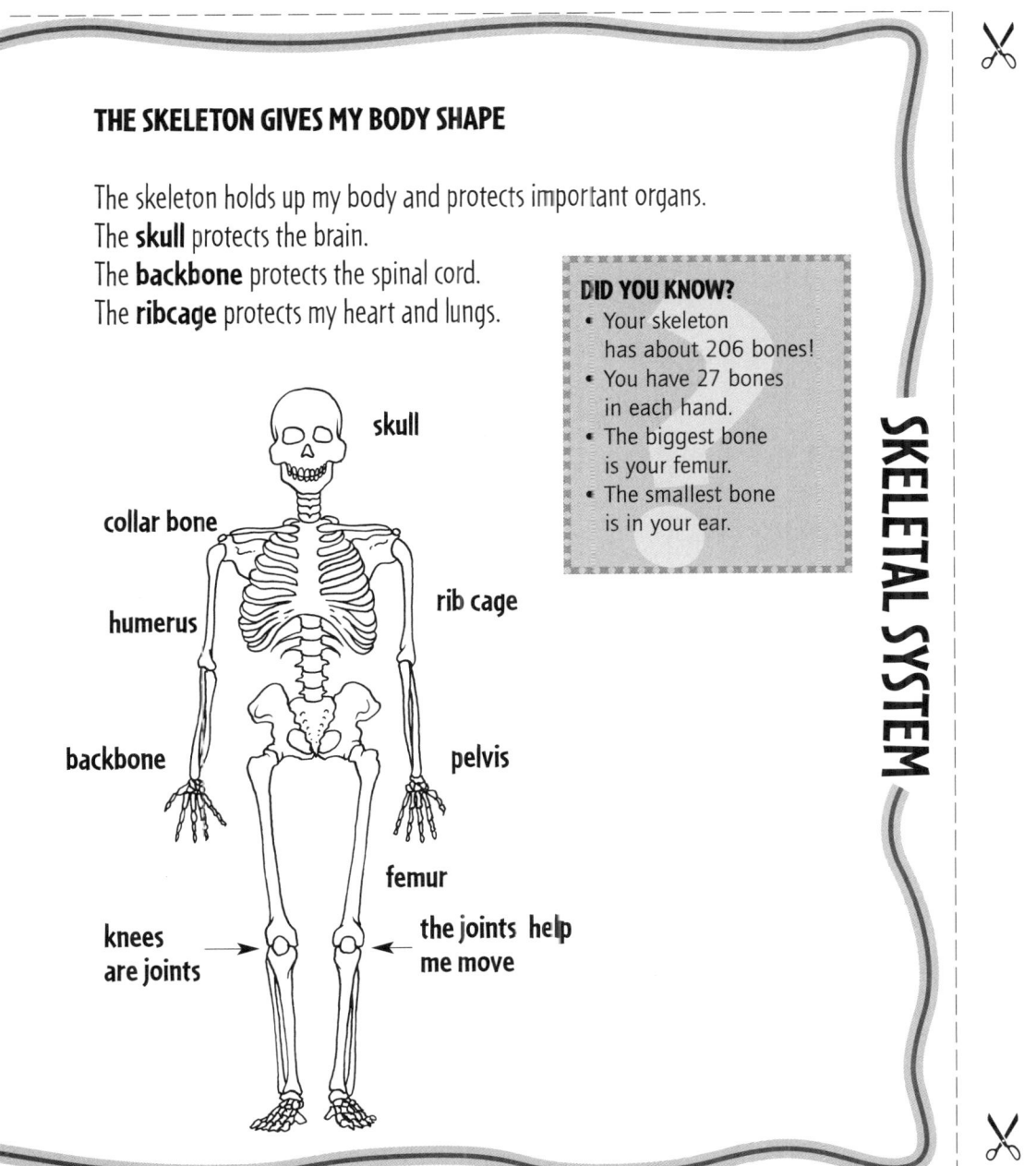

THE SKELETON GIVES MY BODY SHAPE

The skeleton holds up my body and protects important organs.
The **skull** protects the brain.
The **backbone** protects the spinal cord.
The **ribcage** protects my heart and lungs.

DID YOU KNOW?
- Your skeleton has about 206 bones!
- You have 27 bones in each hand.
- The biggest bone is your femur.
- The smallest bone is in your ear.

Labels: skull, collar bone, humerus, backbone, rib cage, pelvis, femur, knees are joints, the joints help me move

SKELETAL SYSTEM

Match the names to the bones.

B-4 WORKSHEET

MUSCLES MAKE ME MOVE

Muscles are under my skin.

Muscles are attached to my bones by **tendons**.

When I want to move, my brain sends a message to my muscles.

Muscles works in pairs:

one muscle gets shorter (contracts) and pulls the bone, the other muscle gets longer and relaxes.

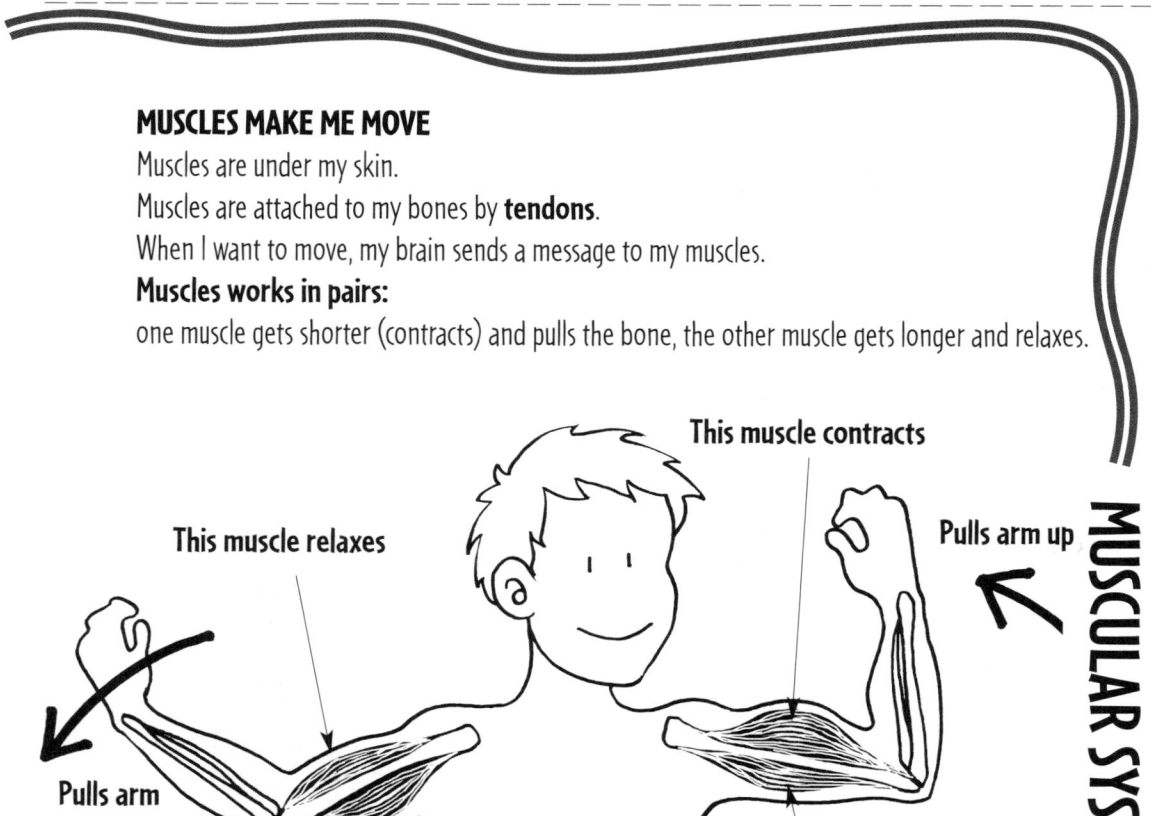

MUSCULAR SYSTEM

Some muscles work **automatically**: chest muscles to breathe and stomach muscles to digest food.

DID YOU KNOW?
- There are about 620 muscles in your body!
- When you smile you move about 30 small muscles in your face.
- When you walk you use about 200 muscles for every single step.

Colour the muscles.

B-5 WORKSHEET

BLOOD AND HEART MAKE UP THE CIRCULATORY SYSTEM

Blood moves oxygen and nutrients around the body and collects waste (carbon dioxide).

The heart is a muscle.
It pumps the blood around the body.

Arteries take the blood away from the heart to the body.
The blood in arteries is bright red and full of oxygen.

Veins take the blood back to the heart.
The blood is purplish red and there is no oxygen in it.

Artery to the lungs
Artery to the body
Vein from the body
Vein from the lungs
Heart muscle

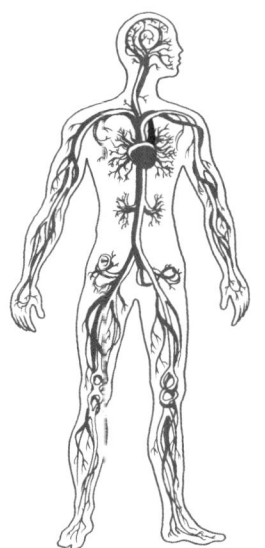

CIRCULATORY SYSTEM

DID YOU KNOW?
- A seven-year-old has 3 litres of blood.
- An adult has about 5 litres of blood.
- A child's heart beats about 100 times a minute.
- An adult's heart beats about 70 times a minute.

Colour the heart and the arteries red. Colour the veins purple.

ALL ABOUT ME • Human body

B-6 WORKSHEET

I CAN BREATHE WITH MY LUNGS

The lungs are big air sacs.

Lungs take in oxygen from the air into the blood and remove carbon dioxide. This happens every time I breathe in and out.

When I exercise I breathe faster because my muscles need more oxygen.

DID YOU KNOW?
- An adult's lungs can hold about five litres of air.
- Adults usually breathe 18 times a minute and more than 25,000 times a day.

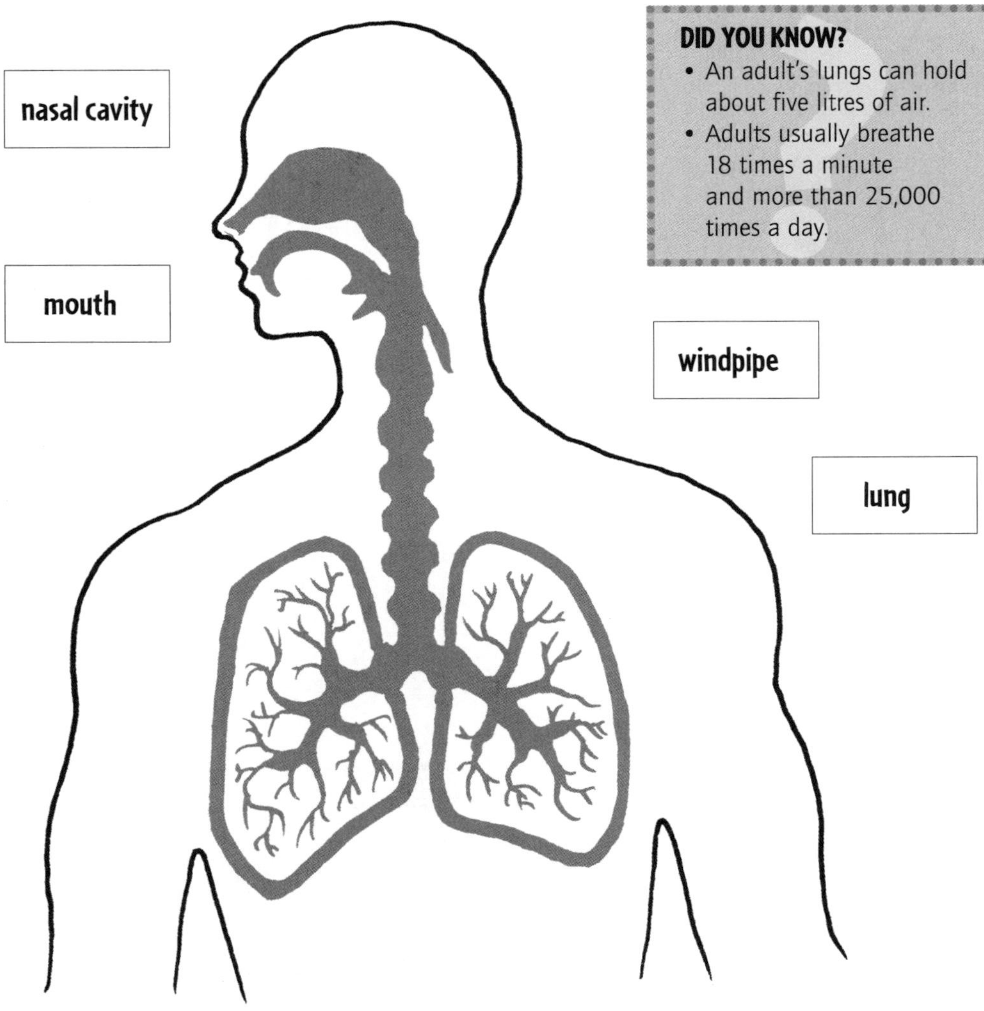

RESPIRATORY SYSTEM

nasal cavity

mouth

windpipe

lung

Match the names to the parts of the respiratory system.

B-7 WORKSHEET

Put the parts of the digestive system in the correct place. Then fill in the gaps in the sentences.

WHERE DOES FOOD GO?

DID YOU KNOW?
- The whole process of digestion lasts about 18 hours.
- Food usually stays in the stomach for about three hours.
- The small intestine is five metres long.

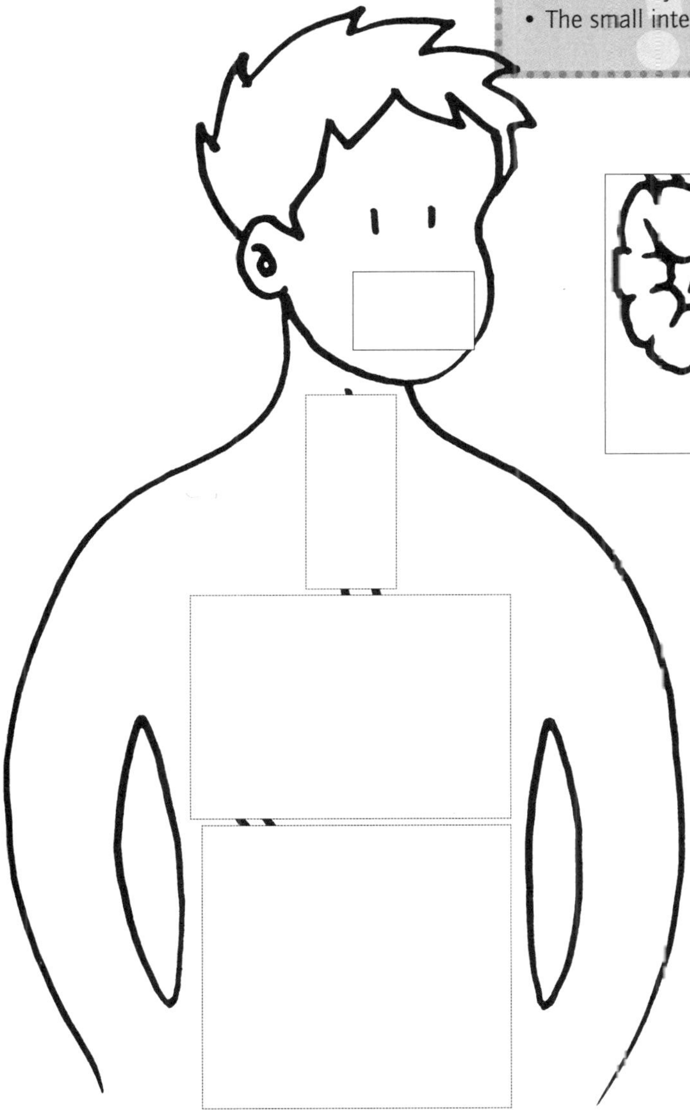

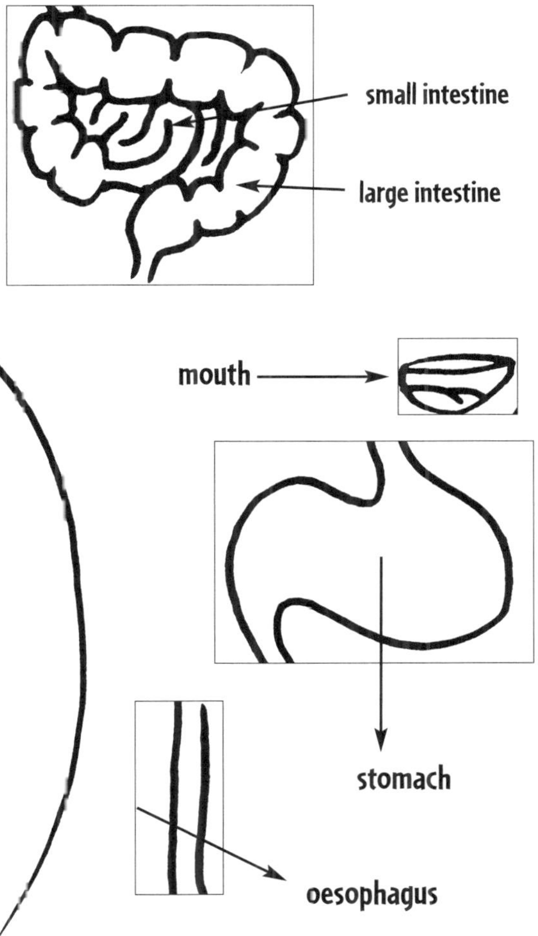

small intestine
large intestine
mouth
stomach
oesophagus

DIGESTIVE SYSTEM

My teeth break the food into small pieces. The food is mixed with saliva in my ....

The food goes down a tube called the oesophagus into my ....

My .... muscles mix the food with special juices to make it very soft.

The food goes from my .... into my ....

Nutrients in the food pass from the .... into my blood. The blood carries the nutrients to every part of my body.

Food that can't be digested comes out of my body when I go to the toilet.

ALL ABOUT ME • Human body

B-8 WORKSHEET

Look at my body!

Colour the picture:
- skeleton ➡ grey
- muscles ➡ pink
- lungs ➡ light blue
- heart ➡ red
- liver ➡ purple
- intestines ➡ green
- brain ➡ brown
- kidneys ➡ orange
- stomach ➡ yellow

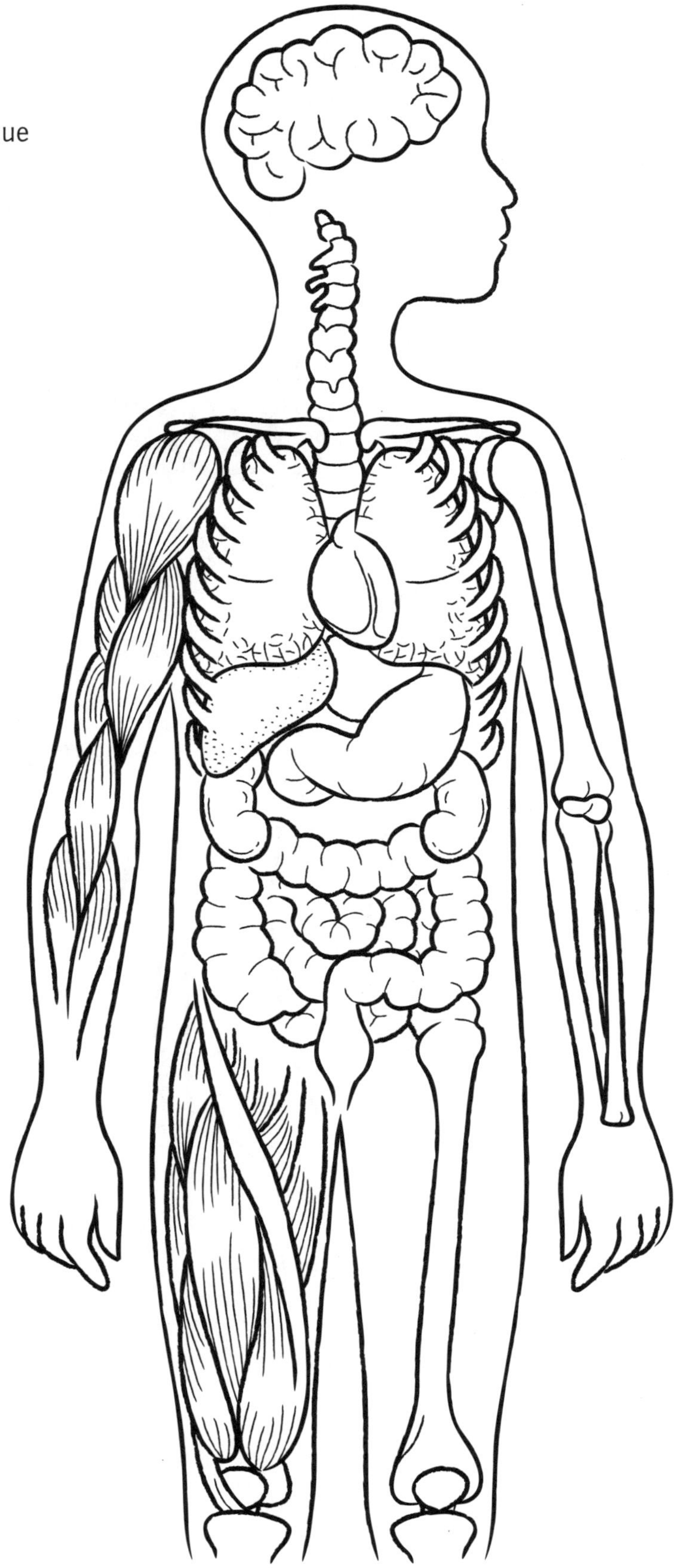

B-9 WORKSHEET

Mr Skeleton

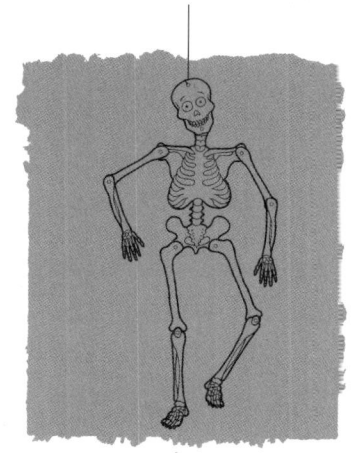

1. Glue the skeleton parts on to cardboard.
2. Cut out the bones.
3. Punch holes on the circle marks.
4. Connect the bones using brass paper fasteners.
5. Attach a short piece of string to your skeleton's skull.

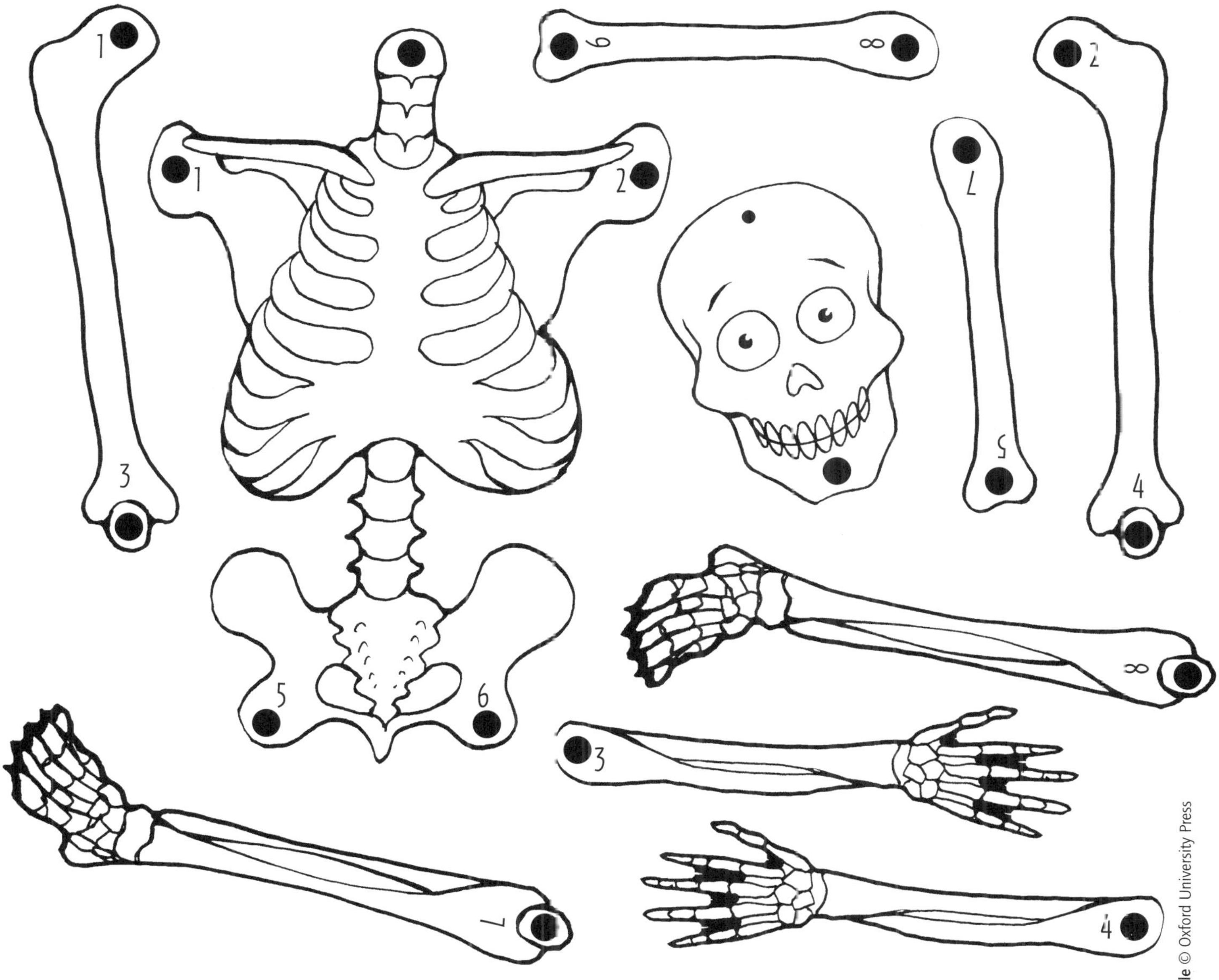

ALL ABOUT ME • Human body

B-10 WORKSHEET

Funny maths

🦶 + 🦶 　　　　 5 + ☐ = ☐ TOES

🐕 + 🐕　　　　 ☐ + 4 = ☐ LEGS

🐘 + 🐘 + 🐘 　 ☐ + ☐ + ☐ = ☐ EARS

😀 + 😀　　　　 ☐ + ☐ = ☐ NOSES

✋ + ✋ + ✋ + ✋ 　 ☐ + ☐ + ☐ + ☐ = ☐ FINGERS

6	BOYS +	4	GIRLS.	→	How many arms in all? ☐
3	DOGS +	4	DUCKS.	→	How many legs in all? ☐
☐	.... +	6	CATS.	→	How many eyes in all? ☐
☐	.... +	☐	....	→	How many feet in all? ☐
☐	.... +	☐	....	→	How many .... in all? ☐

Let's count.

B-11 WORKSHEET

I can move in different ways

1. Cut out the parts of the body.

2. Place the body parts on a sheet of coloured paper to represent different movements (follow your teacher's instructions).

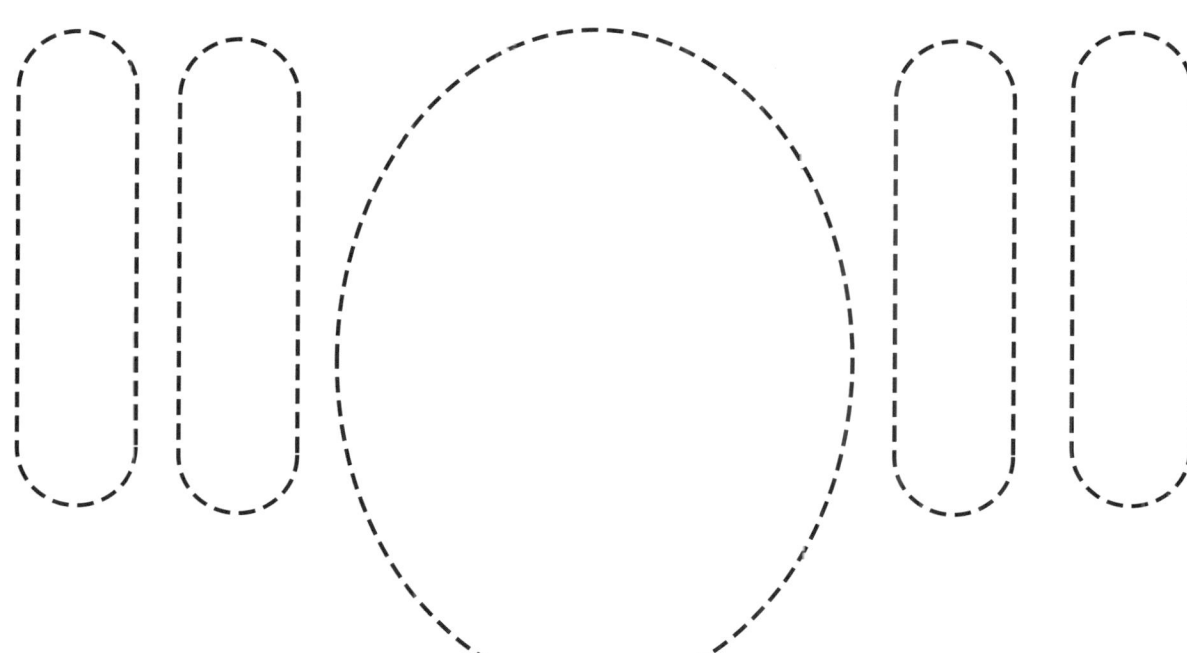

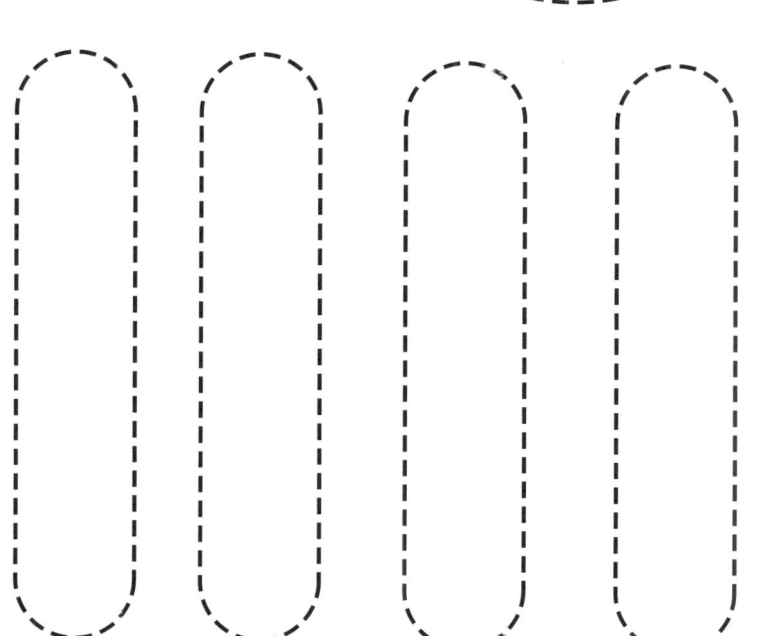

Bodies in art

B-12 WORKSHEET

Read and circle the right words in each sentence.

Ritratto di Jean Hébuterne, A. Modigliani, 1919.

I can see a **man/woman**.
She has got **curly/straight** hair.
She has got a **long/short** nose.
She is **fat/thin**.

Famiglia colombiana, F. Botero, 1999.

I can see a family **in a park/inside a house**.
The girl has got **big/small** eyes.
The mother has got **short/long** hair.
They are quite **thin/fat**.

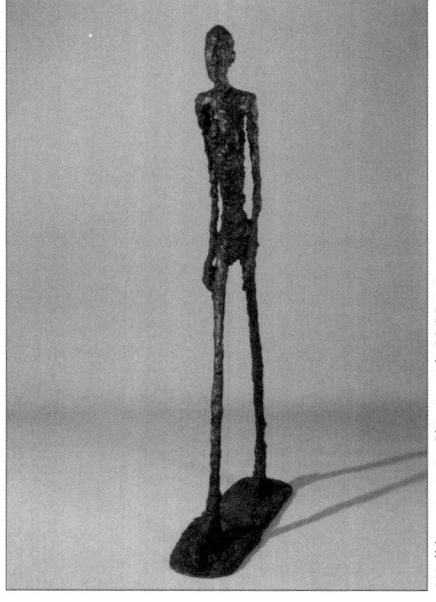

Walking man, A. Giacometti, 1960.

I can see a **man/woman**.
He has got a **thin/fat** body.
He has got **long/short** legs.
He is **sitting/walking**.

Ballerina di quattordici anni, E. Degas, 1880.

I can see a **man/woman**.
I **can/can't** see her eyes.
She looks **old/young**.
She is **dancing/standing**.

THE WORLD AROUND ME

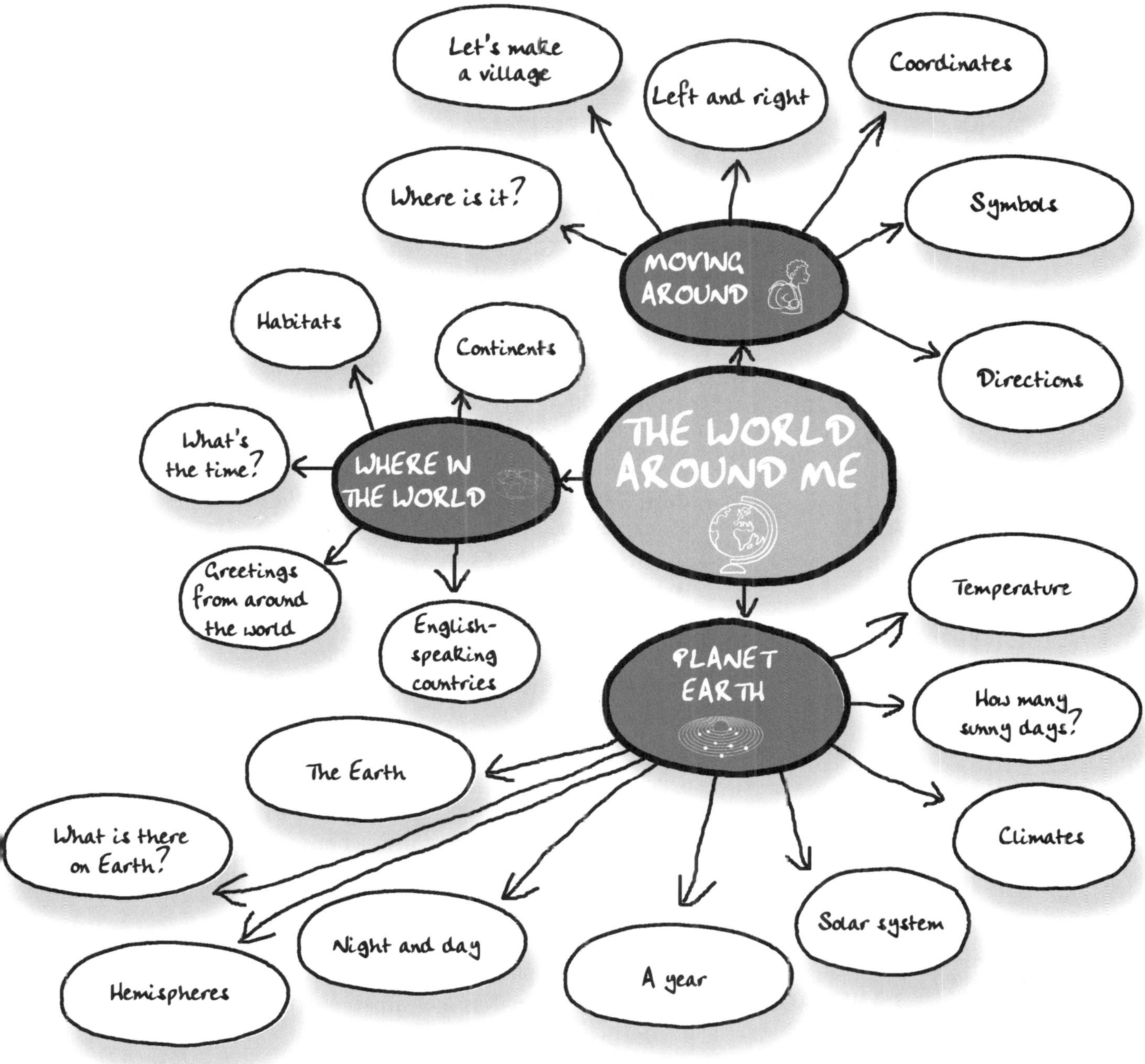

THE WORLD AROUND ME

- **MOVING AROUND**
  - Let's make a village
  - Where is it?
  - Left and right
  - Coordinates
  - Symbols
  - Directions

- **WHERE IN THE WORLD**
  - Habitats
  - Continents
  - What's the time?
  - Greetings from around the world
  - English-speaking countries

- **PLANET EARTH**
  - Temperature
  - How many sunny days?
  - Climates
  - Solar system
  - A year
  - Night and day
  - The Earth
  - What is there on Earth?
  - Hemispheres

CONTENT AREA — THE WORLD AROUND ME

TOPIC — Moving around / Planet Earth / Where in the world

AIMS

- to understand spatial relationships between elements within an environment and recognize the importance of points of reference in making sense of the space
- to understand and use co-ordinates and symbols to locate places on a map
- to recognize key lines of latitude and longitude on the globe (parallels, meridians)
- to use atlases, globes, maps, and plans at a range of scales (e.g. using keys, grids)
- to recognize the Earth as part of a wider solar system
- to identify natural cycles on Earth (day/night/seasons)
- to draw maps using symbols and cardinal points
- to describe where places are (region, country, continent)
- to identify the relationships between the elements of an environment
- to identify key climate change stages in history and their characteristics

LANGUAGE

- to read and understand instructions
- to distinguish between natural and synthetic objects
- to answer simple questions
- to read short informative texts
- to use appropriate geographical vocabulary
- to read and analyse a weather report and talk about the weather
- to compare weather conditions and temperatures
- to describe location by using coordinates and cardinal points
- to describe some physical and political features of continents and countries (environments, climate, states, capitals, borders)

THE WORLD AROUND ME • Moving around

	**VOCABULARY AND STRUCTURES**	Use words and phrases relating to: relative positions (*in front of, behind, near*); directions (*left, right, North, South, West, East*); buildings (*cinema, church, museum, bookshop,* etc.); environments (*hill, sea, mountain range, river, lake, desert, grassland,* etc.); geographical coordinates (*parallels, meridians, prime meridian, equator, tropics*); planets; continents; states; means of transport
	**WHAT CHILDREN NEED TO KNOW ALREADY**	• how to measure • how to use sources of information • how to collect and record evidence • how to analyse evidence and draw conclusions • ordinal numbers and numbers to 100 • buildings and shops; right/left • the structures: *I can; What's the time? Where do you live? Where is …?; What's …? It has got …* • how to use ICT for investigations
	**MATERIALS**	• Atlases • **Worksheets W-1–W-26**
	**CROSS-CURRICULAR ACTIVITIES**	1. *Moving around* 2. *Follow a route* 3. *Planet Earth* 4. *Climates* 5. *Where in the world* 6. ICT 7. Assessment

THE WORLD AROUND ME • Moving around

> Geography is a vast subject, and the range of topics included in the following pages does not claim to represent every aspect of it. The aim is to suggest some practical activities which develop a variety of skills and that teachers can integrate with their geography teaching plans. Activities can be used as support and reinforcement for concepts and skills that have already been acquired by the children. Each topic is organized as a module made up of a range of activities intended to develop certain geographical skills; the teacher can either use all the activities or just choose those that best suit the needs of the class.

1. MOVING AROUND

Time: 6 hour module
Materials: boxes of different sizes, a hoop, **Worksheet W-1**

1.1 WHERE IS IT?

a) Organize a wide range of activities (games in the gym, treasure hunts, route plans) to develop and reinforce the concept of spatial relationships and location (on, under, near, in, in front of, behind, between, on the left, on the right, etc.).

b) Bring in boxes of different sizes. Explain to the children that they have to use them to build a model of the classroom inside a big box. They have to identify where windows and doors are, place the pieces of furniture in the right place, and describe the model: ***Where's the teacher's desk? It's in front of the desks. How many desks are there? There are 24 desks. My desk is next to ...; the blackboard is between the ... and the ...;*** etc.

c) Put the model of the classroom on the floor and get the children to look at it from different view points (from above, from the left side, etc.). Help the children to understand that a map or a plan is a representation of an area seen from above: ***A plan is a picture of something made by looking down on it.*** Tell them to draw a birds-eye view plan of their classroom by looking at the model from above.

1.2 LET'S MAKE A VILLAGE

Explain that the children are going to make a model of the district where the school is or of an imaginary village by using boxes of different sizes. Tell the children to colour each box and turn it into a building (for example, post office, school, bank, etc.). Ask questions about the building each child has made (***What is it? What colour is it? Who lives in the house?***) and get them to agree how to locate the buildings to make a village. Help the children to describe the village: ***Where's the post office? It's in front of/between/*** etc.; ***What colour is the bank? It's yellow. Is it near the school? Yes, it is; No, it isn't!***

1.3 LEFT AND RIGHT

a) Get the children to play the **Knives and forks** game.
  - Split the class into three groups (knives, forks, and spoons).
  - Place a hoop (the plate) in the middle of the gym, or any other empty room, and ask each group to stand by it.
  - Show the children how to mime the cutlery (fork = arms raised and apart; knife = one arm raised and the other one down alongside the body; spoon = arms raised and hands clasped making a circle).

THE WORLD AROUND ME • Moving around

- Help the children to identify the right and left sides of the room in relation to their position and to the hoop on the floor in front of them. You can facilitate the activity by sticking a red label on the right side of the room and a blue label on the left side.
- Explain to the children that they have to follow your instructions: **Knives run to the right, forks run to the left, spoons run to the right.** When you say: **Set the table**, everyone has to run back to the hoop and stand in the right position (knives and spoons on the right of the hoop, forks on the left of it).

b) **Setting the table.** Set a table with breakfast food as shown on **Worksheet W-1**. Ask four children to sit around the table and pretend to be a family, each child playing a different role (mother, father, brother, sister). Divide the other children into groups of three or four and put each group behind one family member. Tell the children to observe and write down the food on the right and on the left of the family member to whom they have been assigned. At the end of the activity get the children to compare the descriptions and draw conclusions (the food on the right of a character is on the left of the one sitting next to him/her, and so on).

c) **Left or right?** Give out copies of **Worksheet W-1** and tell the children to complete it. Check the exercise by asking: **Who's on Robert's left? Who's on Robert's right? What's on Robert's left? What's on Robert's right?**

2. FOLLOW A ROUTE

Time: 3 hour module
Materials: Worksheets W-2 to W-6, digital camera

2.1 COORDINATES

a) Use chalk to draw a simple grid on the floor with numbers across the bottom and letters of the alphabet vertically up the side. Place objects on the chart and ask the children to read the coordinates: **Where's the pen? It's in B2**, etc. You can ask some children to stand on different squares of the chart and ask the others to describe their position: **Mary is standing in A8**.

b) Give out copies of **Worksheet W-2** and ask the children to colour in the squares following the written instructions. At the end of the activity, if they have done it correctly, they should have a picture of a cottage and a tree.

2.2 SYMBOLS

The following activities are aimed at getting the children to use conventional signs on maps.

a) Take the children for a walk in the neighbourhood and ask them to note down the buildings and facilities they see.
- Take photographs and use them to make a map of the area on a poster on which the school and the main streets have been marked previously.
- Ask the children to invent symbols to represent the buildings and other features of the area.
- Tell the children to draw the symbols on cards: ▲ = building; ⚘ = trees; ⚱ = church
- Draw a second map and ask the children to place the symbols on it instead of the photographs.

b) Give out copies of **Worksheet W-3**. Explain to the children that they have to colour in only the symbols that represent buildings and services in the area near the school. Then they have to draw a map of the school area by using the symbols from the key and adding others if necessary.

c) **A tourist map.** Divide the children into pairs or groups of three and give a copy of **Worksheet W-4** to each group; the children have to colour the symbols in the key and draw them where they like on the tourist map (each symbol may be used more than once).

2.3 DIRECTIONS

Discuss, in mother tongue, what a compass is and how it works: *A compass helps you to find directions. Maps are usually made with North at the top and South at the bottom.*

a) Give out copies of **Worksheet W-5** and ask the children to complete the map by following the given instructions.

b) Magic broom hunt. Give out copies of **Worksheet W-6** and explain the instructions. Organize a speed game: the winner is the first child to find the magic broom by following the right route on the map.

3. PLANET EARTH

Time: 6 hour module
Materials: a globe, physical and political maps of the world, **Worksheets W-7 to W-14**, PC

3.1 THE EARTH

Show the children a globe and a physical map of the world and ask them to compare the ways in which the Earth is represented on both of them (draw their attention to how the sea, the land, lakes, rivers, and forests are represented). Tell them to colour the land brown and the sea blue on **Worksheet W-7**.

3.2 WHAT IS THERE ON EARTH?

Brainstorm with the children which kind of environments they know: forest, grassland, desert, hills, countryside, rivers, mountains, sea, islands, etc. Write the names of the environments identified by the children on strips of paper and put them in a bag. Organize the class into groups; ask each group to pick a strip out the bag, read the name of the environment, and agree on a technique to make a display (e.g. collage, pastels, watercolours, images made with a Drawing programme, etc.). When they've finished, each group has to write a short description below their picture, and describe it to the other groups. Then, tell the children to match the names with the environment pictures on **Worksheet W-8**.

3.3 HEMISPHERES

Use a globe to explain to the children that *the Earth is a sphere and imaginary lines go around it. The equator is the biggest circle and it's equidistant from the North Pole and the South Pole* (ask the children to identify and point to the equator, North Pole, and South Pole on the globe). *The equator divides the Earth in half: the top half is the northern hemisphere and the bottom half is the southern hemisphere* (ask the children to point these out on the globe). *'Parallels' are the 90 circles north and 90 circles south of the equator. Meridians are circles that divide Earth in 360° grades from north to south* (get children to identify parallels and meridians on the globe and on a physical map).

a) **Hemispheres.** Give out copies of **Worksheet W-9** and ask the children to colour in the two hemispheres according to the given instructions.

b) **Parallels and meridians.** Children have to write the appropriate names of the parallels, meridians, and Poles next to the corresponding numbers on **Worksheet W-10** (note that the 0 meridian through Greenwich is also known as the prime meridian).

c) **Latitude and longitude.** Give a copy of **Worksheet W-11** to each child and ask them to colour it in according to the instructions.

3.4 NIGHT AND DAY

a) Using a globe explain to the children that *an axis is an imaginary line drawn through the centre of the Earth from the North Pole to the South Pole. The Earth takes 24 hours to*

THE WORLD AROUND ME • Planet Earth

spin on its own axis. We call it a day. When one side is facing the sun, it is daytime. When it is facing away from the sun it's night time. It's advisable to organize some experiments with the science teacher in order to make the concept of the Earth spinning round its axis clear to children. Here is the procedure for making a sundial to record the position of the shadows during the day:

1. Push a long stick into the ground.
2. Every hour put a stone at the end of the shadow.
3. Get the children to make predictions about the results of the experiment (i.e. the length, direction, and position the shadows will fall in).
4. Verify predictions.
5. At what time is the shadow longest?

The length and the position of shadows change. Shadows are long in the morning and evening because the sun is low in the sky. Shadows are short at midday because the sun is high in the sky. The sun doesn't move. It's the Earth that moves!

b) Give a copy of **Worksheet W-12** to each child; tell the children to look at the picture and read the information given. Then, according to their language level, they have to draw or write some activities that can be carried out during the day and others that can be carried out at night in the appropriate boxes.

3.5 A YEAR

a) Brainstorm children's knowledge by asking: *Does the Earth orbit another planet? How many days does the Earth take to orbit the sun? How are the Earth and sun related to the seasons? Why do we have four seasons? What causes our seasons? How does the Earth's tilt affect seasons? Is the season in the northern hemisphere the same as the season in the southern? Nights are longer in winter and shorter in summer. Why?*

b) Collect children's answers, tell them to look at the picture on **Worksheet W-13**, and organize some experiments with the science teacher in order to make the concepts clear: *It takes 365 days for the Earth to orbit the sun. As the Earth orbits the sun and rotates around its axis, not in a perpendicular way but at an angle of 23°, the seasons change. The seasons change according to the Earth's distance from the sun.*

c) Tell the children to read the description of the four seasons on **Worksheet W-13**, write the appropriate season name in each box, and illustrate each season.

3.6 SOLAR SYSTEM

Preparation: revise ordinal numbers.

a) Organize the class into eight groups and give each group the name of a planet. Each group has to prepare a fact-file related to the assigned planet by searching, on the Internet or in science books, for a picture of their planet and some information about it (e.g. dimensions, temperature, and distance from the sun). At the end of the activity, each group has to speak about its planet to the others.

b) Give out copies of **Worksheet W-14** and explain to the children that they have to number the planets from the nearest to the furthest from the sun (1. Mercury; 2. Venus; 3. Earth; 4. Mars; 5. Jupiter; 6. Saturn; 7. Uranus; 8. Neptune). They may be able to answer the questions from their previous research but if not then they will have to look for information in resource books or on the Internet to identify the features of some of the planets and be able to write their names in the appropriate spaces.

(Solutions: a. Venus is the hottest planet; b. Neptune and Uranus are the coldest planets; c. Jupiter is the biggest planet; d. Mars is called the red planet; e. Mercury is the smallest planet.)

4. CLIMATES

Time: over many lessons
Materials: **Worksheets W-15 to W-17**, thermometers, Internet, newspapers

4.1 CLIMATES

Explain to the children that the temperature of any place on Earth depends on its distance from the equator. Ask the children to read the definitions on **Worksheet W-15**, identify which type of climate they refer to, and fill in the gaps using the word bank.

Continental climates have warm summers and very cold winters; Mediterranean climates are hot and dry in summer, rainy in winter; desert climates are very hot and dry; tropical climates are hot all year around and they have only two seasons: a dry season and a wet season; equatorial climates have only one season: hot and wet; polar climates are cold all year around – they have a long cold winter and a short summer. The coldest places on Earth are the areas within the Arctic and Antarctic circles.

4.2 HOW MANY SUNNY DAYS?

Ask the children to keep a record of the weather over a month by using **Worksheet W-16**. Each day, children have to colour in the square corresponding to the weather. At the end of the month ask the children to analyse the data: *How many sunny days? How many rainy days?*

4.3 TEMPERATURE

a) Plan activities with the geography teacher to get the children to find out how a thermometer works. Ask the children: *What do we use thermometers for? We use a thermometer to tell us how hot or cold something is. We can use thermometers to measure the air temperature.*

b) Tell the children to place thermometers in different parts of the school (indoors, outdoors, in the shade, in the sun). At an established time of the day they have to read, record, and compare the temperatures recorded by the various thermometers.

c) Explain to the children that they have to record the outside temperature over a period of time and observe the variation of the temperature in relation to the weather conditions and to the seasons (e.g. record the temperature the first week of each month, or for a whole month). The children can use the chart on **Worksheet W-17** for a monthly record of the temperature and of the weather conditions (you can ask the children to fill in the Worksheet for homework).

d) Another interesting activity is to get the children to compare the temperature in different parts of the world. They have to record the temperature of selected cities for a certain number of days in different seasons by collecting information from newspapers, the Internet, or television. At the end of the experiment, children can read and interpret the data they have collected: *the highest autumn temperature was in ...; the lowest winter temperature was in ...;* etc. (See example on the next page.)

5. WHERE IN THE WORLD

Time: 6 hour module
Materials: globe, **Worksheets W-18 to W-23**, copies of a political map of the world

5.1 CONTINENTS

a) Show the children a globe and ask them to point to the continents on it: *How many continents are there? Do you know their names? Can you point to them on the globe?* Give out

THE WORLD AROUND ME • Where in the world

CITY	Country	AUTUMN									WINTER									SPRING									SUMMER								
		Month: October days:									Month: …… days:									Month: ….. days:									Month: …… days:								
		10	11	12	13	14	15																														
My town ……………	…………																																				
Rome	Italy	20°																																			
Nairobi	…………																																				
Ottawa	…………																																				
Sydney	…………																																				
…………																																					

copies of **Worksheet W-18**; tell the children to colour in the key, write the names of the continents on the map, and colour them according to the colours in the key.

b) Organize a game to get the children to locate some countries and their capitals. Split the class into two or three teams. Hang two or three copies of a world map on the wall or on the board. Give a crayon to each team. Say the name of a country (e.g. Brazil): a child from each group has to run to a world map and colour the right country in (the group can help them locate it). The first team to colour the right country in gets a point. The team that collects the highest number of points by the end of the game is the winner.

c) Get the children to look for interesting information on the Internet about physical features: the longest river in the world; the highest mountain; the biggest ocean; the highest waterfall, etc

5.2 WHAT'S THE TIME?

Give out copies of **Worksheet W-19** and explain to the children that the Earth is divided into 24 different time zones and that it is possible to establish the time in each country in the world starting from the Greenwich 0 meridian. When travelling towards the east you must add one hour to your clock for each time zone; when travelling towards the west you must subtract one hour for each time zone. Ask the children to look at the map on the Worksheet and answer the questions.

5.3 ANIMAL HABITATS

a) Check the children's knowledge about animals and their habitats. Ask them to cut out pictures of animals from magazines or print Clipart from any software. Explain to the children that they have to classify the animals according to the places where they live and then glue them on big posters: **These animals live in hot places/These animals live in cold places.**

b) **Animal habitats.** Give out copies of **Worksheet W-20** and ask the children to find the odd animal out for each habitat.

c) **On land, in water, or in the air?**
- Split the class into groups of four. Pre-teach some vocabulary if necessary (it does/it doesn't …; it has got wings, tail, fins, scales, etc.). Tell each group to think of an animal that lives on land,

in water, or in the air. The other groups have to guess, in turns, what animal it is by asking questions: **Does it live in hot places? Does it live on land? Has it got a tail? Has it got four legs? Has it got wings?** Answers can only be affirmative or negative (**Yes, it does; No, it doesn't; Yes, it has; No, it hasn't**).
- Give out copies of **Worksheet W-21**. Ask the children where the animals live: **Where does a dolphin live? On land, in the water, or in the air?** Explain to the children that they have to cut out the animals at the bottom of the Worksheet and stick them in the right habitat.

5.4 GREETINGS FROM AROUND THE WORLD

a) Brainstorm the names of some countries from different continents with the children (e.g. Great Britain, France, Latvia, Italy, Russia, India, Japan, Mexico, Canada, USA, etc.). Organize the children into groups, say the names of some countries, one at a time, and ask the children to identify them on a big world map. The first team to correctly locate the country gets a point. The team that has the highest number of points at the end of the game is the winner.

b) **Postcards from ...** Ask the children to bring in some postcards, identify the places they come from in an atlas, stick the postcards on a poster, and write next to each of them as much information as they can find about the location: city, country, continent, flag, etc. (As an alternative to postcards you could download pictures from the Internet.)

c) **Weather report.** Explain to the children that they have to read the weather forecast on **Worksheet W-22**, locate the countries on the blank map, and draw the appropriate weather symbol on them.

d) **What's the capital city of ...?** Divide the children into groups of three or four and give a copy of **Worksheet W-23** and an atlas to each group. The children have to search for and write down the names of the capitals for each country and colour in their flags. You can list the English names of the capitals on the board (Paris, Rome, London, Berlin, Dublin, Valletta, Moscow, Istanbul, New Delhi, Peking/Beijing, Tokyo, Cape Town, Wellington, Ottawa, Canberra, Washington, Buenos Aires). At the end of the activity ask: **What's the capital city of ...? What colour is the flag of ...? What country is Wellington capital of?**

e) Introduce vocabulary related to nationalities and get the children involved in a role-play. Make cards with some information on them: name, country, nationality, capital, address. Children pick up a card and interview each other: **Where are you from? What's your nationality? Where do you live? What's the capital city of ...? What's your address?**

5.5 ENGLISH-SPEAKING COUNTRIES

Give out a copy of **Worksheet W-24** to each child and distribute some atlases. Ask the children, in pairs, to identify and write the names of the English-speaking countries under their silhouettes, and check their answers in an atlas.
(Key: A – Australia; B – New Zealand; C – USA; D – Canada; E – Ireland; F – United Kingdom.)

6. Extension activity: ICT

Time: 3 hours

Show the children how to use the Excel programme to record data related to the weather and temperatures and make bar/pie charts. Get the children to record information by using tables.
Here are some examples:

THE WORLD AROUND ME • Where in the world

a) **Where in my part of the world?** (places visited; region; when; who with; interesting experiences)

Places I visited	Region	When	Who	What

b) **Where in the world?** In groups, children have to choose a country and prepare a short description of it.

Country	Continent	Flag	Capital city	Major cities	Major rivers	Major mountains	Neighbour countries	Typical Food	Things to see	How to go there ...

The materials produced could be inserted into children's Portfolios f they have them, along with a description form (Appendix 4).

7. ASSESSMENT

- Progress indicators: **Worksheets W-4/W-5/W-9/W-12/W-18/W-22**
  [**Worksheet W-25**]. How can you go to …? Ask the children to read and colour the best means of transport to use to reach the places given.
- Informal evaluation – notes made on children's comprehension, interaction, and production during the activities (Appendix 1).
- Skills children should have acquired (these can be recorded in the children's ability record (Appendix 2) downloadable from the website):
  - **Content skills:** the child can describe the location of objects; can locate positions on a map by using coordinates; can recognize key lines of latitude and longitude (parallels and meridians); can use atlases, globes, maps, and plans at a range of scales; can draw maps using symbols and cardinal points; can speak about the solar system; can describe where places are (in which region, country, continent); can identify the relationships between the elements of an environment.
  - **Language skills:** the child can read and understand instructions; can answer simple questions; can read short informative texts; can use appropriate geograhical vocabulary; can read and analyse a weather report; can compare weather conditions and temperatures; can describe location by using coordinates and cardinal points; can describe some physical and political features (environments, climate, states, capitals, borders) of continents and countries.
- Self evaluation: Appendix 3. The following statements can be written into the 'What I can do' column:
  I can describe location of objects and places.
  I can find positions on a map using coordinates.
  I can recognize key lines of latitude and longitude.
  I can use atlases, a globe, and maps at a range of scales.
  I can draw maps and use symbols.
  I can talk about the solar system.
  I can use geographical vocabulary and describe some physical and political features of places.
  I can analyse a weather report and compare weather conditions and temperatures.

THE WORLD AROUND ME • Moving around

W-1 WORKSHEET

Left or right?

Who's on Robert's left? ....

Who's on Robert's right? ....

Write a list or draw pictures.

WHAT'S ON ...

ROBERT'S LEFT	ROBERT'S RIGHT

W-2 WORKSHEET

Coordinates

Read and colour the squares.

[Grid with columns A–H and rows 1–10]

GREEN: A6 – A7 – A8 – A9 – A10 – B6 – B7 – B8 – B9 – B10 – C6 – C7 – C8 – C9 – C10
BROWN: B1 – B2 – B3 – B4 – B5
RED: D6 – E6 – F6 – G6 – H6
YELLOW: D5 – E5 – F5 – G5 – H5 – D4 – F4 – H4 – D3 – E3 – F3 – G3 – H3 – D2 – E2 – G2 – H2 – D1 – E1 – G1 – H1
BLACK: F1 – F2
BLUE: E4 – G4

THE WORLD AROUND ME • Moving around

W-3 WORKSHEET

My school area

Colour the symbols of the places that are in your school area.

	church		post office		supermarket		chemist
	bakery		book shop		telephone boxes		post boxes
	bus stop		play area		park		newsagent

Draw a map of your school area using the symbols of the key.

W-4 WORKSHEET

A tourist map

Draw a tourist map:
- colour the symbols in the key;
- copy the symbols on the map as many times as you like.

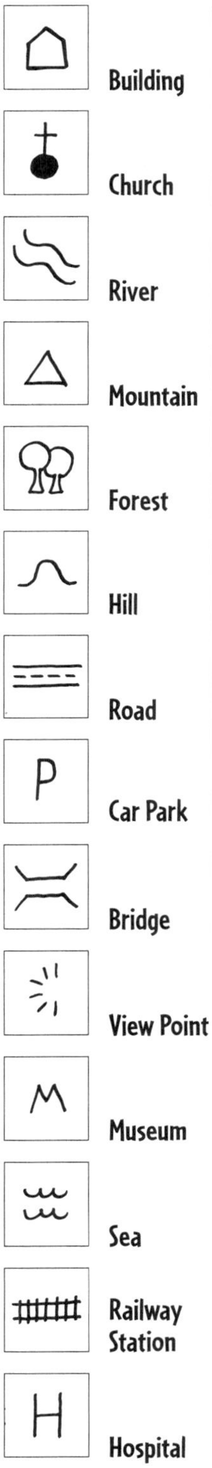

⌂	Building
✝	Church
～	River
△	Mountain
🌳	Forest
⌒	Hill
====	Road
P	Car Park
⊔	Bridge
☀	View Point
M	Museum
～～	Sea
⧈	Railway Station
H	Hospital

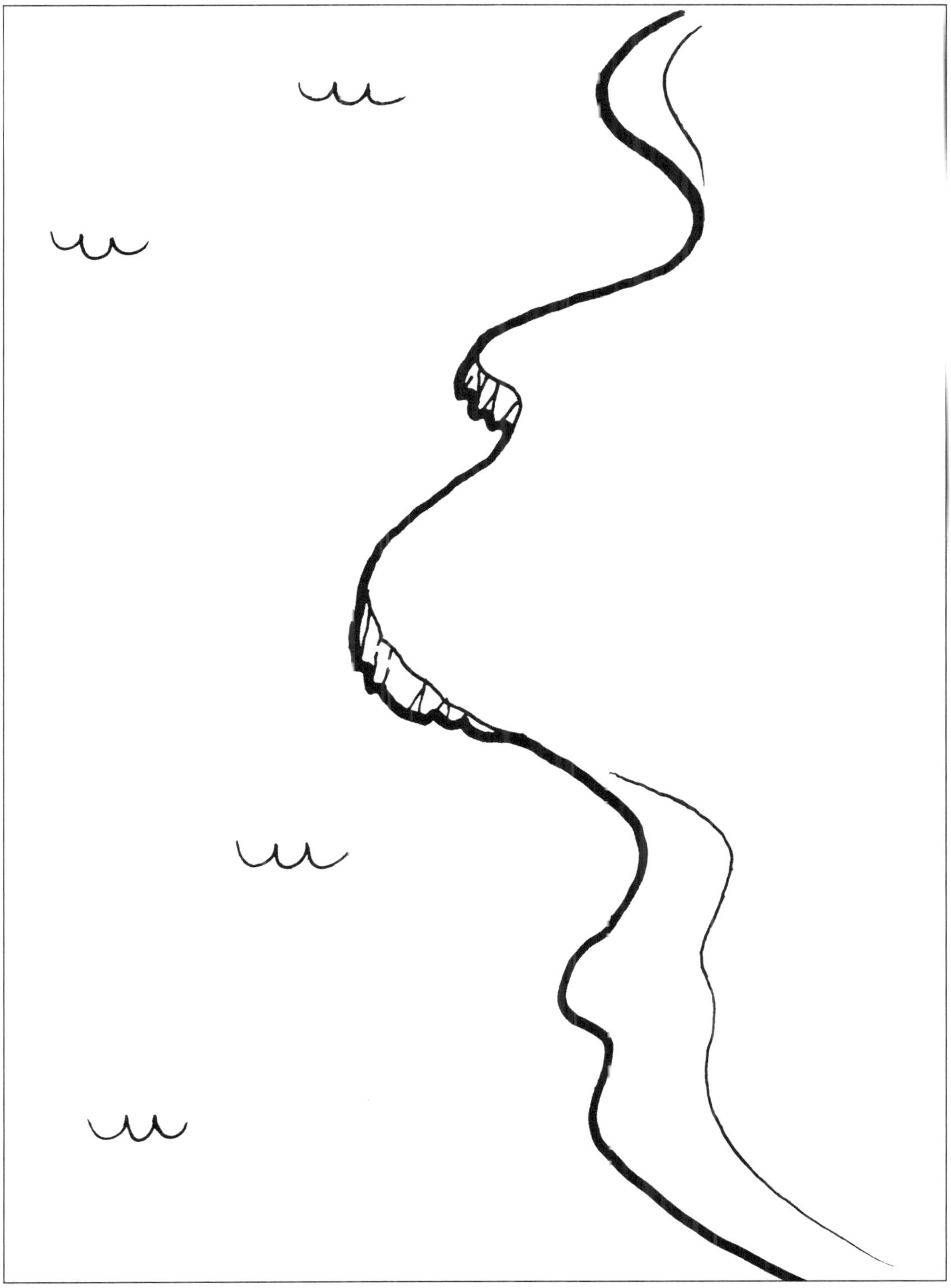

THE WORLD AROUND ME • Moving around

W-5 WORKSHEET

Directions

A COMPASS

A compass helps you to find directions.
Maps are usually made with North at the top and South at the bottom.

Complete the map.
To the East of the school draw a playground.
To the West of the school draw a wood.
To the North of the school draw a football field.
To the South of the school draw a road.

THE WORLD AROUND ME • Moving around

W-6 WORKSHEET

Magic broom hunt

Can you find the witch's magic broom?
Follow the directions.

You are at bat castle.

GO: 4 squares west – 1 square north – 2 squares west – 3 squares north – 2 squares east – 1 square south
2 squares east – 1 square south – 2 squares east – 3 squares north – 3 squares west and 2 squares north.

Where are you now? At .... There's the MAGIC BROOM!!!!!!

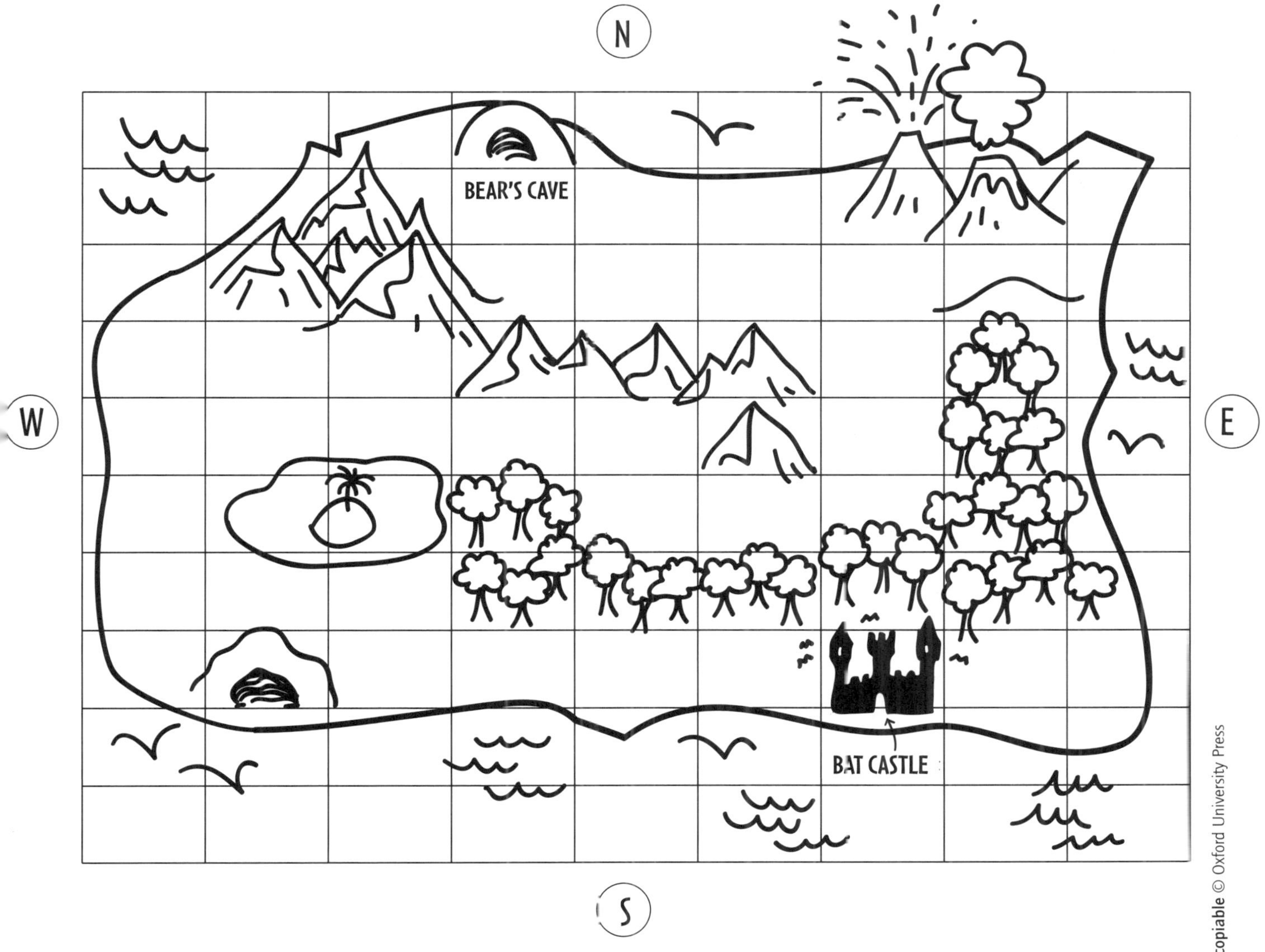

THE WORLD AROUND ME • Planet Earth

W-7 WORKSHEET

The Earth

The Earth is a sphere.
It is round like a ball.
There is land and sea.

Colour the land brown and the sea blue.

What is there on Earth?

island   sea   mountains   river   countryside   hills   lake   desert   forest   grassland

1. ....

2. ....

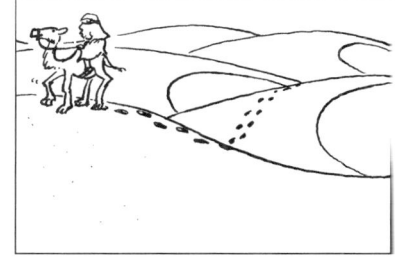

3. ....

4. ....

5. ....

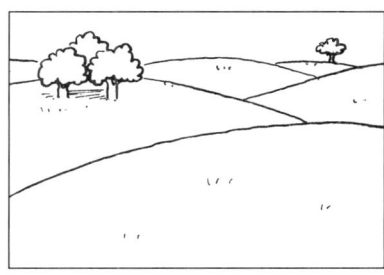

6. ....

7. ....

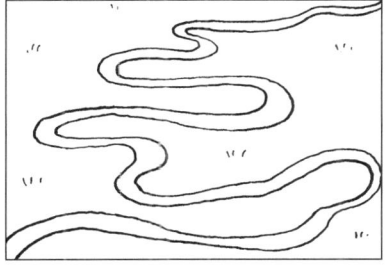

8. ....

9. ....

10. ....

Write the correct name on each picture.

THE WORLD AROUND ME • Planet Earth

W-9 WORKSHEET

Hemispheres

The equator is an imaginary line around the middle of the Earth. It divides the Earth in half: **northern** hemisphere and **southern** hemisphere.

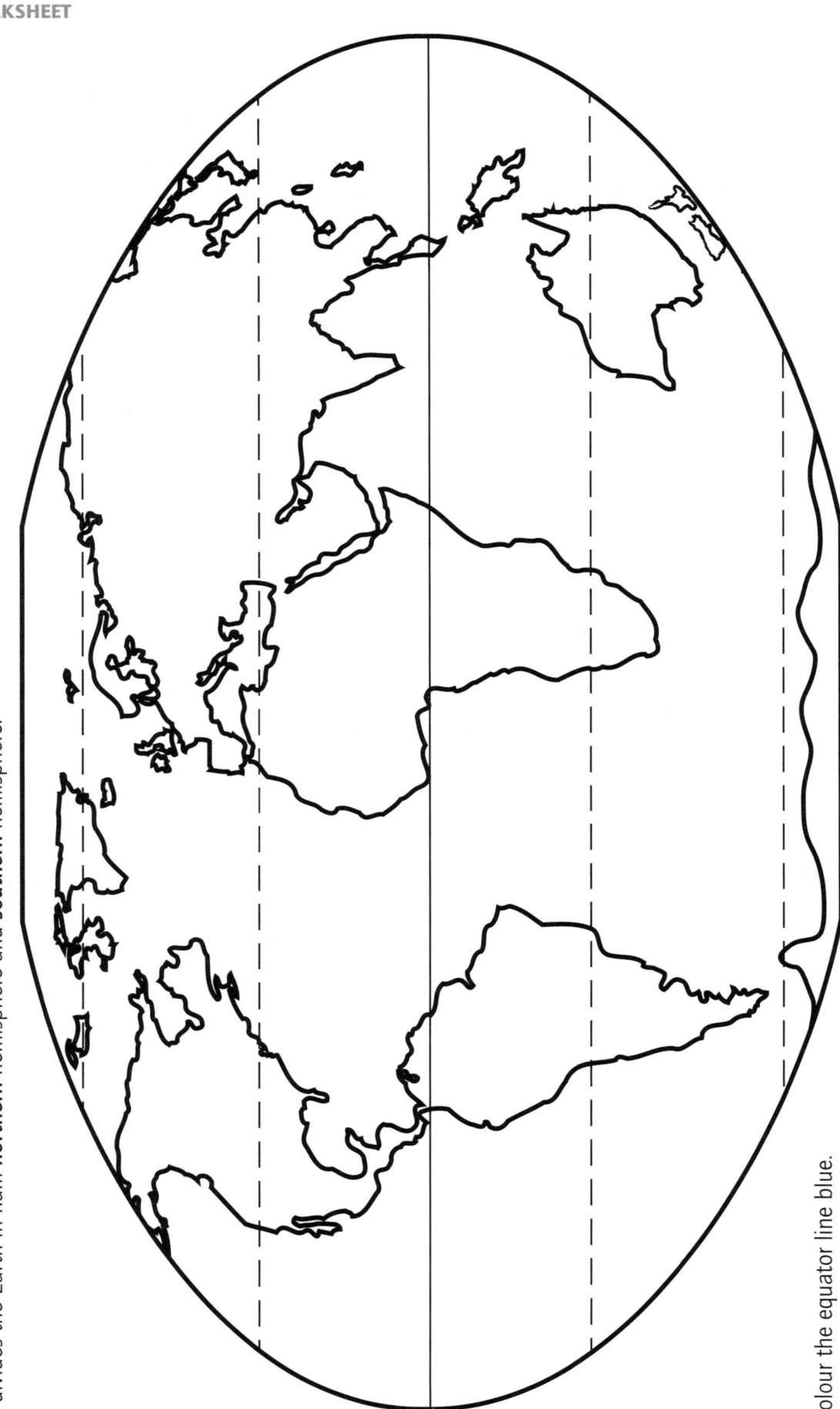

Colour the equator line blue.
Colour the land in the northern hemisphere yellow.
Colour the land in the southern hemisphere orange.

W-10 WORKSHEET

Parallels and meridians

Write the names next to the numbers.

| North Pole | South Pole | Arctic Circle | Antarctic Circle |
| Equator | Tropic of Cancer | Tropic of Capricorn | Prime Meridian |

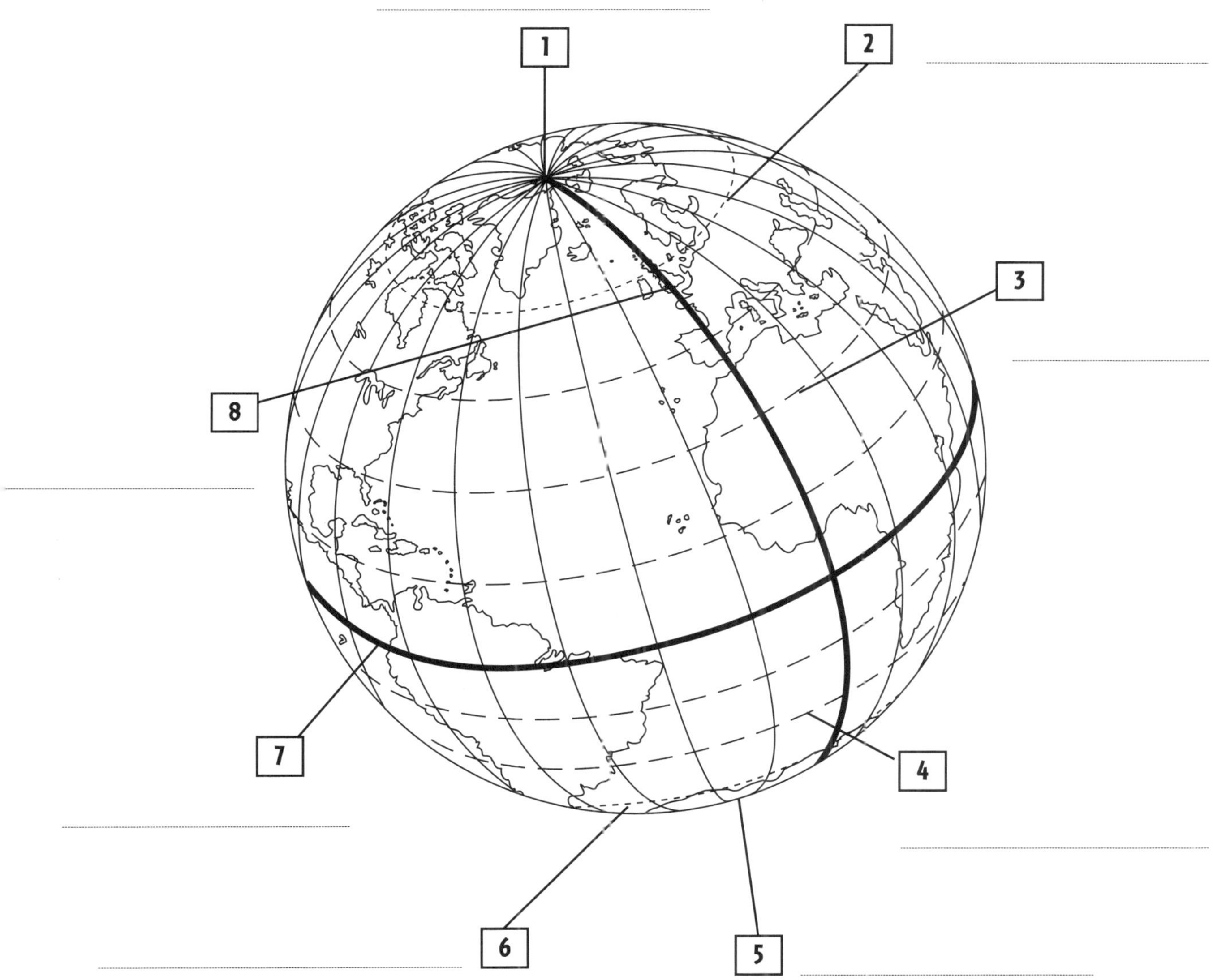

THE WORLD AROUND ME • Planet Earth

W-11 WORKSHEET

Latitude and longitude

Colour the equator green.
Number the lines of **latitude** south of the equator.
Colour the land between 20°N and 40°N yellow.
Colour the land between 40°S and 60°S green.

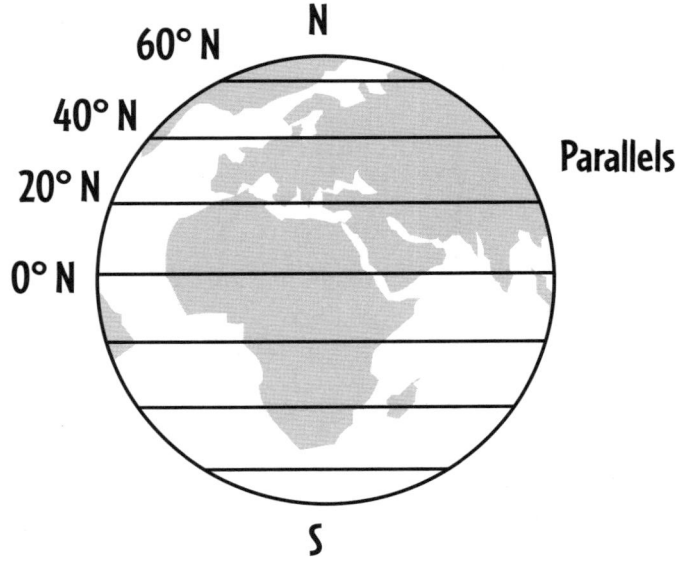

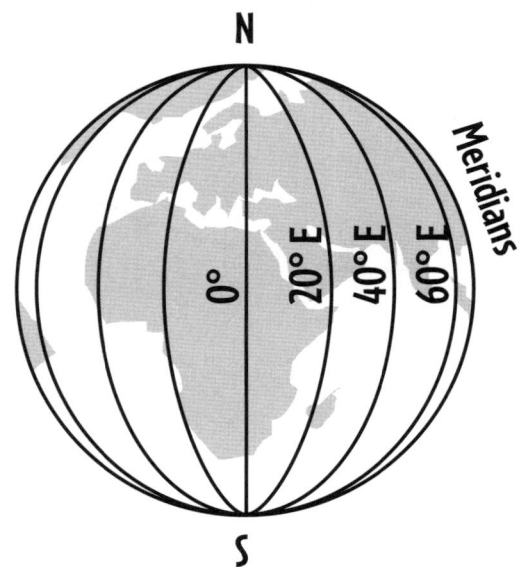

Colour the prime meridian red.
Number the lines of **longitude** west.
Colour the land between the prime meridian and 20°E orange.
Colour the land between 20°W and 40°W pink.

W-12 WORKSHEET

Night and day

The Earth takes 24 hours to spin round once.
When our part is facing the sun it is daytime.
When our part is facing away from the sun it's night-time.

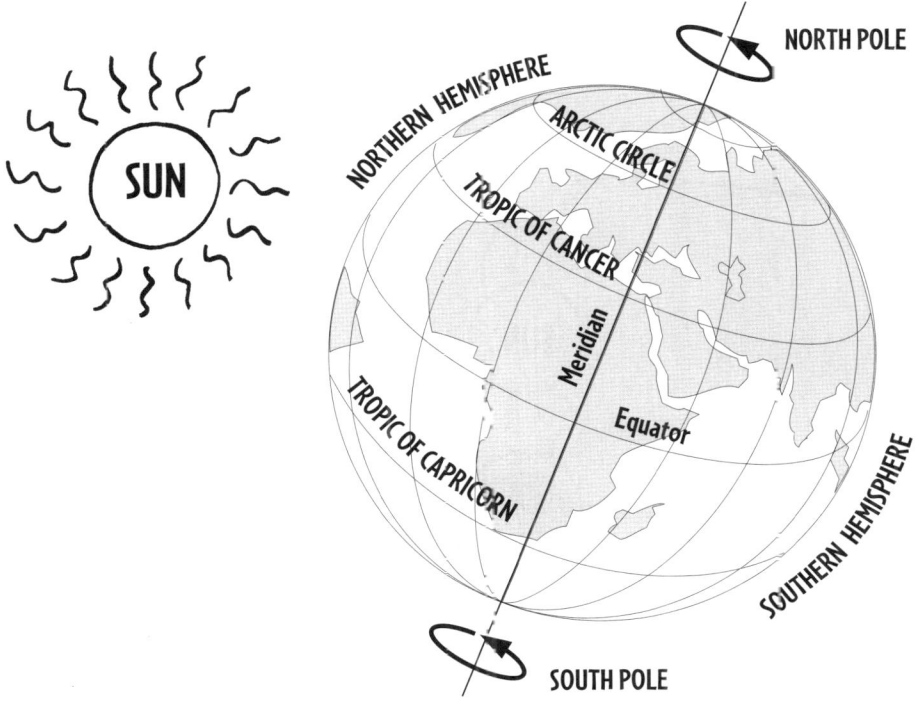

Draw some pictures of daytime and night-time activities.

DAYTIME	NIGHT-TIME

A year

The Earth takes **365 days** to orbit the sun.
As the Earth moves around the sun the **SEASONS** change.

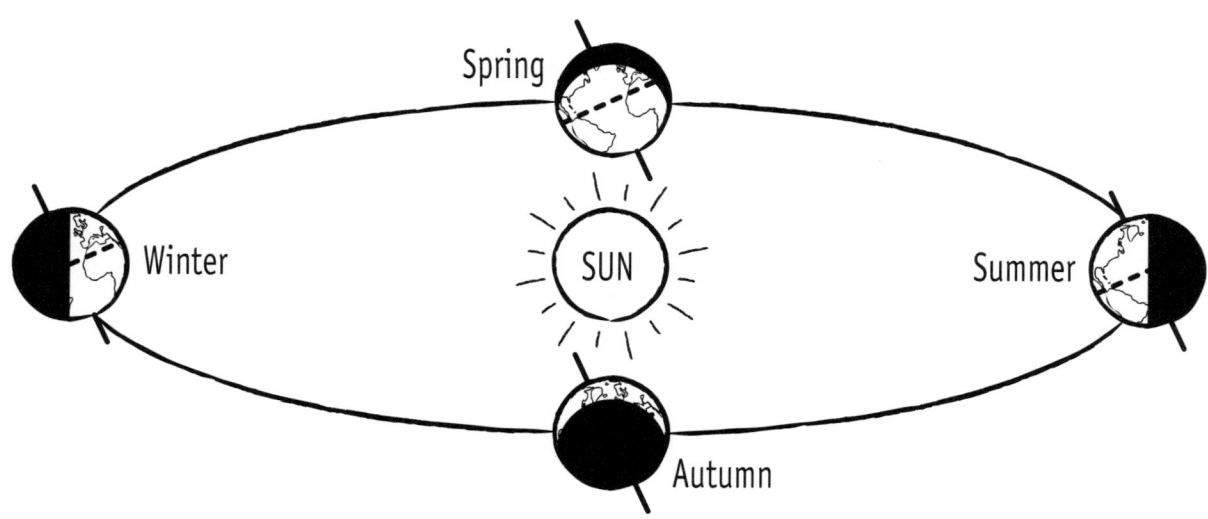

Read, write the name of the seasons, and draw pictures.

....
It's the coldest season of the year.

....
Green leaves from some trees turn red, orange, and brown.

....
The weather gets warmer, flowers open, and gardens become colourful.

....
It's the hottest season of the year.

The Earth in the solar system

Eight planets orbit the sun.
The Earth is the third planet from the sun.

Number the planets from the nearest to the furthest from the sun.

1st .... 2nd .... 3rd ....

4th .... 5th .... 6th ....

7th .... 8th ....

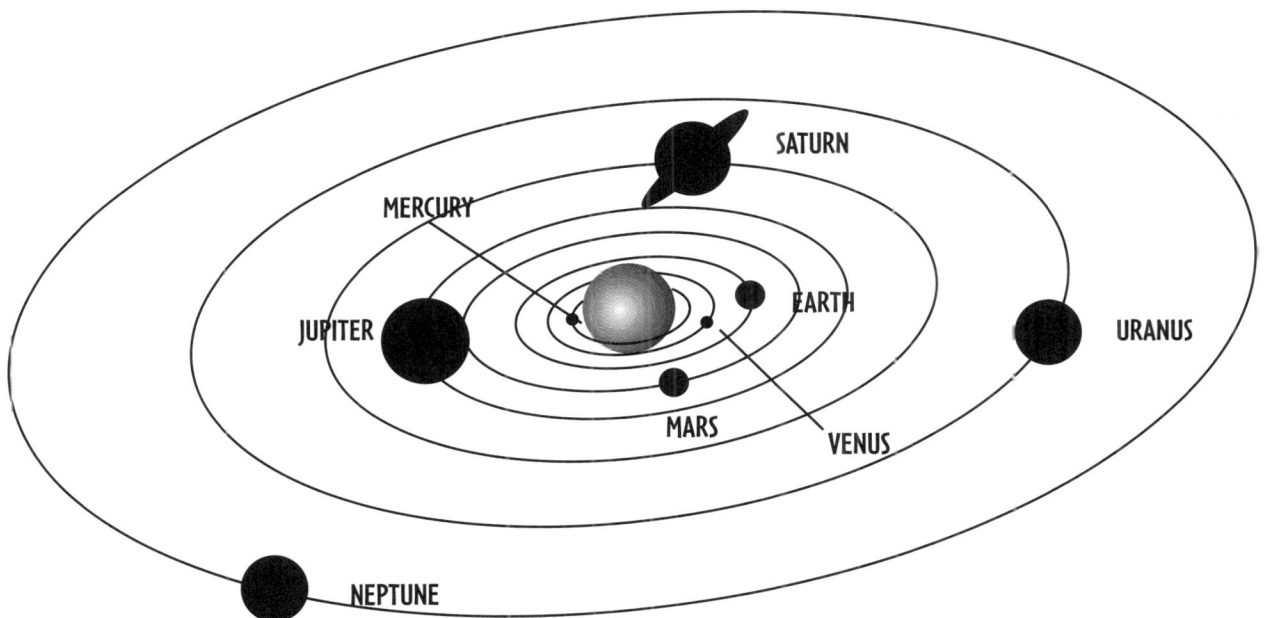

Complete with the right planet.

a. _____ is the hottest planet (+500°C).

b. _____ is the coldest planet (−200°C).

c. _____ is the biggest planet (diameter: 142,984 km).

d. _____ is called the red planet.

e. _____ is the smallest planet (diameter: 4,878 km).

W-15 WORKSHEET

Climates

| POLAR | MEDITERRANEAN | EQUATORIAL | DESERT | TROPICAL | CONTINENTAL |

ANTARCTICA IS THE COLDEST PLACE ON EARTH — −89°C in 1983

Fill in the gaps:

- .... climates have warm summers and very cold winters.
- .... climates are hot and dry in the summer, mild and rainy in winter.
- .... climates have only one season: hot and wet.
- .... climates are hot and have two seasons: a dry season and a wet season.
- .... climates are very dry and hot.
- .... climates are cold and have two seasons: a long cold winter and a short summer.

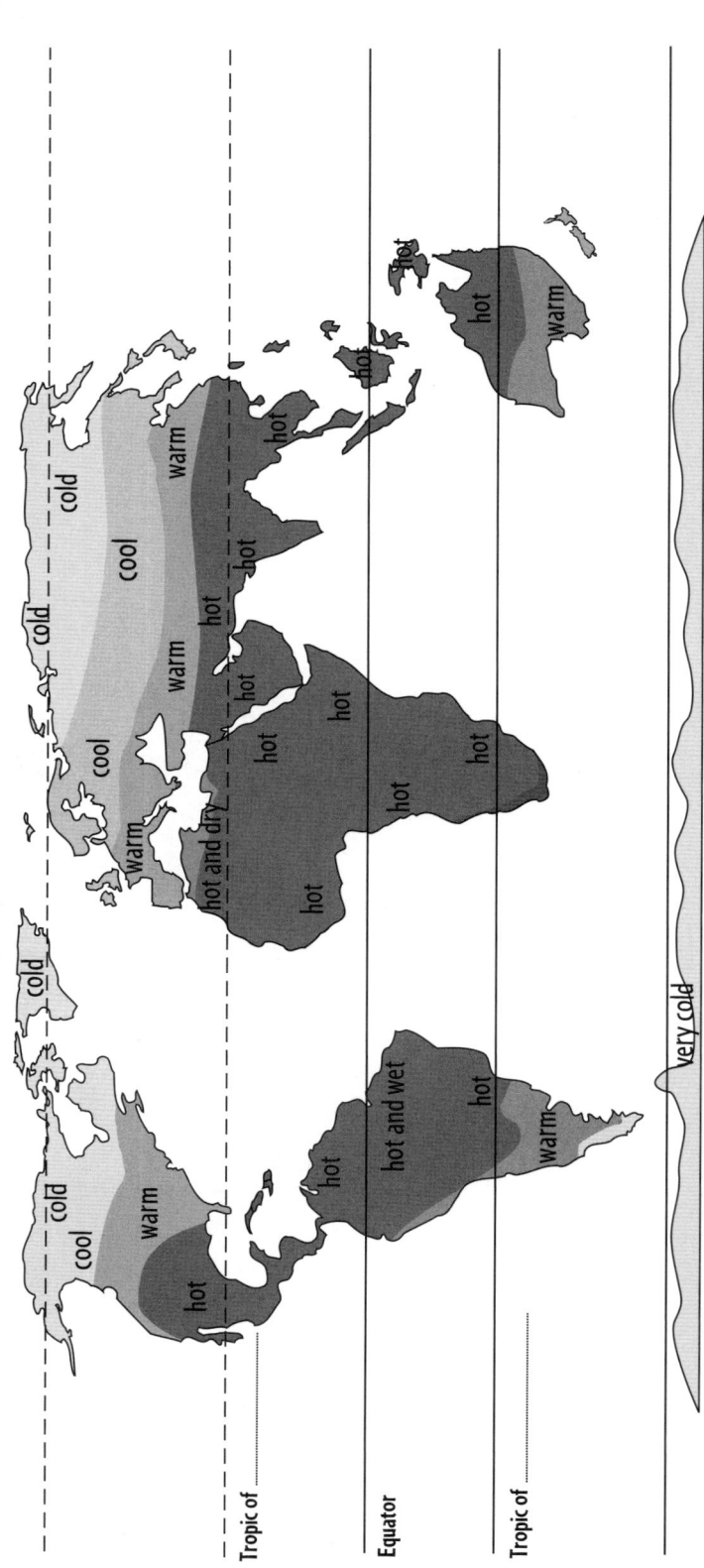

THE WORLD AROUND ME • Planet Earth

W-16 WORKSHEET

How many sunny days?

Month: ....

THE WORLD AROUND ME • Planet Earth

W-17 WORKSHEET

Month ....

 Highest temperature this month.

 Lowest temperature this month.

1 ☀ 14°C	2 °C	3 °C	4 °C	5 °C	6 °C	7 °C
8 °C	9 °C	10 °C	11 °C	12 °C	13 °C	14 °C
15 °C	16 °C	17 °C	18 °C	19 °C	20 °C	21 °C
22 °C	23 °C	24 °C	25 °C	26 °C	27 °C	28 °C
29 °C	30 °C	31 °C				

This month we had:

.... sunny days   .... rainy days   .... cloudy days

.... windy days   .... foggy days   .... snowy days

.... changeable days

W-18 WORKSHEET

THE WORLD AROUND ME • Where in the world

Continents

Write the names of the continents on the map. Colour the key and colour the continents using the same colour.

☐ NORTH AMERICA ☐ SOUTH AMERICA ☐ OCEANIA ☐ ANTARCTICA ☐ AFRICA ☐ ASIA ☐ EUROPE

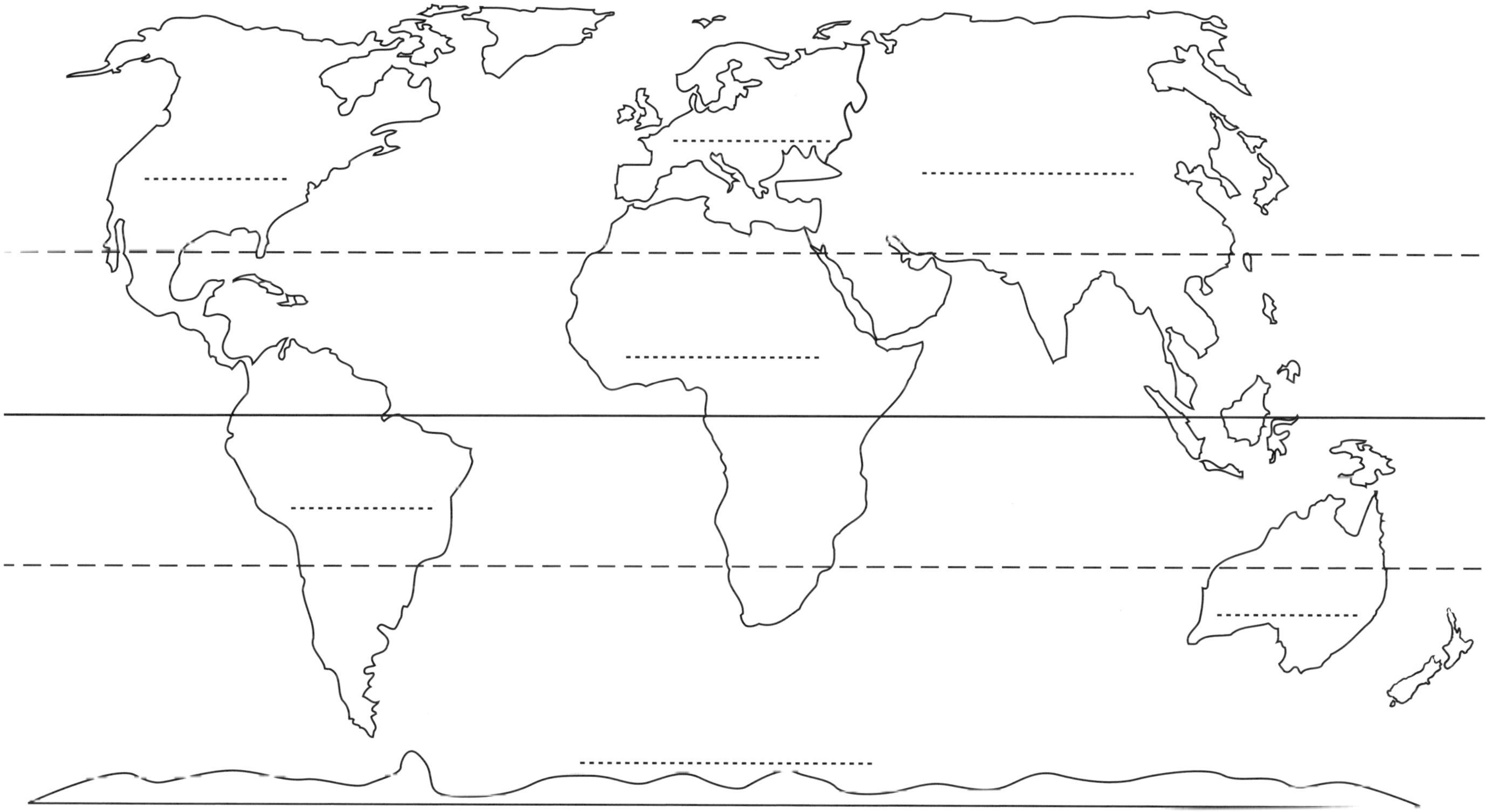

161

Photocopiable © Oxford University Press

THE WORLD AROUND ME • Where in the world

W-19 WORKSHEET

What's the time?

The Earth is divided into 24 time zones starting from the prime meridian.
Going one zone east we have to add 1 hour.
Going one zone west we have to take away 1 hour.

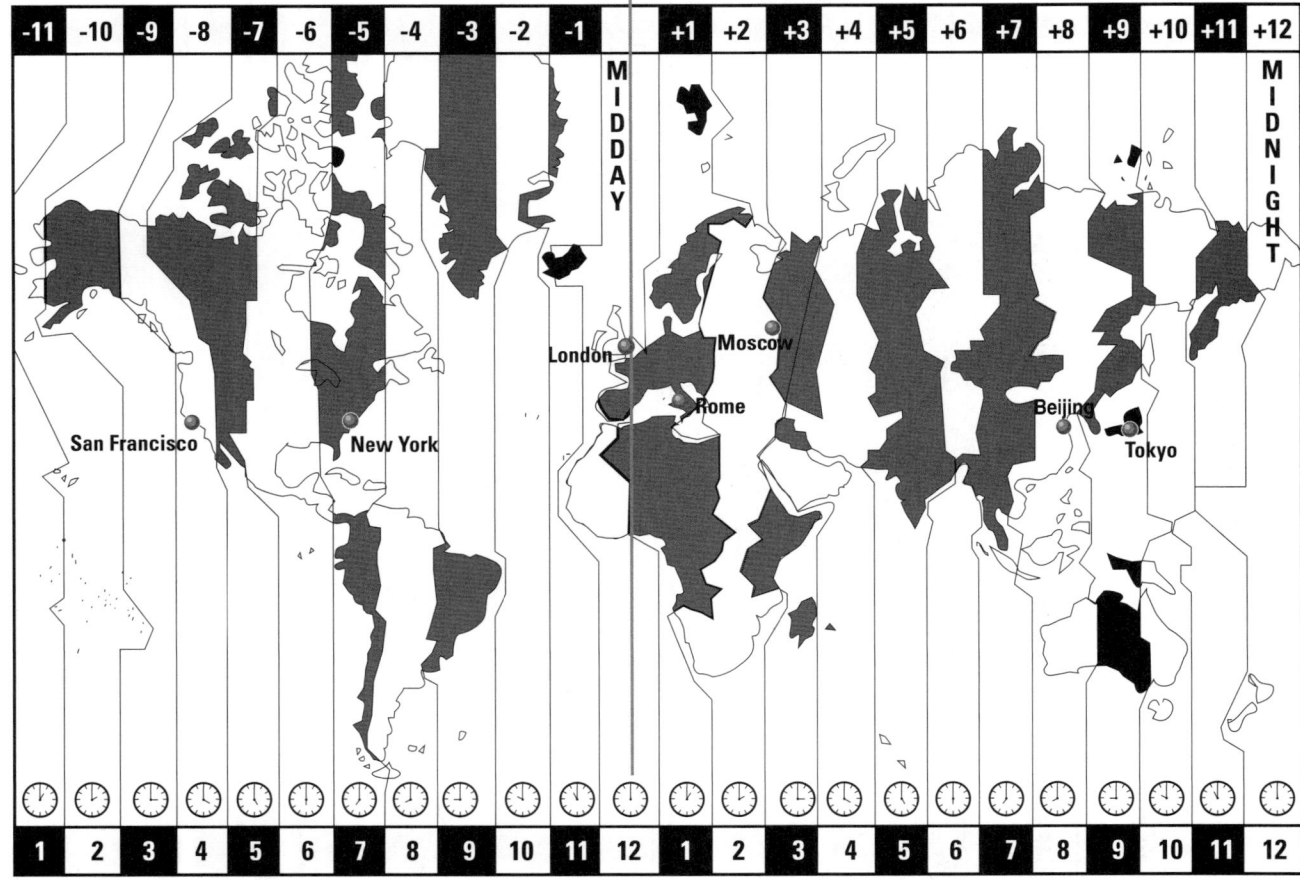

When it's 1 p.m. in London, what's the time in:

- New York? ....
- San Francisco? ....
- Tokyo? ....
- India? ....
- Moscow? ....
- Mexico? ....
- Beijing? ....

THE WORLD AROUND ME • Where in the world

W-20 WORKSHEET

Animal habitats

Put a (circle) around the animals that are in the wrong habitat.

THE JUNGLE

THE ARCTIC

THE DESERT

163

THE WORLD AROUND ME • Where in the world

W-21 WORKSHEET

On land, in water, or in the air?

Cut out and glue the animals in the right places.

dolphin 	tiger 	rabbit 	butterfly 	bee 
cat 	octopus 	parrot 	sea horse 	monkey 

THE WORLD AROUND ME • Where in the world

W-22 WORKSHEET

Weather report

Read the weather report below.

It's sunny in Australia.	It's cloudy in northern Brazil.	It's sunny in southern India.
It's snowy in northern Canada.	It's foggy in Ireland.	It's snowy in Japan.
It's rainy in southern Africa.	It's windy in central Russia.	It's changeable in Iceland.

Draw the symbols in the right place on the world map.

SUNNY	RAINY	WINDY	FOGGY	SNOWY	CLOUDY	CHANGEABLE

THE WORLD AROUND ME • Where in the world

W-23 WORKSHEET

What's the capital city of ....?

Fill in the table.

Flag	Country	Capital city
	USA	
	Australia	
	France	
	Italy	
	Russia	
	Germany	
	Turkey	
	India	
	China	
	United Kingdom	
	Republic of Ireland	
	Japan	
	South Africa	
	New Zealand	
	Canada	
	Argentina	
	Malta	

Photocopiable © Oxford University Press

W-24 WORKSHEET

English-speaking countries

Write the names of the English-speaking countries (you can use your atlas).

Australia – Canada – USA – United Kingdom – Ireland – New Zealand

A

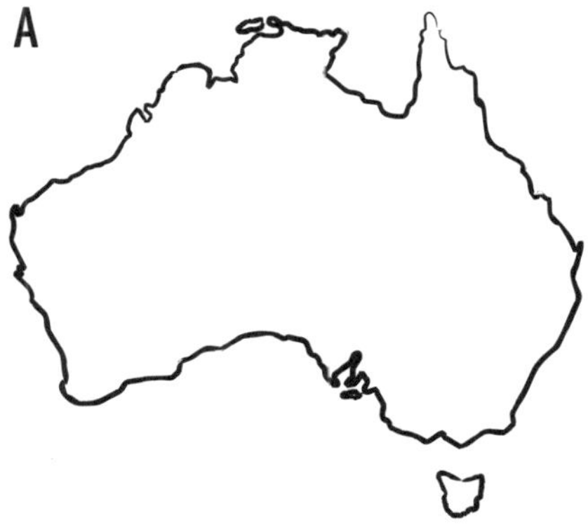

B

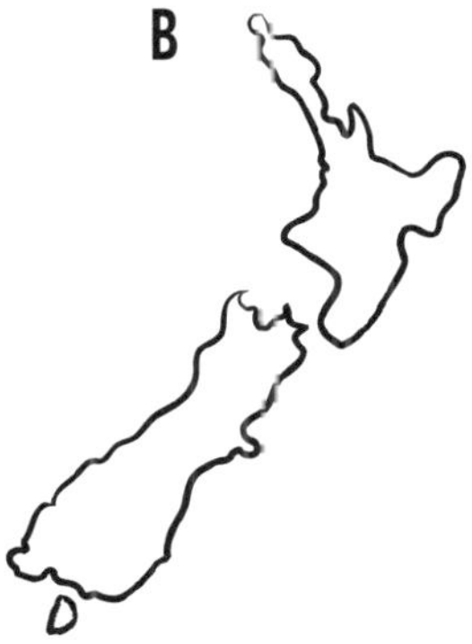

C

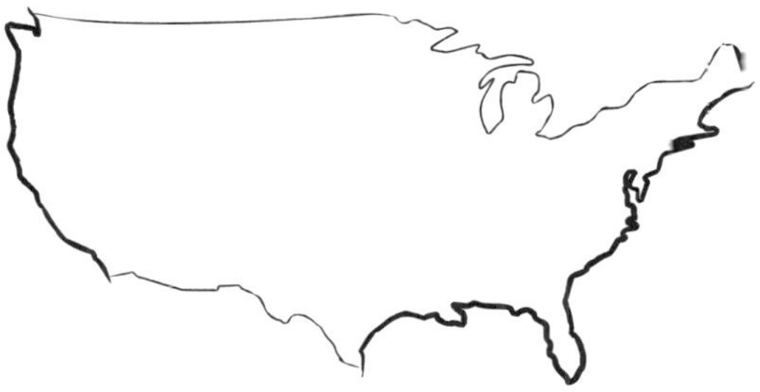

D

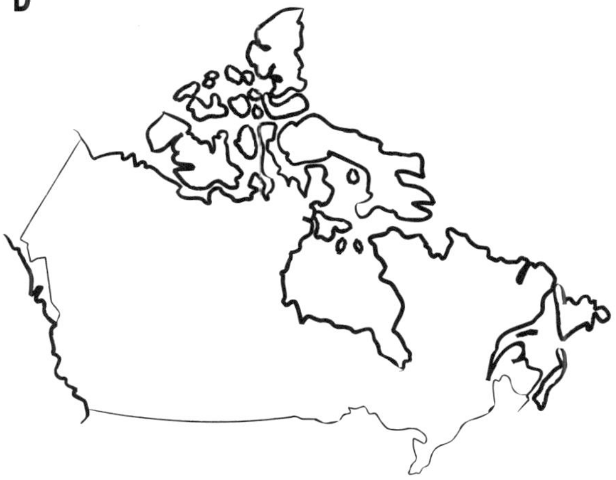

E

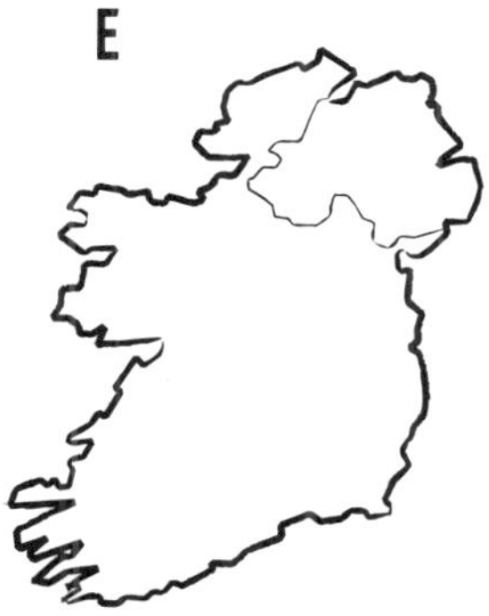

F

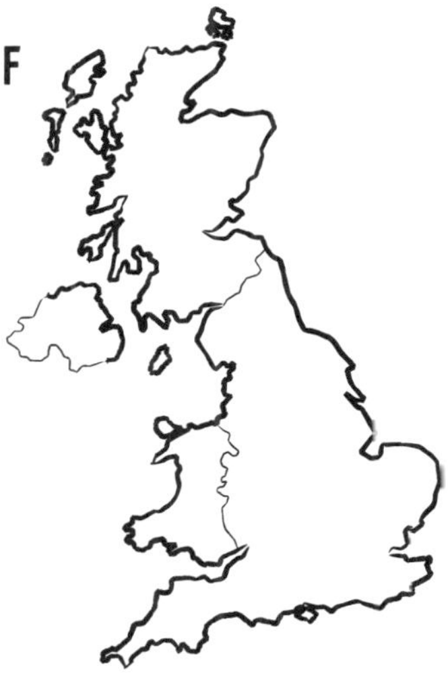

A) ______________________ B) ______________________

C) ______________________ D) ______________________

E) ______________________ F) ______________________

 **THE WORLD AROUND ME** • Where in the world

W-25 WORKSHEET

How can you go to ... ?

I CAN GO TO SCHOOL

  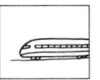

on foot   by car   by bus   by train   by plane   by ship   by spaceship

I CAN GO TO THE CAPITAL OF MY COUNTRY

  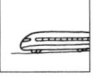

on foot   by car   by bus   by train   by plane   by ship   by spaceship

I CAN GO TO PARIS

on foot   by car   by bus   by train   by plane   by ship   by spaceship

I CAN GO TO LONDON

 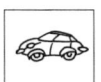 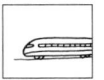  

on foot   by car   by bus   by train   by plane   by ship   by spaceship

I CAN GO TO NEW YORK

on foot   by car   by bus   by train   by plane   by ship   by spaceship

I CAN GO TO TOKYO

on foot   by car   by bus   by train   by plane   by ship   by spaceship

I CAN GO TO THE MOON

on foot   by car   by bus   by train   by plane   by ship   by spaceship

CAN YOU GO TO MARS?   **YES**   **NO**

Read and colour the right means of transport.

TIME TRAVELLING

 **CONTENT AREA** # TIME TRAVELLING

	**TOPIC**	Dinosaurs Egyptians Romans
	**AIMS**	• to put events on a timeline • to identify features of historical periods • to reconstruct events using a variety of sources • to make comparisons and identify similarities/differences between historical periods
	**LANGUAGE**	• to read and understand instructions • to answer simple questions • to research information in simple texts • to describe objects, situations, animals • to use appropriate vocabulary related to events of the past
	**VOCABULARY AND STRUCTURES**	Use words and phrases relating to: dinosaurs (names, body parts, diet, dimensions); geometrical shapes; numbers (*How many?*); directions (*left/right*); games; personal tastes (*Do you like? I like/I don't like*); hobbies (*My favourite sport/hobby is …*); family relations; descriptions (*I have got, It has got, This is my …*)
	**WHAT CHILDREN NEED TO KNOW ALREADY**	• names of some body parts • basic vocabulary related to colours, numbers, adjectives • structures: *I can, I like, I am*
	**MATERIALS**	• resource books, websites, paper, cardboard, paints, glue • **Worksheets T-1–T-19**
	**CROSS-CURRICULAR ACTIVITIES**	1. *Dinosaurs* 2. *Egyptians* 3. *Romans* 4. Art 5. ICT 6. Assessment

The following plan is not intended to cover the whole range of history as a discipline, which will have to be taught in mother tongue and linked to the national curriculum. The activities suggested in three thematic fields (Dinosaurs, Egyptians, Romans) should be seen as a possible supplement to the subject curriculum and can be used to support and reinforce concepts and skills that children have already acquired.

TIME TRAVELLING • Dinosaurs

1. DINOSAURS

Time: 5 hour module
Materials: resource books, Internet, **Worksheets T-1 to T-7**

1.1 PREPARATION
- Brainstorm the children's knowledge about dinosaurs and revise vocabulary related to animal body parts: *What do you know about dinosaurs? Do you know the names of some of them? When did they live? What did they feed on? How did they defend themselves?*
- Ask the children to look for pictures of dinosaurs in books, videos, and websites, or use toy dinosaurs which can easily be found in shops: *Dinosaurs lived millions of years ago. Look at this dinosaur. Is it big? Is it small? What's its name? How many legs has it got? Look at its tail. Is it long? Is it short?*

1.2 DINOSAUR PUPPETS
Ask the children to make puppets by sticking pictures of dinosaurs to a pencil or stick (see **Worksheet T-1**). The 'dino-puppets' can be used for different activities (games, puppet shows ...).

1.3 MIXED-UP DINOSAURS
The dinosaurs on **Worksheet T-1** can also be used to make mixed-up dinosaurs. Tell the children to cut out the pictures of the dinosaurs and cut their bodies in three parts (heads and necks, bodies and legs, tails); they can then make new dinosaurs by putting together body parts from different dinosaurs and giving them a new name: *My dinosaur has got a Triceratops' head, a T-Rex's body, and a Stegosaurus' tail. It's called ...*

1.4 WHO ARE YOU? [GAME]
Choose a piece of music; ask each child to choose a dino-puppet and move freely to the rhythm of music. When you stop the music, all the children who have the same dinosaur have to gather together and answer the question: *Who are you? I'm a T-Rex ... I'm a Stegosaurus.* Children have to change the dino-puppet after two turns.

1.5 WHAT'S MISSING?
Give out copies of **Worksheet T-2**. Explain the work palaeontologists do to the children and that they are going to pretend to be palaeontologists. Tell the children they have to cut out the pieces of a dinosaur skeleton, make the puzzle, glue the skeleton into their exercise books, and draw the missing parts of the body.

1.6 WE ARE ALL DINOSAURS
Organize the class into groups of three or four; give each group a name of a new dinosaur and ask them to look for information about the assigned dinosaur using various sources (resource books in English, websites, etc.). Each group has to record the information on a poster and afterwards introduce its dinosaur to the class. Help the children to make simple comparisons: *Some dinosaurs are very big and slow; some dinosaurs are very small and fast; some dinosaurs walk on four legs; some dinosaurs walk on two legs.*

TIME TRAVELLING • Egyptians

Dinosaurs	How long	Weight	Tail	Neck	Food	Other information
Apatosaurus	22 metres	35 tonnes	long	long	carnivore	4 short legs small head

1.7 WHO IS IT?
Clear a space between the desks and tell groups of three children to take turns to mime a dinosaur while the rest of the class has to guess its name. Older children with a higher level of English can play a more difficult variation of the game: they can describe the features of the dinosaur instead of miming it: *I have got four short legs; I have got a big head; I like plants; I have got three horns on my head. Who am I?*

1.8 CARNIVORE OR HERBIVORE?
By using the information they have collected through the previous activities, children should be able to colour in the appropriate food for each dinosaur on **Worksheet T-3**.

1.9 TRICERATOPS AND T-REX
Ask the children to read the information about the two dinosaurs on **Worksheets T-4** and **T-5** and circle the correct words to complete the sentences.

1.10 WE ARE ALL DINOSAURS
Get the children to make a book about dinosaurs. Give a copy of **Worksheet T-6** to each child. Tell the children to complete the sentences by inserting the missing words, colour in the pictures, and to make the book as shown in the picture.

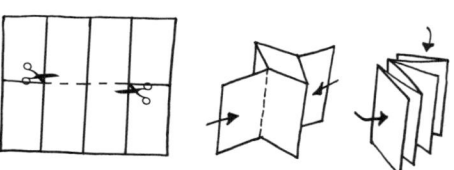

1.11 Extension activity: MATHS
A geometrical dinosaur
Revise geometrical shapes by using blocks and tell the children to draw a dinosaur using only circles, squares, rectangles, and triangles. When they have drawn their dinosaurs, they must count how many circles, squares, rectangles and triangles they have used and write the numbers underneath the picture.

2. EGYPTIANS
Time: 5 hour module
Materials: Worksheets T-7 to T-12

2.1 WELCOME TO ANCIENT EGYPT
It can be very useful to get the children to make a booklet about ancient Egypt as an assessment tool and a project carried out jointly with the history teacher. Children can staple together the shaped cut-outs from **Worksheets T-7 to T-12** to make a booklet.
- [**Worksheet T-7**]. Children should have learnt about Egyptian mummies in history lessons. Ask them to colour in the book cover and cut it out along the dotted lines.

- [**Worksheet T-8**]. Explain to the children that they have to look at the map of Ancient Egypt and fill it in with the missing information.
- [**Worksheet T-9**]. Revise with children how numbers were written in Egyptian times (from the lowest to the highest and from left to right. For example, the number 315 was written in this way: first came the units (5 ≡), then the tens (10 ∩), then the hundreds (300 ℘ ℘ ℘), and finally the thousands). Tell the children to identify, read out, and write the numbers on the Worksheet.
- [**Worksheet T-10**]. Ask the children if they remember what hieroglyphics are: *Egyptians wrote using pictures called Hieroglyphics. The pictures represented word signs or sound signs.* Tell the children to read the words on the Worksheet and write their name in the cartouche from left to right.
- [**Worksheet T-11**]. Ask the children to solve the puzzles. *How many pyramid shapes can you see in this picture?* (27). *Can you find the right way to the king's room?*
- [**Worksheet T-12**]. The Egyptians used to decorate the walls of their palaces, houses, and tombs with drawings depicting either scenes of everyday life or stories of gods and kings. Archaeologists have managed to learn a lot about the daily life of the Egyptians thanks to these pictures. Tell the children to draw pictures of scenes from their own everyday lives on **Worksheet T-12**. Draw a mind map like the one below on the board to help children organize their ideas.

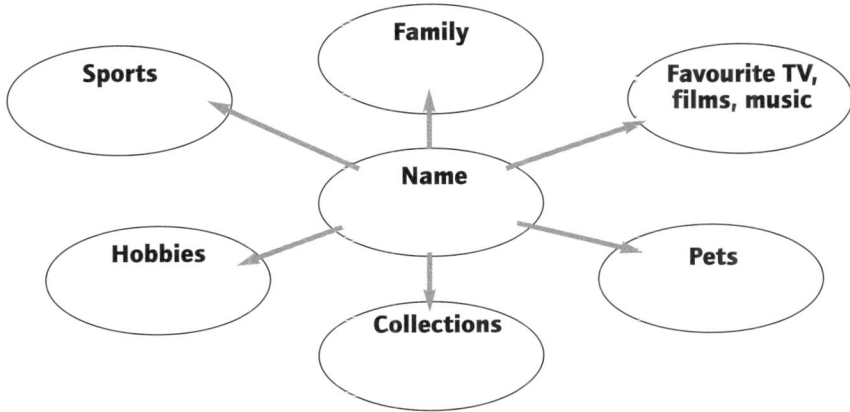

3. ROMANS

Time: 5 hour module
Materials: Worksheets T-13 to T-19, old socks, sticks, rags

3.1 NEWS FROM ANCIENT ROME

As for ancient Egypt, the children can make a booklet about the Romans by using the shaped cut-outs from **Worksheets T-13 to T-19**. The booklet can be used as an assessment tool and a final product of studies carried out jointly with the history teacher.

- [**Worksheet T-13**]. The children should know that the Colosseum, in Rome, is one of the most famous Roman buildings. Ask the children to colour in the booklet cover and cut it out along the dotted lines.
- [**Worksheet T-14**]. **The Roman Empire.** Tell the children to find out how big the Roman Empire was by joining up the dotted borders and colouring the map orange.
- [**Worksheet T-15**]. **Going to school.** Ask the children to think about the main differences between school today and in Roman times. They can then complete the Worksheet by drawing pictures: *Roman schoolchildren wrote on wax tablets with a pointed stick called a stylus. Roman books were rolls of paper called scrolls. Today we have exercise books and books; we use pens and Arabic numbers.*

- [Worksheet T-16]. **Going shopping.** Discuss differences between shopping in Roman times and today with the children. *In Roman times there were no doors or windows. At the forum there was a market once a week where Romans could buy fruit, vegetables, meat, fish, wine and olive oil. Today there are supermarkets, shopping centres*, etc. Ask the children to complete the Worksheet with the missing words and draw fruit and vegetables in the baskets.
- [Worksheet T-17]. **At the baths.** Baths were a place where Romans could meet their friends, enjoy themselves, and relax. Tell the children to look at the picture, identify the objects, characters, and rooms mentioned, and colour them in.
- [Worksheet T-18]. **Mosaics.** The Romans used to adorn walls, floors and pavements with mosaics, using small pieces of coloured stone. Explain to the children that they have to draw the outline of an animal or a flower and then make a mosaic by covering it with little pieces of coloured paper.
- [Worksheet T-19]. **Fun and games.** Lessons in Roman times used to end in the early afternoon, therefore children had plenty of time for their favourite games (dice, checkers, fighting with wooden swords, throwing the javelin). The adults' favourite games were chariot racing and the gladiator combats, which were held in circuses and arenas: *Chariot races were very popular. Charioteers were in four different teams: Reds, Greens, Blues and Whites. The horses had to race around the track seven times. The winner won a bag full of gold. Gladiators were slaves or prisoners. They had to fight each other or wild animals.* Tell the children to match each game on the Worksheet with its name and find the odd one out.

3.2 A CHARIOT RACE

Show children how to make a horse by using a stick and a sock filled with rags, as shown in the picture opposite. Organize a chariot race in the playground or in the gym. The children should be divided into four teams, each of which wears one of the four colours used by the ancient Romans (Reds, Greens, Blues, Whites). They have to do seven laps on their horses. The winner is the first to cross the line after seven laps.

4. Extension activity: ART

Time: 2 hours
Materials: paper, paint, crayons, newspapers, glue, stapler, cardboard box, aluminium foil

4.1 ART EXHIBITION

Prepare an exhibition of three-dimensional mummies the same size as the children. Divide the children into small groups. Each group has to trace the outline of a classmate on a sheet of paper folded into two in order to make two identical cut-outs. Tell the children to draw and colour in the face of the mummy on one of the two cut-outs and then paint the rest of the body. Then, they have to staple the two cut-outs together, on one side only, to make an empty body and fill it with balls of crumpled newspaper. When the body is filled up, children have to seal the open side of the mummy with glue, tape, or staples.

4.2 A ROMAN SHIELD

Explain to the children that the Roman army was very big and very well organized. A soldier wore a helmet, a shield, a sword, armour, a red tunic, and strong sandals (see picture). Give children these instructions for how to make a Roman sword and shield:

1. Cut a rectangle out of a cardboard box and paint it red.
2. Decorate the shield as you like.
3. Make a handle with some cardboard.
4. Tape it to the back of the shield.
5. Cut out a sword from cardboard and wrap it in foil.

5. Extension activity: ICT

The children can use the Internet to find information, pictures, monuments, and museums related to the three historical periods.

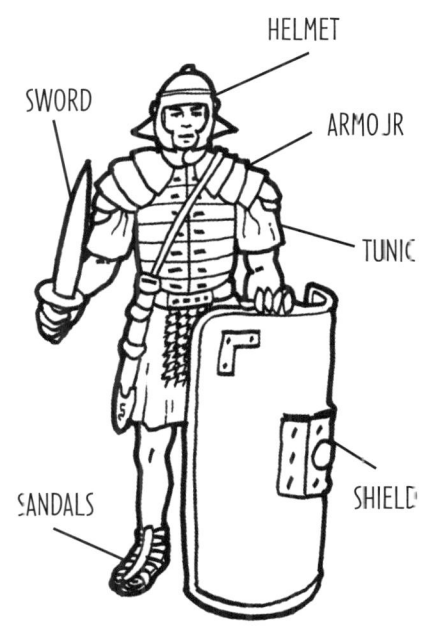

6. ASSESSMENT

- Progress indicators: all the Worksheets
- Informal evaluation: notes made on children's comprehension, interaction, and production during the activities (Appendix 1).
- Skills children should have acquired (these can be recorded on the children's ability record (Appendix 2) downloadable from the website)
  - Content skills: the child can place historical events on a timeline; can identify features of historical periods; can reconstruct events using a variety of sources; can make comparisons and identify similarities/differences between historical periods.
  - Language skills: the child can read and understand instructions; can answer simple questions; can identify information in simple texts; can describe objects, situations, and animals.
- Self evaluation: Appendix 3. The following statements can be written into the 'What I can do' column:
  I can place historical events on a timeline.
  I can identify features of historical periods
  I can make comparisons and identify similarities or differences between historical periods.
  I can find out information from texts.
  I can reconstruct events from a variety of sources.

T-1 WORKSHEET

Dinosaur puppets

Colour and cut out the dinosaurs, glue them on a pencil or a stick to make puppets.

TIME TRAVELLING · Dinosaurs

T-2 WORKSHEET

What's missing?

Paleontologists study dinosaur fossils.
Pretend to be a paleontologist: cut out the pieces, make the puzzle, glue it into your exercise book, and draw the missing parts of the dinosaur's skeleton.

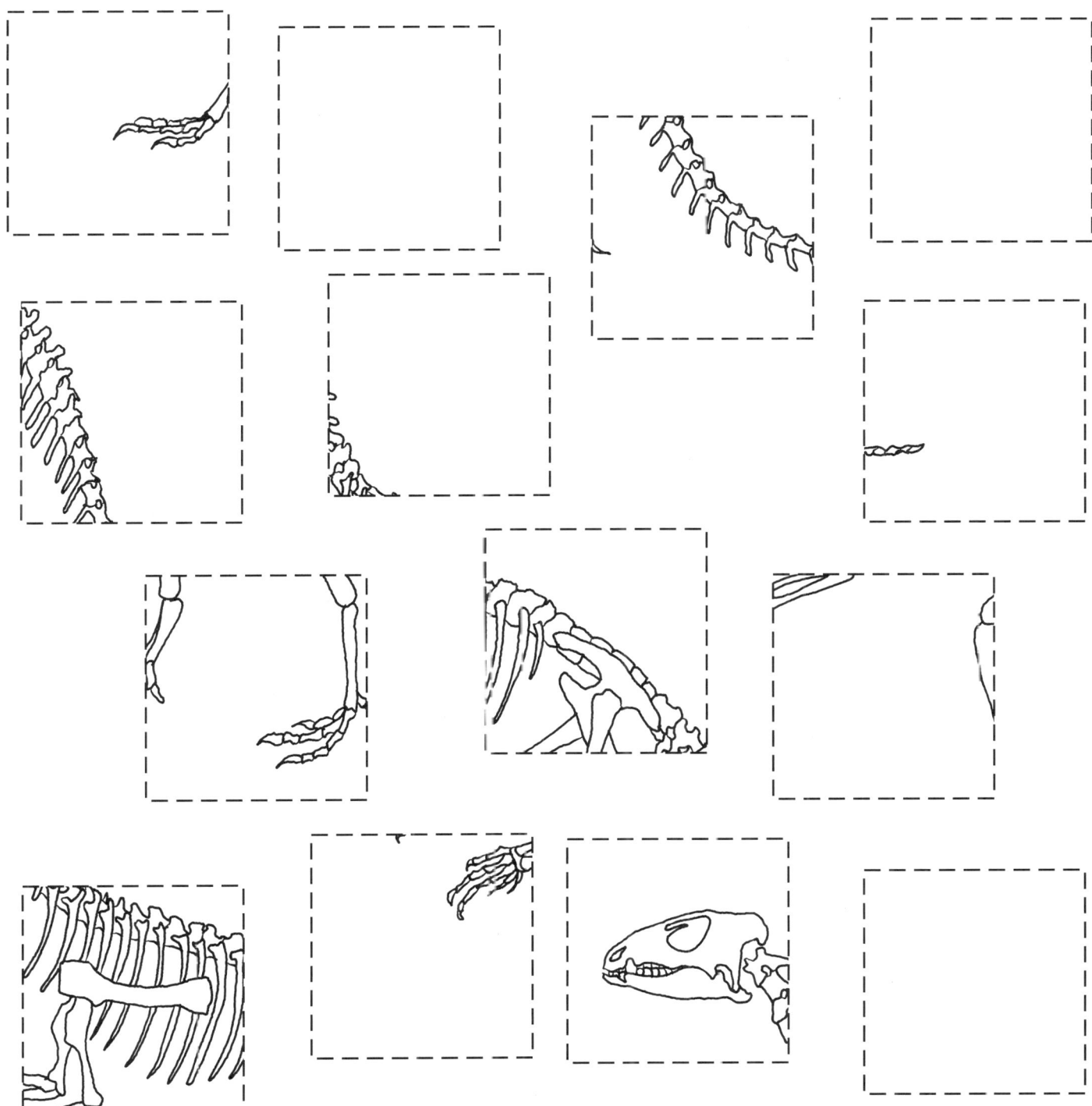

TIME TRAVELLING • Dinosaurs

T-3 WORKSHEET

Carnivore or herbivore?

Colour the right food for each dinosaur.

DINOSAURS	FOOD
Triceratops	
Velociraptor	
T-Rex	
Diplodocus	
Allosaurus	
Stegosaurus	

Photocopiable © Oxford University Press

T-4 WORKSHEET

Triceratops

Read about Triceratops. Tick (✔) the correct word to complete the sentence.

> Hello! I'm a triceratops. I'm big.
> I have got a big head, short legs, and a short tail.
> I have got three horns. I have got flat teeth.
> I walk on four legs. I eat leaves and bushes.
> I lay big eggs.

TAIL

HORNS

BEAK

1. I am
   - [ ] big
   - [ ] small

2. I have got
   - [ ] two horns
   - [ ] three horns

3. I have got a ___ head
   - [ ] big
   - [ ] small

4. I walk on
   - [ ] four legs
   - [ ] two legs

5. I have got ___ teeth
   - [ ] sharp
   - [ ] flat

6. I eat
   - [ ] plants
   - [ ] meat

7. I have got ___ legs
   - [ ] long
   - [ ] short

8. I
   - [ ] have babies
   - [ ] lay big eggs

Photocopiable © Oxford University Press

TIME TRAVELLING • Dinosaurs

T-5 WORKSHEET

T-Rex

Read about T-Rex. Tick (✔) the correct word to complete the sentence.

SCALY SKIN

Hello! I'm king of the dinosaurs. I'm big. I have got a long tail, two long legs, and two short arms. I have got sharp teeth and claws. I have got scaly skin. I walk on two legs. I eat small dinosaurs.

TEETH

CLAWS

1. I am
   ☐ big
   ☐ small

2. I have got
   ☐ horns
   ☐ claws

3. I have got
   ☐ long
   ☐ short
   arms

4. I walk on
   ☐ four
   ☐ two
   legs

5. I have got
   ☐ sharp
   ☐ flat
   teeth

6. I eat
   ☐ plants
   ☐ meat

7. I have got
   ☐ long
   ☐ short
   legs

8. I have
   ☐ furry
   ☐ scaly
   skin

Photocopiable © Oxford University Press

T-6 WORKSHEET

We are all dinosaurs

I'm an AN_____AURUS.
I like _____.
I've got _____ on my body.
I walk on ___ legs.
I'm 10 metres long.
I weigh __ tonnes.

5 – plants – four – spikes

I'm an O_____ OR.
I like _____.
I've got a _____ on my head.
I walk on ___ legs.
I'm 2 metres long.
I weigh __ kilograms.

Eggs – two – 20 – crest

I'm an AL___AURUS.
I like _____.
I've got _____ teeth.
I walk on ___ legs.
I'm 5 metres long.
I weigh __ tonnes.

two – sharp – meat – 2

I'm a D_____US.
I like _____ and _____.
I've got a _____ neck.
I walk on ___ legs.
I'm 27 metres long.
I weigh __ tonnes.

25 – four – long – leaves – plants

My favourite dinosaur is

This book belongs to
....

I'm a V_____ OR.
I like _____.
I've got _____ teeth.
I can ___ very fast.
I'm 2 metres long.
I weigh __ kilograms.

113 – sharp – animals – run

WE ARE ALL DINOSAURS

I'm a S_____AURUS.
I like _____ and _____ on my body.
I've got bony _____ on my body.
I walk on ___ legs.
I'm 9 metres long.
I weigh 1,400 kilograms.

plates – four – leaves – plants

Photocopiable © Oxford University Press

TIME TRAVELLING • Egyptians

T-7 WORKSHEET

Colour and cut out.

WELCOME TO ANCIENT EGYPT

T-8 WORKSHEET

Read and fill in the gaps.

Rocky and sandy desert

Sunny and hot

1400 B.C.

Egypt

Nile

A TRIP TO ANCIENT EGYPT

Date: ....
Place: ....
Land: ....
Climate: ....
River: ....

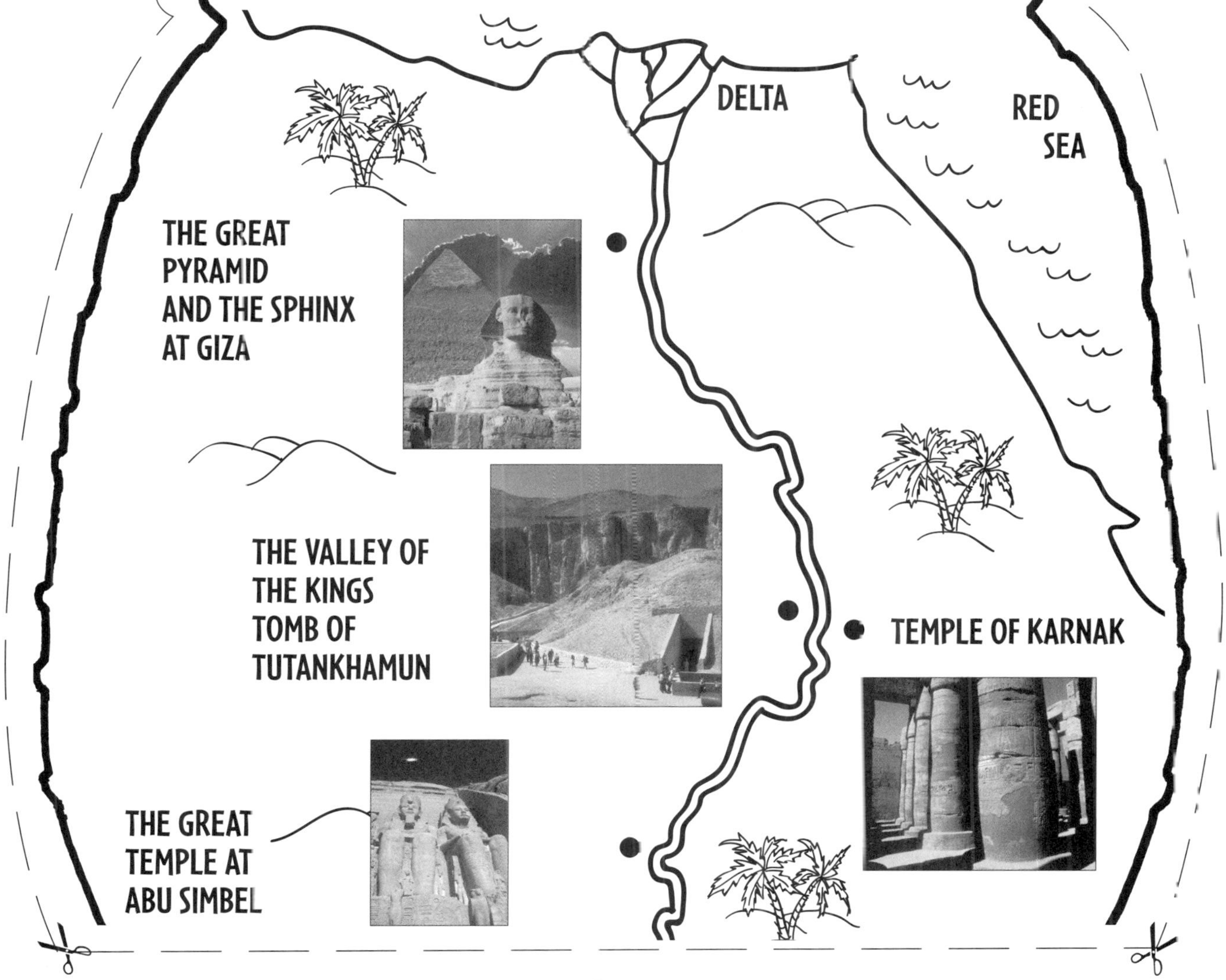

DELTA

RED SEA

THE GREAT PYRAMID AND THE SPHINX AT GIZA

THE VALLEY OF THE KINGS TOMB OF TUTANKHAMUN

TEMPLE OF KARNAK

THE GREAT TEMPLE AT ABU SIMBEL

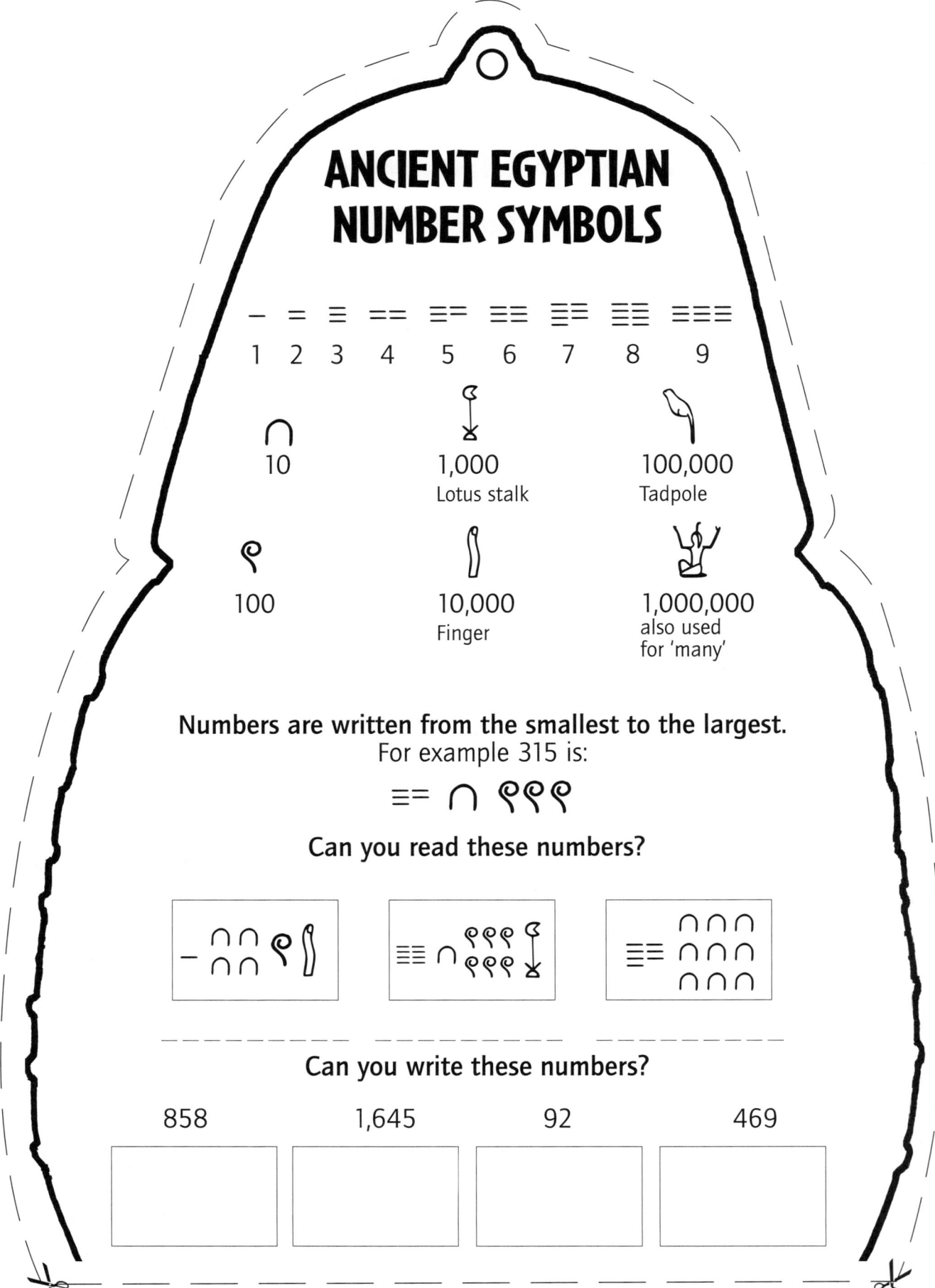

T-10 WORKSHEET

TIME TRAVELLING • Egyptians

EGYPTIAN WRITING

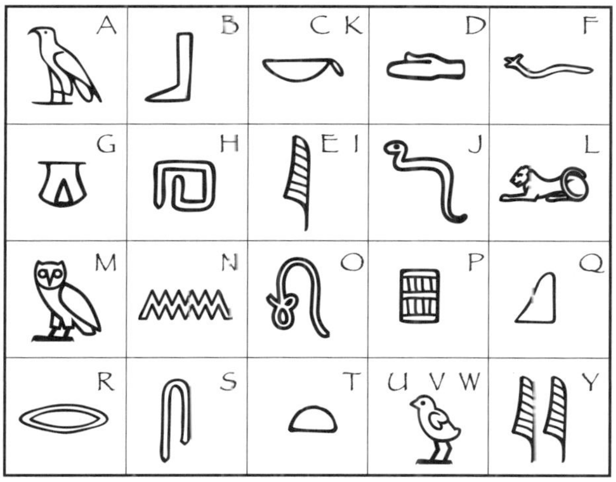

Can you read these words?

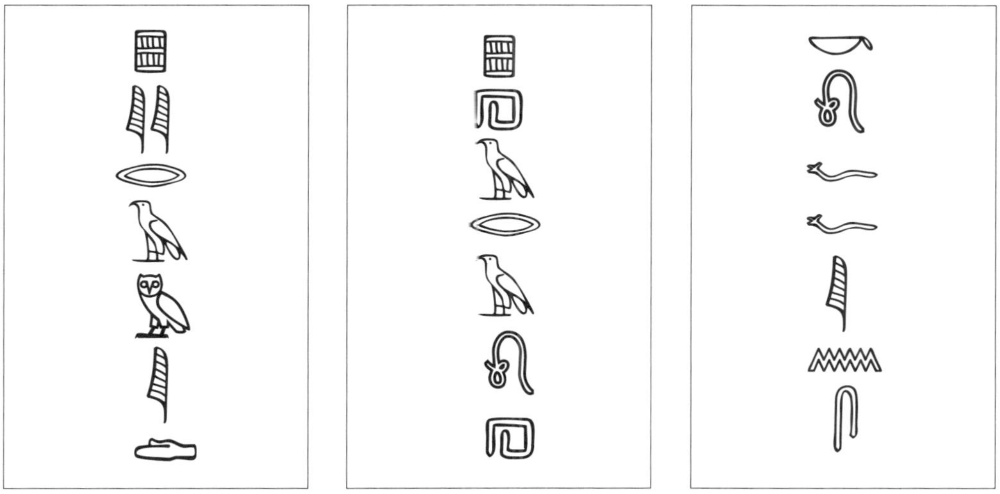

Write your name in the cartouche from left to right.

TIME TRAVELLING • Egyptians

T-11 WORKSHEET

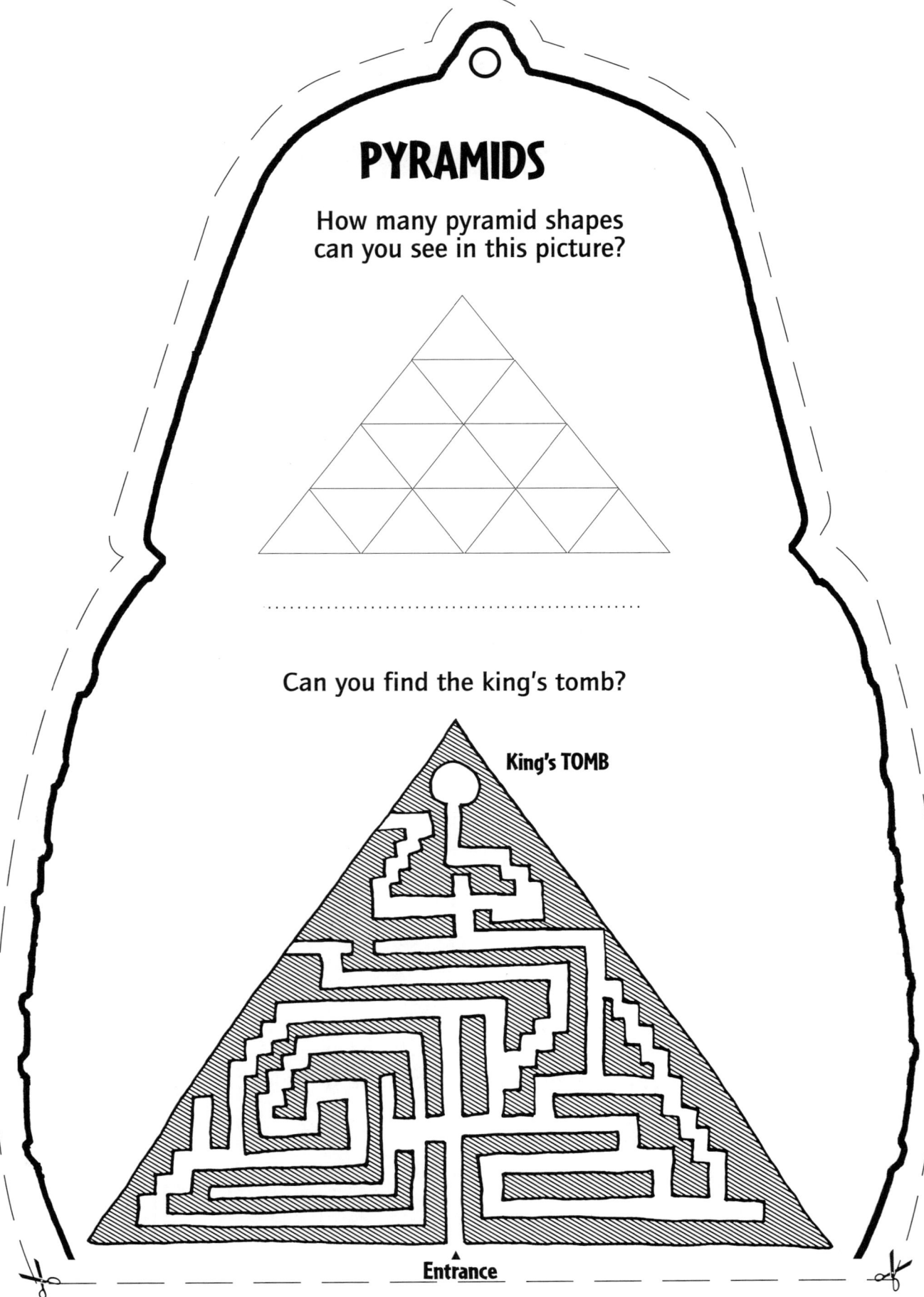

PYRAMIDS

How many pyramid shapes can you see in this picture?

....

Can you find the king's tomb?

King's TOMB

Entrance

T-12 WORKSHEET

TOMB PAINTINGS

Paintings on the walls of the tombs tell us about life in ancient Egypt (farming, clothes, animals, hairstyles, boats ...).

A PAINTING ABOUT MY LIFE

Make a drawing about your life (the place where you live, your family, your hobbies, ...). Use simple colours like blue, red, and green.

TIME TRAVELLING • Romans

T-13 WORKSHEET

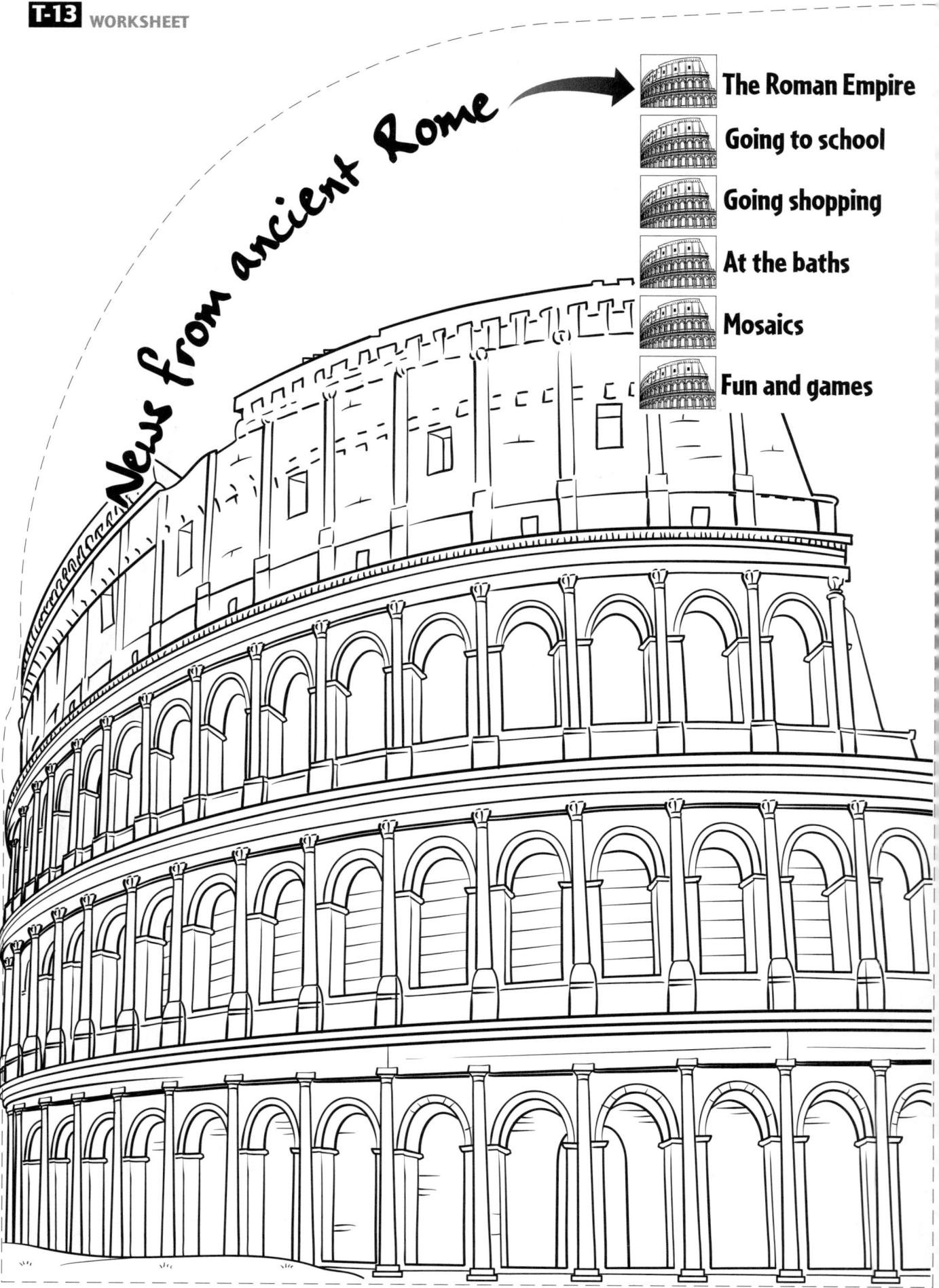

News from ancient Rome

- The Roman Empire
- Going to school
- Going shopping
- At the baths
- Mosaics
- Fun and games

T-14 WORKSHEET

TIME TRAVELLING • Romans

The Roman Empire 2000 years ago

Trace the borders of the Roman Empire. Colour them orange.

TIME TRAVELLING • Romans

T-15 WORKSHEET

Read and draw.

Going to school

IN ROMAN TIMES

 wax tablets

 stylus

 scroll

I II III IV
V VI VII
VIII IX X   Roman numbers

TODAY

 exercise book

pen

 book

 Arabic numbers

Photocopiable © Oxford University Press

TIME TRAVELLING • Romans

T-16 WORKSHEET

Going shopping

In a Roman street
Fill in the gaps with the missing words.

| PHARMACIST | CLOTH | BAKER | WOMAN |

| A .... is baking bread in the oven. | A .... merchant is selling material for a tunic. | A .... is selling hot food. | A .... is selling herbs. |

At the market
Read, draw, and colour the fruit and vegetables.

191   Photocopiable © Oxford University Press

TIME TRAVELLING • Romans

T-17 WORKSHEET

At the baths

Roman towns had public bath houses with hot, warm, and cold baths.

Heating system

a. The cold room was called the **Frigidarium**. Can you see where it is? Colour it blue.
b. The hot room was called the **Caldarium**. Can you see where it is? Colour it red.
c. Spot three Romans having a **massage** and colour them pink.
d. How many **statues** can you see? . . . .
e. Can you see a man wearing a **toga**? Colour him grey.
f. The Romans used oil and hot soap to wash their bodies. Can you spot four **pots of oil**? Colour them yellow.

192

Photocopiable © Oxford University Press

T-18 WORKSHEET

Mosaics

Rich Romans decorated floors with mosaic pictures using small pieces of coloured stones.

This mosaic, *Beware of the dog*, was buried in Pompeii when Mount Vesuvius erupted in A.D. 79 and was discovered many centuries later.

Draw the outline of a picture (animal or flower).
Cut coloured paper in small pieces and glue them on the picture to make your mosaic.

TIME TRAVELLING • Romans

T-19 WORKSHEET

Fun and games

- Wooden swords  
- Javelin
- Sticks and ball  
- Hoops 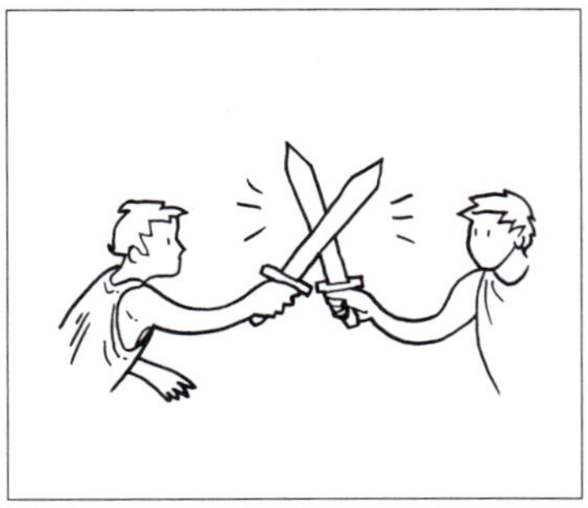
- Chariot races 
- Dice
- Checkers  
- Gladiators

Match each game to its name. Spot the odd one out.

Photocopiable © Oxford University Press